Development Perspectives

MALCOLM ADISESHIAH
(1910-1994)

Development Perspectives

MALCOLM ADISESHIAH MEMORIAL LECTURES

Edited by

R. SRINIVASAN

Malcolm & Elizabeth Adiseshiah Trust
Chennai, India

ACADEMIC FOUNDATION
NEW DELHI

www.academicfoundation.org
www.academicfoundation.com

First published in 2015
by

ACADEMIC FOUNDATION
4772-73 / 23 Bharat Ram Road, (23 Ansari Road),
Darya Ganj, New Delhi - 110 002 (India).
Phones : 23245001 / 02 / 03 / 04.
Fax : +91-11-23245005.
E-mail : books@academicfoundation.com
www.academicfoundation.org
www.academicfoundation.com

in association with
Malcolm & Elizabeth Adiseshiah Trust, Chennai, India.

Cataloging in Publication Data--DK
Courtesy: D.K. Agencies (P) Ltd. <docinfo@dkagencies.com>

Development perspectives : Malcolm Adiseshiah memorial lectures / edited by R. Srinivasan.
pages ; cm
ISBN 9789332701779

1. Economic development--Social aspects--India. 2. India--Economic policy. I. Srinivasan, R., editor. II. Malcolm & Elizabeth Adiseshiah Trust.issuing body.

DDC 338.954 23

Typeset by Italics India, New Delhi.

Printed and bound by The Book Mint, New Delhi.
www.thebookmint.in

CONTENTS

Editor/Contributors

Editor:

R. SRINIVASAN, is an Associate Professor in Econometrics, University of Madras. He has more than 25 years of experience in teaching and research in economics. He was a member of the State Planning Commission (2006-2011) and many other policy making and academic bodies. His researches have been in the areas of public finance and regional economics. His special interest in teaching of economics led him to organise periodic workshops for teacher of economics in schools and colleges to explore new teaching techniques and to reform economics curriculum. He has been extensively contributing on economic issues for both print and television media.

Contributors:

BINA AGARWAL, Professor of Development Economics and Environment, University of Manchester, UK. She is a well known economist and her pioneering research contributions in understanding the women's land rights enlarged the research agenda on gender inequality. She also explored the intra-family gender inequality in India and other southeast Asian countries, and the interface between gender inequality and environment sustainability.

AMITA BAVISKAR, Associate Professor, Sociology Unit, Institute of Economic Growth, New Delhi. Her research interests include the adverse impact of development projects on the marginalised sections such as the tribals in forests and the slum dwellers and migrants in the urban areas. Cultural politics of environment and development is the central aspect of her research, and she continues to explore India's development paradigms and the conflicts over natural resources.

RAJEEV BHARGAVA, Professor, Centre for the Studies of Developing Societies, Delhi. An erudite scholar and political theorist, he has formal academic training in economics and political science. His theoretical works include books on *Individualism in Social Science* and *What is Political Theory and Why Do We Need It?* His works on secularism gave a new and refreshing perspective to the debate not only in India but also in academic circles all over the world.

C.P. CHANDRASEKHAR, Professor, Centre for Economic Studies and Planning, School of Social Sciences, Jawaharlal Nehru University, Delhi. One of the critiques of the economic reforms in India, he is an acknowledged economist and public intellectual. His research works on financial sector in India gave a new perspective to analysis of financial sector reforms in the country and the global financial system. His writings throw open alternate sources of data and imaginative interpretation of official database from alternative perspectives.

SATISH DESHPANDE, Professor, Department of Sociology, Delhi University, Delhi. He has formal training in both economics and sociology, and has made prominent contributions to our understanding of caste in India. The description of lower castes as 'hypersensitive' and upper castes as 'invisible' shows his imaginative and thoughtful research conclusions on the caste and social hierarchy in India. His deep inquiries into caste and its implications have led to his advocacy of enumerating caste in the Census and to the construction of an index which captures disadvantage from a multi-dimensional perspective.

RAMACHANDRA GUHA, Distinguished Historian and Writer, India. His earliest writings on Himalayan ecology established him as an erudite scholar in India. As a contemporary historian, his works on Mahatma Gandhi and India after Independence are not only insightful but also contributed to the cause of secularism and egalitarian social order in India. As a writer on cricket India, he is well known outside the academic circles to the enthusiasts of the game all over the world.

DIPANKAR GUPTA, Distinguished Professor and Director, Centre for Public Affairs and Critical Theory, Deparment of Sociology, Shiv Nadar University, Uttar Pradesh. An erudite scholar and a well known sociologist, Prof Gupta has given path breaking research works on understanding rural India, particularly its complexities in agrarian communities, caste system and its evolution in embracing the non-farm characters. His popular writings bring out the abilities of a public intellectual in him and encourage the general public for a well informed public debate.

GOPAL NARAYAN GURU, Professor, Centre for Political Studies, School of Social Sciences, Jawaharlal Nehru University, Delhi. As a political scientist, he initiated fresh thinking in the political and social discourses on Dalits and more particularly on Dalit Women. His methodological innovations in gathering facts and utilising philosophical debates to analyse the India's social structure and its hierarchy are well known. Prof Guru elevated the debates on Dalit issues to higher philosophical plane, substantiated by undisputable facts.

PRATAP BHANU MEHTA, President, Centre for Policy Research, New Delhi. A high ranking political scientist, Prof Mehta has distinguished himself with finest research on contemporary political issues, blending philosophical inquiry, theoretical insights, and empirical reality. His research interests are around the issues of nexus between state and citizens, inequality and positive discrimination. Through the writings, he shows the pervasive and persistent inequalities that have resulted in altering the expectations of the people from the state and have posed problems in the achievement of essential goals through collective action.

SHARMILA REGE (1964-2013), Professor of Sociology, University of Pune, Maharashtra. Combining theory with activism, she carried out research on gender and caste, thus taking new paths to analysing sociological issues crossing disciplinary boundaries and structures. Her works on Dalit Feminist Standpoint have been acknowledged by her peers as groundbreaking in understanding feminist politics in India. Prof Rege has left a rich literature and research agenda for the young scholars of social science to take forward.

JANDHYALA B.G. TILAK, Professor and Head, Educational Finance, National University of Educational Planning and Administration, New Delhi. One of the pioneers of research in economics of education in India, Prof Tilak has touched all the aspects of this important facet of development. From his earliest works on returns to education to the latest on financing education in India and the issues in higher education such as opening up this sector to foreign competition, show his deep involvement in debating the contemporary development issues with passion and perspective.

YOGENDRA YADAV, Professor (on leave), Centre for the Studies of Developing Societies, Delhi. He is a prominent political scientist in the country and well known even to the common man for his untiring efforts to research and disseminate his findings on democratic institutions such as election. As a teacher, he was actively involved in preparing textbooks for school children in NCERT. Now he is an active politician, putting his research into action.

Foreword

Dr Malcolm S. Adiseshiah, eminent educationist, economist, Parliamentarian, philanthropist and an institution builder, foresaw the need for research in development studies to understand development issues in a holistic manner using inter-disciplinary approach. He founded the Madras Institute of Development Studies (MIDS) in 1970, now a well known Indian Council of Social Sciences Research Institute. The Malcolm & Elizabeth Adiseshiah (M&EA) Trust was established in 1999 with financial contributions from Malcolm Adiseshiah and Elizabeth Adiseshiah. One of the major activities of M&EA Trust is presentation of Malcolm Adiseshiah Award every year to a scholar below the age of 60 in recognition of his or her achievements in the field of development studies. So far 13 eminent social scientists delivered Malcolm Adiseshiah Memorial lectures. The Trust could not get the final version of the first lecture and hence decided to publish the remaining 12 lectures to make them accessible to researchers, students and policymakers.

All the 12 lectures focus on development issues and use multidisciplinary approach. The lecturers are distinguished scholars with expertise in the fields of economics, education, environment, history, political science, policy studies and sociology. Ten papers deal with development themes such as gender inequality, educational policy, culture and agriculture in rural India, cultural politics of environment and development, global imbalances, social justice, religious diversity, caste and castelessness, Dalit studies, and Dalit rights over natural resources. Two papers deal with methodological issues in historical approach and survey research. Thus the themes are multidisciplinary in nature and reflect contemporary social concerns, especially distributive equity. I am sure that this book will stimulate further research on development issues and policies and will be of immense use to students, researchers and policymakers in all social science disciplines.

The Trust is grateful to Professor C.T. Kurien, an eminent economist, founder trustee and past Chairman, M&EA Trust, and long-term associate of Professor Adiseshiah, for writing a note on Dr Adiseshiah. The Trust appreciates the excellent editorial work done by Dr R. Srinivasan, a M&EA Trustee. I would like to thank Dr H.B.N. Shetty, Executive Trustee, M&EA Trust, for his sincere and untiring efforts in publishing this book. Finally, I thank the Academic Foundation for their efforts in bringing out this publication in short time.

— U. Sankar
Chairman,
Malcolm & Elizabeth Adiseshiah Trust

PROFILE

Malcolm Adiseshiah
(1910-1994)

"In the years following independence, India was sending forth in triumph into the world a noble set of its choice citizens with enlightened ideas of society and civilization. It was the era which saw India emerge as one of the leading nations of the Third World. Malcolm Adiseshiah, with his unflagging perseverance and indomitable courage, is among the most eminent of those early emissaries." These are the opening sentences of a biographical sketch of Dr Malcolm Adiseshiah in the volume of essays and reflections his colleagues and admirers brought out on his 80th birthday in 1990 (*Economy, Society and Development*, 1991, which those interested may look up for a more detailed account). That this was not an exaggerated claim can be seen from the fact that for over two decades from 1948 Adiseshiah was a top official of UNESCO, including its Deputy Director-General from 1962 to 1970. Those who were familiar with the UNESCO's functioning of the 1950s and 1960s would also testify that it was Malcolm Adiseshiah who converted that organisation which in its early years was something of a limited club of the so-called advanced countries of the world into a truly global body, concerned not only with the science and culture of the affluent, but primarily with the education and development of the vast majority of human beings.

Adiseshiah was born in Vellore where he also had his early education in the Voorhees School and College. He then moved to

Loyola College in Madras from where he took a B.A.(Hons) degree in Economics. After teaching at St. Paul's College, Calcutta, for a brief period, he went over to England for the doctoral programme in the London School of Economics and the Cambridge University. With a doctorate he returned to India in 1940 as Professor of Economics in the Madras Christian College. He left the College in 1945 and worked with the World University Service in Geneva before moving to UNESCO.

On his retirement from UNESCO in 1970, he returned to India and Tamil Nadu determined to devote the rest of his life in the service of his country, especially in the spheres of economic development and education. Together with his wife, Elizabeth, they had registered a Trust in Paris for these purposes setting aside a substantial portion of their resources also to carry out their mission. So was founded the Madras Institute of Development Studies (MIDS) late in 1970. When, in 1972, Adiseshiah became a member of the newly constituted Tamil Nadu Planning Commission, he used the Institute for his studies pertaining to the state. It is noteworthy that the first study done through the Institute, which later came out as its first publication also, was "Income Earning Trends and Social Status of the Harijan Community in Tamil Nadu".

That was symbolic of Adiseshiah's commitment to use his privileges and resources in the service of others, especially the least privileged in society. All through his life he was led by the conviction that knowledge had a liberating and uplifting role and hence making knowledge available to others was a sacred duty. And he used every opportunity he came to have to convert this conviction into action. He was the Vice-Chancellor of the Madras University from 1975 to 1978 and during this short period he introduced the semester system and granted autonomy to selected colleges, making the University the pioneer in the country for this innovative scheme. He was nominated to the Rajya Sabha in 1978 and he made use of the opportunity to initiate a programme of adult literacy in the country, and push it with vigour, especially in Tamil Nadu. He was Chairman of the MIDS from its inception till his death in 1994. Through his own prolific research output and the contacts he had in the country and the rest of the world, he enabled the Institute to gain recognition as a major centre for social science research. He chaired many other institutions and professional bodies in Tamil Nadu and the rest of the country. Whatever he took up, he was a man of vision and action, always dreaming and always acting, and by his commitment always exhorting others to join him.

Trained as an economist Adiseshiah continued his involvement with the subject all through his life. His students, some of whom like Prof K.N. Raj, who later on became actively associated with the teaching of economics, policy making and institution building, still recall what a tremendous inspiration Adiseshiah was to them. In his quasi-autobiographical work published under the title *Let My Country Awake*, Adiseshiah recalls how the teaching of economics, first in Calcutta and then in Madras, was a learning experience for him also. He records that his own economics was shaped "in the villages of Bengal and South India with their rural service centres where we [he and his students] worked out the economics of hand-pound rice, hand-made paper, handloom textiles, crop rotation and rural credit, rural medicine, sanitation, adult literacy and curriculum reform" and that "it was there that I found the testing ground for the many ideas and plans that I carried with me to UNESCO in Paris and from there to the four corners of the earth." The same texture of intimate links with real life became the distinct feature of all his writings subsequently and that made his commentaries on economic issues distinctly unique. In UNESCO, he never wrote a mission report about any country without familiarising himself with the specifics of each situation, practically always through visits and personal contacts of many kinds.

Back in India, the many scholarly papers he wrote, his incisive editorials on the economic situation in Tamil Nadu, in the country and in the international arena that he wrote every month from 1971 till 1994 in the *Bulletin: Madras Development Seminar Series* (MIDS Bulletin) and the *Mid-Year Review of the Indian Economy* that he authored for several years (published by the Indian International Centre) were received with wide acclaim and are still considered to be very weighty professional contributions.

Malcolm and Elizabeth Adiseshiah had decided that after their life time their properties would be devoted for the continuation of the work they were doing. Elizabeth Adiseshiah passed away in 1986 leaving all her property to her husband. In his Will, Malcolm Adiseshiah bequeathed their residential property to the MIDS and stated that the rest, the financial assets, should be used to set up a new trust for conducting programmes in the broad area of economics—teaching and research, both fundamental and applied, and that the trust should be named Malcolm and Elizabeth Adiseshiah Trust.

In life through tireless work and in his Will through a rare gesture worthy of emulation by the affluent in our land, Malcolm Adiseshiah demonstrated his commitment to the spread of knowledge and the upliftment of the less privileged. Truly was he one of the most outstanding and humane personalities of our time.

— Prof C.T. Kurien
Founder Trustee and past Chairman,
Malcolm & Elizabeth Adiseshiah Trust

Introduction

The Malcolm and Elizabeth Adiseshiah Trust, Chennai, instituted the Malcolm Award in 2000, soon after the formation of the Trust in 1999. Malcolm Adiseshiah himself a development economist, encouraged scores of development thinkers in the country primarily through Madras Institute of Development Studies (MIDS), where he invited the best academics from all social sciences to work on development issues in India and in Tamil Nadu. He also encouraged many other academics, both young and old, through comments on their works in various forma. The Trust thought that this tradition should continue and hence this Award.

The Malcolm Lectures are delivered every year on his death anniversary in his memory. These lectures are delivered by the recipients of the Malcolm Adiseshiah Award. So far, 13 Malcolm Adiseshiah Lectures have been delivered and 12 of them are included in this volume. The first lecture was delivered by Abijit Banerjee and the Trust is not in possession of the transcript of that lecture. We have presented the lectures in the chronological order. Though development is the common theme of all these lectures, the issue explored in each lecture is unique and many of the experts have taken up inter-disciplinary approaches. For instance, the 2006 lecture on Dalit studies by Sharmila Rege is quite different from the 2013 lecture on Dalits rights for exploiting natural resources by Gopal Narayana Guru, as you will know that they have chosen to explore two different aspects of the most depressed community. Secularism, survey research and caste politics are the themes of the three Malcolm Adiseshiah Lectures presented by three political scientists namely Rajeev Bhargava, Yogendra Yadav and Satish Deshpande.

So too every economist in this list has discussed distinct aspects of development.

Distribution is an inseparable aspect of development discourses. Malcolm Adiseshiah Lecture 2002 by Bina Agarwal, "Gender Inequalities: Neglected Dimensions and Hidden Facets" initiated debate on addressing gender bias in economy. Intra-household differences, social norms and evolving new norms to control women have contributed to gender inequalities in society. Based on her own previous research findings and on similar such works across the globe, she unravelled the gender inequalities based on unequal property rights, inequalities in social norms and facilitated by these two, new norms are created to further the gender inequalities in society. Reducing gender inequalities requires changing women's perception of self-interest and enhancing her bargaining power. The latter requires women to come together as a larger group to gain power. Her suggestion to enhance women's bargaining power through collective action, with proactive indulgence of the state and CSOs (civil society organisations) is essential. This, she considers as a challenge for gender economics and for the social sciences more generally.

Third recipient of the Malcolm Adiseshiah Award Jandhyala B.G. Tilak, delivered the Malcolm Adiseshiah Lecture, "State, Households and Markets in Education" in 2003. The perspectives of education differ between the three agencies—the state has a long term public good approach, individual's aim is to maximise life-time earnings and market works with still shorter term objective of profit maximisation. The state expenditure on education was not adequate to provide quality education to all children currently enrolled, therefore, other laudable objectives of attaining universal school education and increasing expenditure on education to six per cent of GDP (gross domestic product) had to wait for larger allocation in future. As the state's expenditure on education declined, households were compelled to spend on it. The government policy to facilitate private investment in educational sector not only increased the number of colleges and universities but also reduced the quality of education imparted. Further, the growth of education sector in different parts of the country was also uneven. The civil society should have compelled the state to commit its own revenue to provide free and compulsory good quality education to all its citizens, otherwise the private sector would continue to hold the state and households to ransom.

Dipankar Gupta's Malcolm Adiseshiah Lecture 2004, "Whither the Indian Village?: Culture and Agriculture in Rural India" was on the changing characteristics of Indian villages, particularly when they were alienated from the agricultural sector. Declining agriculture, increasing non-farm sector in villages, land fragmentation, declining caste domination and the cultural implosion have taken away the prospects of development for both cultivators and landless labourers in the villages. While caste system is collapsing, caste identity is gaining currency. Agitations are not between agricultural labourers and landlords, they are now by the farmers as a whole, as agriculture is recognised as 'a relatively unrewarding profession'. Non-farm workers in villages are employed in such sectors both within and outside the villages and both cultivators and landless labourers are in this category, reflecting the prolonged distress in agriculture. Prof Gupta concludes, "Agriculture is an economic residue that generously accommodates non-achievers ... From rich to poor, the trend is to leave the villages, ...this is what India's villages are telling us whether or not we are inclined to listen to these rustic murmurs."

Narrating various conflicts over environment and development in India, Amita Baviskar, delivered the Malcolm Adiseshiah Lecture 2005, "Cultural Politics of Environment and Development: The Indian Experience". Emphasising the interconnectedness between environment and development, she says that environment represents both material and symbolic resources. The ecological and social limits of growth are the basis for cultural politics of environment and development. This conceptualisation is critical to understand the hegemony of knowledge, social practices, working of state institutions, and other forces that create inequality. The rich are able to buy the scarce common property resources, while the poor have not received enough. Therefore, the real cost of protecting the environment is borne by the poor, who are displaced or disallowed to use the common property resources. The middle class, described by Amita Baviskar as the intelligentsia should study the limits of consumerism of the rich in order to address the issues of poverty and environment. It is also essential for the intelligentsia to support the cultural politics that brings various groups together to pursue a common cause.

Arguing for a separate 'Dalit studies' in higher educational institution is the central theme of the Malcolm Adiseshiah Lecture 2006, "Dalit Studies as Pedagogical Practice: Claiming More than Just a 'Little Place' in the Academia" delivered by Sharmila Rege. Both the colonial power and nationalists considered the knowledge in India as Hindu and *brahmanical*. In this identification, the original intellect of the Dalits was erased from the public knowledge. Based on the discourses of Phule, Dr Ambedkar, Shahu, and the other recent writings by various Dalit movements, she underlines the importance of questioning the misrepresentation of Dalits by the dominant classes. Dalit studies should draw from all the social sciences the theortical and empirical explorations, equally the experiences of social struggles also should be incorporated. Importantly, the continuous interactions between the academia and social movements should continue to evolve the dalit studies as pedagogical practice.

Distinguished public intellectual and historian Ramachandra Guha delivered the Malcolm Adiseshiah Lecture 2007. His views on the unwritten history of Independent India was the theme of the lecture, "The Challenge of Contemporary History". His complaint that while social scientists generally concentrated on issues in Independent India, the historians faithfully carried out research on pre-independent India. Thus, 1947 divided historians from others in terms of the researching issues. He went on to elaborate and draw the attention of fellow historians about the need to write on modern Indian history because, 1947 turned the country into a single, large, multi-religious, multi-cultural, multi-linguistic country experiencing four revolutions simultaneously, namely the urban, industrial, national and democratic. Every region or state has experienced different levels of development and socio-political changes that should be captured through all forms of historical writing from biographies to social histories. Of course, the historians and the readers would be biased as participants in these events and lack of access to historical records would be another major constraint. Nevertheless, the availability of official records and print media resources in libraries and museums and oral histories of associates of personalities and witnesses should form a rich sources of historical research. He drew the attention of all social scientists to combine historical research with analysis of contemporary evidence on developmental issues.

Reflecting on his long experience in survey research, Yogendra Yadav's Malcolm Adiseshiah Lecture 2008 was, "Whither Survey Research? Reflections on the State of Survey Research on Politics in most of the World". Malcolm Adiseshiah Lecturers have always been raising serious questions and pointing to new vistas in development studies. True to this tradition, Yogendra Yadav encountered some of the serious charges against the use of survey research in political science. The use of survey research in global South is often described as a transplantation of that technique from the global North. Mere use of a technique without any theoretical and methodological adaptation has paid little dividend in terms of theoretical conceptions for the South and that would lead to parochial universalism, according to Prof Yadav. He has pointed out that there could be efforts to transform the survey method for the developing countries. Conception of survey research as an art, without claims of scientificity, it can serve as a tool to capture the changes in mass political behaviour and opinions. Strengthening the sampling techniques, conceptualising issues in the language of the subjects and creating a protocol for fieldwork, could go a long way in transforming the survey research suitable to our democracy.

That there were no alternatives to the otherwise illegitimate international reserve currency, that is US Dollar was the reason for its continuance as such, was the main argument that C.P. Chandrasekar put forth in his Malcolm Adiseshiah Lecture for 2009, "Global Imbalances and the Dollar's Future". He traced the growth of US Dollar as the international reserve currency since the World War II. Initially, the faith in it was because of the gold standard that US preserved and that faith continued even after it broke away from this arrangement in 1970s and during the times it lost the economic competitiveness to other developing countries thereafter. In 1980s, the US could coerce the other developed countries at least in three instances to stabilise US Dollar, which was subject to secular depreciation along with extreme volatility. The liberalised exchange rate regimes in the developing countries since the 1990s facilitated the US to get its CAD (current account deficit) financed by liberal support from these countries, mainly China, who were maintaining current account surplus with the US. The inability of the Euro and Yen or SDR (special drawing rights) to substitute the US Dollar as an international currency, sustains the supremacy of it till now.

In the Malcolm Adiseshiah Lecture 2010-"The Politics of Social Justice" Banu Pratap Mehta addressed two issues, namely the limited set of instruments for attaining social justice and the continuance of caste in the politics of social justice. He narrated that democracy has allowed inequality to grow mainly because the instruments such as taxation, industrial capital, land reforms and the state's welfare programmes have been used with limited success. He opined that even in the case of such limited success, "they enhance the ethic of individuation, mobility and competition rather than a politics of inequality. It is therefore possible to articulate a discourse of improvement, but there is no locus of social justice." The political equality enshrined in the Indian Constitution has thrown a veil on the social and economic inequality. This has brought caste as an axis of equality at the central to Indian politics. Prof Mehta described how inequality has only promoted the struggle for power in Indian politics with little impact of social transformation. He concluded that though class mobility was possible, with continuance of caste as a defining institution in political landscape, we had to fight oligarchy and populism to address social inequality.

Like many of his predecessors, Rajeev Bhargava, the recipient of the Malcolm Adiseshiah Award 2011, chose to deliver a lecture on a contemporary issue with historical accounts, "Political Responses to Religious Diversity in Ancient and Modern India." After defining the diversity of religion and diversity within religion, emphasising that both the forms exist in India, he underlined that the form of secularism being practiced in India was different from the western and liberal forms of securalism. He listed eight features of Indian secularism, like recognition of multiple religions, inter-religious and intra-religious domination, existence of multiple values of peace, toleration, liberty and/or equity, recognition of public character of religion, intervention of state in religious matters with principled distance, state showing necessary hostility and active respect for religion, balancing between multiple and ambiguous and equally important values. Prof Bhargava argued the essence of Ashoka's Dhamma giving shape to "the ambition of a new public morality widely endorsed by all affected groups...though not guaranteed to succeed, gave the hope for a durable principled coexistence between groups engaged in fierce verbal disputes' as the base of 'toleration' that could promote amicable collective living."

Satish Deshpande was the recipient of Malcolm Adiseshiah Award for Development Studies 2012. In his Lecture, "Caste and Castelessness in the Indian Republic: Towards a Biography of the 'General Category'", he emphasised the need to engage the emergence and rise of the notion of castelessness and its main form of appearance in everyday life, namely the 'general category'. He traced the history of various attempts to abolish/annihilate caste system in India, both in the pre-indepedence and post-independence periods and finally how the Mandal movement and reservation for OBCs (other backward classes) brought back the recognition of caste, particularly the OBCs who were hitherto under the 'general category'. Now the upper caste elite have started to clamour for a casteless society, concealing their caste identities in the context, of caste enumeration in Census. In this context, he raised questions such as how one's caste might block life chances and how castelessness would increase it? At the same time, we are also ignorant of the 'processes and modalities, the concrete ways in which an upper caste identity secretes and synergises the dispositions and embodied competences that add up to that abstract term, 'advantage'. Thus, he argued for a creating detailed biographies of the various castes in the general category.

2013 Malcolm Adiseshiah awardee Gopal Narayana Guru, delivered the Malcolm Adiseshiah lecture, 'Two Locations of

Injustice: Present and Posterity". In this lecture, he problematised the Dalit's demand for exclusive rights to exploit nature. Such a demand was first raised by the Dalit Indian Chamber of Commerce and Industry. 'For-profit exploitation' of nature by the Dalits may put them on equal footing with other corporate entities, but it will definitely work against the common Dalits, who are dependent on the nature for livelihood and who are also protectors of nature. While emphasising the need to restore the land rights for the Dalits, Prof Gopal has underlined the conflict of justice between the present and posterity with regard to natural resources in this lecture. Rather he argued that the common Dalit should resist the forces from within and outside that exploited the nature for profit, rendering injustice to the posterity, at the same time without benefiting the common Dalits then.

Apart from 'development' being the overarching theme of all these lectures, one would also find the contemporary relevance of the issues that have been discussed. More importantly inequalities of all forms, gender, religion, community and space have been the major subjects of discussion in these lectures. Every lecture exposes the academic scholarship and commitment of the expert to the chosen theme. The lectures are balanced in terms of theoretical queries, empirical analysis and in many instances inputs are drawn from socio-political movements and such other institutions.

— R. Srinivasan
Trustee,
Malcolm & Elizabeth Adiseshiah Trust

1

BINA AGARWAL[1]

Gender Inequalities

Neglected Dimensions and Hidden Facts

Dr Adiseshiah's engagement with the issues of inequality, poverty, environmental degradation and agrarian transformation has a special resonance for me, since these are also concerns I share. Equally, I find myself in strong agreement with him on the importance of framing these questions within a political economy and interdisciplinary perspective. My paper will thus focus centrally on these aspects which preoccupied him for so many years. In this I will seek to weave together several aspects of my work—some past, some current, some empirical and some theoretical.

Gender Inequality

Rural women in northwest India, married to strangers miles away from their birth villages, use folk songs to decry their estrangement from the green pastures of their childhood homes—homes to which their brothers, who inherit the ancestral land, have automatic access. I quote excerpts from two folk songs:

> To my brother belong your green fields
> O father, while I am banished afar.
>
> Always you said
> Your brother and you are the same
> O father. But today you betray me...

---

1. This is a slightly revised version of the Malcolm Adiseshiah Memorial Lecture 2002. In particular, this version includes examples of recent developments on women's land rights in China and the transition economies, which were not part of the original lecture. In an early form, some of these ideas were also presented in a public lecture I gave at Barnard college, Columbia University in December 2001, when I was based there as the Hirschorn visiting professor.

My *doli* leaves your house, O father
My *doli* leaves your house.
These dowry jewels are not jewels
But wounds arounds my neck, O father.
My *doli* leaves...[2]

Women in Sri Lanka, by contrast, traditionally inherited immovable property, and sometimes their husbands moved in with them. But according to folklore such a husband was advised to always keep a walking stick, an umbrella, and an oil lamp handy. Why? In case his wife evicted him when he was ill and in the rain, in the middle of the night! And some wives indeed did so.

Both examples depict gender inequality. In the first, the woman has no property and social norms require her to join her husband—a dislocation she sees as banishment. In the second, the man has no property and social norms allow him to join his wife, but in a home from which he can easily be evicted. In the first example, the woman is the less equal, in the second the man.

These examples illustrate several things. They highlight that gender inequality and indeed gender in general, is a relational category. And although most times we are grappling with woman's disadvantaged position, in rare cases men too might occupy that position. In particular, these examples highlight the importance of women's property status and enabling social norms in determining gender relations.

Compared with other inequalities such as those of class or race, gender inequality also has some distinct features. One, it dwells not only outside the home but also centrally within it. Mainstream economic theory has long treated the household as a unitary entity in relation to both consumption and production. The unitary household model assumes that all household resources and incomes are pooled, and family members either share common interests and preferences, or an altruistic household head (who represents the household's tastes

2. These verses are taken from folk songs sung by women in northwest India when the bride leaves her parent's home on marriage. *Doli* means a palanquin. I am grateful to Veena Das for sharing the second song with me.

and preferences and seeks to maximise households utility) ensures equitable allocation of goods and tasks (see also, Agarwal, 1997).

Most people know from personal experience that this is not how real families behave. But academically too, in recent years, virtually every assumption of the unitary household model has been challenged effectively through empirical evidence, including assumptions of shared preferences and interests, pooled incomes, and altruism as the guiding principle of intra-household allocations. Gender, in particular, is noted to be an important signifier of differences in interests, preferences, endowments and allocations. And in alternative 'bargaining models' of the household, bargaining power rather than altruism is seen as guiding intra-household allocations.

Two, gender inequalities stem not only from differences in economic endowments between women and men but also from social norms and perceptions, that is, the inequalities are also ideologically embedded. While norms and perceptions impinge on other social inequalities like race and caste as well, gendered norms and perceptions cut across these categories and exist additionally.

Three, gender inequalities not only pre-exist, new ones can arise from the foundations of the old ones, and people with prior advantage can set in place rules that perpetuate that advantage, such as rules governing new institutions now being promoted to manage common pool resources. Although based on principles of cooperation, such institutions can effectively exclude significant sections, such as women, from their decision-making bodies and their benefits. In other words, gender inequality can be in the process of constant recreation in new forms.

Gender inequality is thus a vast subject with a vast literature on it. But some aspects are more neglected and hidden than others. And it is on these aspects that I will now focus, namely:

(i) Inequality in command over property—a notably neglected dimension.
(ii) Inequalities in social perceptions and social norms, the workings of which are often hidden but which have visible economic outcomes.

The former is a significant material form of inequality, the latter a significant ideological form.

(iii) New inequalities arising in emergent institutions through the interaction of the above two dimensions of pre-existing inequalities. This will also throw light on the process of inequality creation.

In addition, I will illustrate how gender inequalities are simultaneously constituted in several arenas: the family, the community, the market and the state. And the bargaining approach provides a promising analytical framework for understanding how both the material and the ideological aspects of gender inequality can be challenged within these arenas.

Gender Gap in Command Over Property

The Nature of the Gap

Consider first the issue of property. Economists have long emphasised the importance of property rights for incentives and efficiency. But relatively few have looked at the gender gap in command over property. And although there has been some progress on this count in recent years, it still remains a largely neglected issue. Economic analysis and policies concerning women continue to be preoccupied with employment, and relatedly with education.

In the process, inequality in command over property has largely been neglected. Yet it is this aspect of inequality which remains one of the most important forms of persisting economic inequality between women and men—one which has a critical bearing not only on women's economic well-being but also on their social and political status.

The idea of 'command' over property is more complex than it appears on the surface (for a detailed discussion, see Agarwal, 1994). First, it takes us away from the narrow legalistic way in which many think of property rights. Command over property implies not merely rights in law, but effective rights in practice. Equality in legal rights to own property need not guarantee equality in actual ownership.

This is especially true of inheritance where the gap between law and practice can be vast.

In India, for example, legally women enjoy significant inheritance rights, even if unequal to men's (Agarwal, 1994). In practice, only a small percentage of women inherit. A sample survey of rural widows in 1991, by development sociologist Martha Chen, found that only 13 per cent of the surveyed women with landowning fathers inherited any land as daughters. And only 51 per cent of widows whose deceased husbands owned land, inherited any. Thus, 87 per cent of daughters and 49 per cent of widows with legal claims did not inherit (cited in Agarwal, 1998).

Second, property advantage can arise not only from ownership but also from effective control over it. Ownership alone does not always guarantee control. In many countries, even when women inherit they do not fully control what they receive. Some obstacles are social. For example, some cultures restrict women's interactions in the public sphere and hence their ability to manage their property effectively. Other barriers can be legal. For instance, in Sri Lanka's Jaffna Province, a married Tamil woman, under local law, needs her husband's permission to lease out or sell her own property. Similar laws prevailed earlier in parts of Europe. The distinctions between law and practice, and between ownership and control are thus especially critical for women.

Third, property advantage can stem not only from private property but also public property. For instance, in most societies today, control over wealth-generating public property is largely in male hands, be they managers in large corporations, or heads of government bureaucracies. Even in the former socialist USSR, although private property ownership was abolished, decision-making over public property remained mostly with men.

Four, men (as a gender, even if not all men as individuals) also largely control the instruments through which existing property advantages get perpetuated, such as institutions that enact and implement property laws (e.g. Parliaments and law courts) and the mechanisms of recruitment into bodies which control property.

Fifth, command over property can also significantly influence the institutions that shape ideas about gender, such as the media, and educational and religious bodies. Predominantly male control over these institutions can thus affect the persistence of negative ideological assumptions about women's needs, work roles, capabilities, and so on.

Seen in this broad way, gender inequality in command over property is thus important globally, in both developing and developed countries. However, which form of property is important can differ by context, and in large parts of the developing world, arable land has a pre-eminent position, as outlined below.

The Importance of Land

In largely agrarian economies, arable land is the most valued form of property. It is wealth creating, livelihood sustaining and status enhancing. For most rural households it provides security against poverty. Traditionally, it has been the basis of political power and social status. For many, it is even linked with personal identity and rootedness. And it has a permanence that few other assets possess. That is why people often end up spending more on litigation over ancestral land than its economic value would justify. It is notable that even in parts of central Europe today, as urban labour markets stagnate, people are returning to land and rural livelihoods for survival, as recent work on Uzbekistan shows (see Kandiyoti, 2003).

While the links between access to land, economic well being and social status are well recognised at the household level, their importance specifically for women has largely been neglected in both research and policy. The United Nations (UN) has long claimed that women own only one per cent of the world's property, but they provide no data to back this claim. In fact, in most countries, large-scale surveys do not collect gender-disaggregated data for land or other assets. (Nepal is a recent exception where such data are now being collected in their census.) Hence, in order to estimate women's access to land we still have to depend mostly on small-scale surveys or village-level studies. These sources show, as noted, that few women own arable land and even fewer effectively control some. Why is this the case?

First of all, there are the noted biases in inheritance. Second, even government transfers of public land instead of narrowing the gender gap in private property tend to widen it, by transferring titles almost solely to men. This is true not only in India but in many other countries. In the Latin American agrarian reforms of the 1960s to the 1980s, for instance, less than 15 per cent of the beneficiaries across eight countries were women. Recent shifts toward joint titling remain regionally uneven (Deere and de Leon, 2001).

In China, again, although the law promises gender equality in use rights in the distribution of household responsibility land, in practice, a range of gender inequalities can emerge. For instance, since most women leave their village on marriage, and land re-adjustments are infrequent, many have to wait long periods for land to be allotted for them in their husband's village. They also face special problems on divorce or widowhood (see e.g. Li, 1999). These problems could get compounded following the 1998 Land Management Law (LML) which has restricted readjustments by extending the duration of the household responsibility contract from 15 to 30 years (Li, 2003; Brown, 2003). According to Li (2003: 4), figures derived from a survey undertaken by the All-China Women's Federation and the State Statistics Bureau of 2000, showed that 70 per cent of people without their own land were women, and among these women, 20 per cent had never held land, while the others had lost their land on marriage, divorce, or reallocation. It is as yet unclear to what extent the 2003 Rural Land Contracting Law (RLCL) can redress these gender inequalities.[3]

Studies also show that typically officials get the husband to sign the contract for the family's land use allotments (Li, 1999), embodying the assumptions of the unitary household.

3. For instance, on the one hand the RLCL further limits the practice of land readjustments, especially on account of population change. On the other hand, under this law, a collective cannot reassign land that is allotted to a woman if she later marries out of the village, unless the collective in her marital village allots land to her. Similarly, a collective cannot reassign land allotted to a woman during her marriage, if she divorces, unless she receives a new allotment in the village where she lives after divorce (Brown, 2003).

The third source of land is potentially through the market. But in many countries rural land markets are limited, and, in any case, given women's fewer financial resources, their access to land either by purchase or lease is substantially more restricted than men's. Support from the state or from NGOs (non-governmental organisations) can enhance this access, say, through the provision of subsidised credit to groups of women,[4] but only to a limited extent.

Implications of Women's Unequal Access to Land

The social and economic implications of this gender inequality can be wide-ranging. Millions of women in Asia, Africa and Latin America depend critically on land for a livelihood. The process of agrarian change under which labour shifts from agriculture to non-agriculture has been slow and gender-biased. In many countries, more men than women have moved to non-farm jobs. Hence, a disproportionate number of those left dependent on land are women. In India today, relative to 53 per cent of male workers 75 per cent of female workers are in agriculture. And the gender gap is growing (Agarwal, 2003).

As more men shift to non-farm work, *de facto* female-headed households will also grow: estimates for India and Bangladesh already range between 20 per cent and 35 per cent. Many of these women bear growing responsibilities for running the farm, but can be seriously constrained by inadequate land rights.

Indeed a lack of effective land rights affects both welfare and productive efficiency. This is discussed in depth in my land rights book and recent papers (e.g. Agarwal, 1994; 2003), so I will only touch on some aspects here.

(i) Welfare: Consider first, the welfare effects. These can be both direct and indirect. There is ample evidence that a household's property status does not automatically define the well being of all its members. First, there is persistent gender inequality in the distribution of gains from household resources. In South Asia, this

4. The excellent work of the Deccan Development Society, an NGO working in Medak District in Andhra Pradesh, is a case in point (for details, see Agarwal, 2003).

impinges even on allocations for food and health care. Land solely in men's hands therefore does not guarantee female welfare.

Women without their own land also face high risks of poverty in case of desertion, divorce or widowhood. In parts of South Asia, often widows deprived of their property shares by family members are found doing wage labour on the farms of well-off brothers or brothers-in-law. In Bangladesh, widows living as dependents of male relatives are found to face much greater mortality risks than those heading their own households, and presumably owning some independent assets.

In China, similarly, in practice (even if not in law) divorced women tend to lose their land allotments in their husbands' villages and may not easily get land allotted for them in their parental village when they return there, leaving them effectively landless and poverty prone. This is especially likely following the above mentioned 1998 LML which restricts the frequency and scope of land readjustments. This is likely to have negative implications for women marrying into another village or returning to their birth villages on divorce or widowhood (Brown, 2003; Li, 2003).

Hence, in most countries, to the extent that women, even of propertied households, own no property themselves, their class position remains vicarious: a well-placed marriage can raise it, divorce or widowhood can lower it. Direct land access would provide a more certain means of welfare improvement and poverty reduction.

Second, land access would increase women's entitlement to family welfare. For elderly women, owning land can improve support from kin. As many elderly people say in India: "without property children do not look after their parents well" (Caldwell *et al.*, 1988: 191).

Third, land access has interlinked livelihood effects. For instance, it can improve credit and employment access. In South Asia, those with land are more likely to obtain credit and put it to viable use. In rural labour markets, those with land are found more likely to get employment and higher wages. Also, even a small plot is found to be a critical element in a diversified livelihood system. It can be used not just for crops, but also to grow trees for fruit or fuelwood, or fodder for animals, or to set up a vegetable garden or a micro-enterprise. The landed are found to get much better returns than the landless, even in rural non-farm activity.

Fourth, assets in women's hands can have inter-generational benefits. For a start, women are found to spend a much larger part of their earnings on family needs than men (Dwyer and Bruce, 1989). Several studies also show a positive link between children's welfare and the mother's assets. In Brazil, the effect on child survival probabilities was found to be almost 20 times greater when asset income accrued to the mother than when it accrued to the father (Thomas, 1990). In rural India, children were found more likely to attend school and get medical care if the mother had assets (Duraiswamy and Malathy, 1991; Duraiswamy, 1992). On children's education, similar results obtain for Bangladesh, Indonesia and Ethiopia (Quisumbing, 2003). It is no coincidence that in South Asia the best social indicators on health, education and fertility are found in Kerala in India and Sri Lanka in general—regions where women historically enjoyed notable rights in land and other property.

(ii) Efficiency: Welfare apart, in several contexts there can be efficiency gains from gender equal land access for several reasons. First there is the issue of incentives. These are found to matter not only at the household level but also at the intra-household level. In Kenya, for instance, the introduction of new weeding technology was found to raise crop yields on women's plots by 56 per cent—plots from which women controlled the output, but it raised yields only by 15 per cent on the men's plots where too women weeded but men got the proceeds (Elson, 1995). Second, there can be gender differences in preferences and efficiency of land use. In Burkina Faso, due to their choice of cropping patterns, women achieved much higher values of output per hectare on their own plots than did their husbands on theirs (Udry *et al.*, 1999). Similar research is needed in other regions.

(iii) Empowerment: Last but not the least, land is found to empower women socially. It adds to their voice, their sense of identity and their self-confidence. This is perhaps most graphically revealed in the voices of women themselves. In the 1970s Bodhgaya movement in Bihar, when landless women in two villages received land for the first time, after an extended land struggle in which they and their

households had participated, they movingly recounted how having land of their own had given them the strength to speak and walk (Alaka and Chetna, 1987). Women in China responded in similar ways when the Agrarian Reform Law of 1947 gave them separate land deeds for the first time, as described by Hinton (1972) (see also Croll, 1978).

Also, in our study based on a sample of some 500 households in Kerala, a colleague and I found a dramatically lower incidence of marital violence where the woman owned land or a house than where she owned neither (Agarwal and Panda, 2003).

Indeed in mainly agrarian economies there are many pointers that enhancing women's land access would help improve not just equity but also family welfare, production efficiency, and women's bargaining power and sense of empowerment.

Having said this, however, I need to emphasise four points. One, there is scope for more empirical analysis in different regions of the world on the welfare and efficiency links of women's property status. For instance, are the links between women's land access and incentives noted in Kenya also found in Asia or Latin America, where the pattern of family based farming is different? Are the links between the mother's assets and child survival found in Brazil as important in Africa or Asia? Does women's ownership of property serve as a deterrent to domestic violence in other regions as well? Two, although for illustration I have focused on land, my general purpose is to highlight the importance of property as such. In other contexts, a house may be as critical for women's economic and social security. Three, ownership confers only one form of right, but use rights or rights of control are also important. Indeed in public property, what matters is not ownership but managerial control—the ability to make rules, be it for government run enterprises or for the management of local common pool resources, such as forests.

Four, it appears imperative that countries formulating new property laws do not repeat old biases. In post-apartheid South Africa, in Central Asia, in Central and Eastern Europe, as well as in China, scholars are already expressing concern about the creation of new gender inequalities in land and other assets (see e.g. Walker,

2003, Kandiyoti, 2003, Verdery, 1996, Li, 2003). To move toward such equality often requires taking into account the social context within which the laws will be implemented, since many laws which might in principle be gender-neutral can become unequal due to pre-existing social biases.

Social Perceptions

The second form of gender inequality I explore now is ideological, as embedded in social perceptions and social norms. Although difficult to quantify and often hidden, these inequalities can affect economic outcomes for women in virtually every sphere, be it property rights, employment or intra-household allocations. And they remain understudied and under-theorised.

First consider perceptions. There can be, and often is, a divergence between what a person actually contributes, needs, or is able to do, and perceptions about her contributions, needs or abilities. In particular, a person's contributions and needs may be undervalued because of her gender or race, or both. This affects outcomes in the market, the family, the community and the state (for elaboration see Agarwal, 1997).

In the labour market, for instance, gender, like race, often defines perceptions about abilities. The work women do is often labeled as 'unskilled' and that which men do as 'skilled', even if the tasks require equal skill. Or women are perceived as having lesser ability or commitment; or as being supplementary earners and men as being the breadwinners. Such assumptions often underlie discriminatory hiring and pay practices. Women on account of their gender may thus be paid less than men with the same abilities, for the same tasks.

Perceptions also guide intra-family allocations. For example, who gets what is often justified by referring to a person's contributions or needs. But a person's contributions may be undervalued because of gender, or because the work is less 'visible'. Home based or unwaged work done mostly by women is often less valued than work which is more 'visible' in physical or monetary terms.

Female members would thus receive less than males because their contributions to the household are perceived as being less—what

Amartya Sen terms "perceived contribution response" (Sen, 1990). Equally, women and girls may receive less because they are seen as needing less—what I term "perceived need response" (Agarwal, 1997). Systematic undervaluation of women's contributions or needs in systems where these are important distributive principles can thus reinforce gender-related deprivation. And such undervaluation is not confined to developing countries. Research on American households 'indicates that women doing paid work have more bargaining power than housewives, because housework is culturally devalued (England and Kilbourne, 1990). Indeed, the Western feminist debate on 'wages for housework' arose from the recognition that unwaged work was 'invisible' and thus perceived as having little value.

Perceptions similarly influence community responses, and can hinder women's participation in collective activity. For instance, in my current research on forest management in the villages of India and Nepal, men typically exclude women from decision-making because they perceive them as making little contribution. Some characteristic responses are: "Women can't make any helpful suggestions." Or, "women are illiterate. If they come to meetings, we men might as well stay at home..." I found that often the men who said this were themselves illiterate. Hence, their response clearly had more to do with their 'perceptions' about gender differences in abilities rather than with 'actual differences' in abilities.

The government's public policy is similarly affected by perceptions. For instance, that governments transfer land almost solely to men, even when women are significant farmers, has much to do with perceptions about, rather than the universal fact of male responsibility and female dependency. Similarly, perceptions can make women's public presence invisible. For instance, in matrilineal Meghalaya, when I asked officials why even in this society where traditionally women had property claims, they did not allot land to women, I was told: "Women can't come to our office to fill out papers." Yet outside their windows numerous women traders were selling their wares!

Indeed perceptions underlie many assumptions in economic analysis and policy. They both constitute gender inequality in ideational terms and can lead to gender unequal material outcomes.

Social Norms

Like perceptions, gendered social norms embody an important form of ideological inequality. Conventionally few economists explicitly recognised the importance of social norms. Recent literature on social capital emphasises the positive side of social norms. Social norms are seen to reduce transaction costs and enhance economic efficiency.

But are all social norms good? Not at all. Many social norms can also have a 'dark' side, especially for women. Such norms enter almost every sphere of activity both within and outside the home. Within the home, norms define the gender division of labour and goods. For instance, everywhere norms define housework and childcare as mainly women's work, and in many rural areas this is also the case for firewood collection and cattle care. Hence, firewood or fodder shortages adversely affect women more than men. Domestic responsibilities also undermine women's ability to participate in public decision-making, which may involve lengthy meetings at inconvenient times. Hence, a common response by rural women is that they don't have time to sit around for several hours in a meeting in the middle of the day.

Again, in north India, norms determine that males should eat before females and/or get more and better quality food. This makes for gender differences in nourishment and growth (Agarwal, 1994). This is also the case in parts of China. For instance, Elizabeth Croll (2004: 145) quotes a young girl as saying: "My mom, no matter what happened, always considered my elder brother first and ignored me. At the table, she kept putting food into my brother's bowl and not mine, as if I were not her own child."

Social norms can similarly discourage women from asserting their rights, including in property. For instance, in northwest India social norms often dictate that a 'good' sister should forfeit her claim in parental property in favour of her brother.

Outside the household again, social norms restrict women's earning options by discouraging (or even preventing) them from working outside the home, limiting the range of tasks they may perform, placing double burdens of work on them, institutionalising lower wages for them, and so on. For instance, in many societies, norms restrict women's mobility and public interaction. In northern South Asia women of 'good character' are expected to avoid village spaces where men congregate. Hence while male farmers can sit in teashops and strike deals with other men for hiring labour or selling their crop, women farmers cannot do the same (Agarwal, 1994). Similarly, a fear of reputation loss or reprimand from families makes women uncomfortable going to public meetings, unless men invite them. As a group of women in north India told Britt (1993: 148): "The meetings are considered for men only. Women are never called" (see also Agarwal, 2001).

Social norms also govern female behaviour. This can range from high female seclusion to more subtle gendering, such as the expectation in many societies that women will be soft spoken and less visible. Women fish traders in parts of south India, if found haggling loudly, risk being dubbed as 'masculine' and losing social status. Women in public meetings often sit on one side or at the back of the meeting space where they are less visible and audible, making them less effective in public forums. Again, in most societies, norms dictate that women rather than men relocate on marriage or job shifts. In both India and China, it is the woman who is usually expected to leave her natal home and go to the husband's village or home after marriage.

Basically gendered social perceptions and social norms embody inequalities which are hidden, sometimes difficult to name, often impossible to quantify. Yet they centrally affect material outcomes for women, impinging both on their employment status and their property status.

Emergent Inequalities: Community Forestry

Gender inequalities in property endowments, norms and perceptions form the bedrock of pre-existing material and ideological disadvantage. And their persistence can create new inequalities. Consider examples from my current research on community forestry and collective action in India and Nepal, where I have done detailed fieldwork (see, Agarwal, 2000; 2001).

Forests and commons have always been important sources of basic needs such as fuelwood, fodder and other items for rural households. But because women often lack private property resources such as land and since social norms make firewood and fodder gathering mainly women's responsibility, their dependence on the commons is greater than that of men.

Traditionally rights in local forests were based on village citizenship. Access to these communal resources thus mitigated, to some degree, inequalities in private property. However, to reduce deforestation, today governments in many countries (including developed ones such as the Scandinavian countries and Canada) are involving communities in local forest management. Certainly, across South Asia today, CFGs (community forestry groups) are mushrooming. Most are state-initiated under the Joint Forest Management (JFM) programme launched in 1990, in which government and villagers share the costs and benefits from protection. There are over 64,000 JFM groups in India alone, in addition to self-initiated groups.

The JFM groups have a two-tier management structure: a GB (general body) which can draw members from the whole village and an EC (executive committee) of 9-15 persons. Both bodies, interactively, define the rules for forest use, the punishments for abuse, and the methods of protection and benefit distribution. Who has a voice in the GB and EC bears centrally on who gains or loses from these initiatives.

These groups were based on modern ideas of cooperation and participation and are meant to include all villagers, but effectively many have excluded significant sections such as women from their decision-making and main benefit sharing. For instance, in many

Indian states the criteria for GB membership is one person per household. Although technically gender neutral, it is usually men alone who join, since they are seen as the household heads.

But even where women can become members, few attend the meetings due to restrictive social norms and perceptions. Some women's groups explained this to me as follows (see, Agarwal, 2001):

Men don't listen. They feel they should be the spokespersons.

When we open our mouths, men shout us down.

Or take a male response: "I am a man, I attend the meeting. If I am prepared to make the female members of my family act according to what I say, why should they attend the meeting?"

These 'participatory exclusions' as I term them, that is, exclusions within seeming participative institutions, have other negative consequences. Without women's participation, the rules framed for forest use tend to take little account of their concerns. Typically CFGs ban forest entry. This affects women more than men. Men mostly use the forest for small timber for agricultural implements or house building—both are sporadic needs, and purchase is also an option. Women need the forests almost daily for firewood and fodder, and for most women firewood purchase is not an option both because they have limited control over cash, and because firewood is not easily available for purchase in the rural areas. Hence, women are the worst affected by the ban on entry.

In some regions women who before forest closure spent 1-2 hours for a headload of firewood ended up spending 4-5 hours after closure, and journeys of half a kilometer grew to 8-9 kilometers (Sarin, 1995). And although over time the forests have regenerated, the strict bans on extractions often continue. Firewood extractions are sometimes as low as 10-15 per cent of sustainable limits (Agarwal, 2002). Hence even several years into protection, firewood shortages persist in most cases. Paradoxically, as some poor women in one Indian village told me: "Earlier too there was a shortage but not as acute".

Most women have switched in varying degrees to using crop waste and some even use weeds as cooking fuel. These firewood substitutes take more time to ignite and keep alight, thus increasing cooking time. They also seriously increase smoke-related health risks, both for women and for infants playing in smoky kitchens.

Benefits from the regenerated resource are, however, largely male controlled. To begin with, any cash generated typically goes into a community fund controlled by men and mostly used for purposes from which women do not usually benefit, such as for purchasing rugs, drums or community utensils which the men use or lease out, or for travel to other villages, etc. Where benefits are distributed in cash or kind, entitlements are linked to membership and often also to contribution to protection. Thus non-member households, that are mostly the poor, are excluded, with the exclusion especially affecting poor women. Also, implicitly embodying the assumptions of a unitary household, benefit shares are on a household basis, so even if both spouses are members they get only one share.

Inequities arise too from the distributive principles followed. Distribution can be market determined (willingness to pay) or by contribution or need. While seemingly neutral, these principles have notable gender (and class) bias since people differ in their ability to pay or to contribute, or in their needs. In practice, distribution is usually by contribution and sometimes by sale. Sales adversely affect women more than men, since women have fewer financial means. But even distribution by contribution can prove inequitable where social norms bar women from making specific types of important contributions, such as doing patrol duty.

Not surprisingly, women especially the poor, often resent the closures. Some common responses are: "What forest? ... Since the men have started protecting it, they don't even allow us to look at it!" Or "the community forest belongs to the men, we own nothing." The new arrangements are thus creating a system of property rights in communal land which, like existing rights in privatised land, are strongly male centred and inequitable.

Here new gender inequality is being created through male control of public property and the rules that govern its use. All the rules are gender neutral on the surface. But they become unequal when filtered through the prism of pre-existing inequalities. Hence, membership by one person per household translates to one man per household. A lack of private property resources increases women's dependence on common pool resources. Both norms and perception restrict women's participation and voice in rule making and implementation. And much of this remains hidden, since most evaluations still deem the CFGs to be success stories of decentralised management and participative community involvement.

Reducing the Inequalities

How can the noted inequalities be reduced in both their material and ideological forms. A promising analytical framework for examining the prospects for change is that of bargaining. In terms of this framework, women's ability to change rules, norms, perceptions and property distribution in a gender-progressive direction would depend especially on their bargaining power with the state, the community and the family, as the case may be (for a detailed discussion, see Agarwal, 1997).

Traditionally economists have applied ideas about bargaining within the game-theoretic mode and with little attention to gender. Recent interest in intra-household gender dynamics has yielded some interesting formulations of bargaining models, but with little application to extra-household arenas or to qualitative factors. In my discussion, at least two types of shifts from this standard approach appear necessary: First, taking account of qualitative factors such as social norms and perceptions which have particular gender implications. Second, extending the framework to include non-household non-market arenas, such as the state and the community. Both extensions need a less restrictive formulation than that of a formal game-theoretic model. Here it is useful to distinguish between a bargaining 'approach' and formal models. A bargaining approach that is not constrained by the structure that formal modeling requires would allow us to more freely apply concepts such as bargaining power to new arenas; and also allow us a freer engagement with qualitative factors.

In the present discussion, applying the bargaining approach to interactions within three major arenas—the state, the community and the family—is especially relevant. It is relevant whether we are concerned with land rights, or changing social norms, or with community forestry. Consider community forestry by way of illustration.

Some CFG rules, such as eligibility to GB membership are made at the state level, others that relate to forest closure are made at the community level. And social norms, perceptions, and property endowments are constituted in all three arenas. What would affect women's ability to bargain effectively in these arenas? A key element would clearly be women's own attitude to seeking change, as discussed below.

Women's Attitudes or Socio-economic Constraints?

One influential view has been that a notable barrier to improving women's situation can be their lack of perception of self-interest. Nobel Laureate Amartya Sen, for instance, has argued that one reason for persistent gender inequality in intrafamily allocations in traditional societies is women's lack of perception of self-interest, or what he terms false perception and Marxists term false consciousness. He notes: "...acute inequalities often survive precisely by making allies out of the deprived. The underdog comes to accept the legitimacy of the unequal order and becomes an implicit accomplice" (Sen 1990: 126).

But the question is, how can one tell? Observationally, it is difficult to infer from people's overt behaviour whether they are conforming to an unequal order because they accept its legitimacy, or out of fear, or because they lack other options. Empirical work which probes women's covert responses, suggests that a lack of options is especially relevant.

There are numerous examples of women's 'everyday resistance' to intra-household inequalities. In Bangladesh, a number of studies have found many instances of rural women secretly trying to earn some cash by selling small amounts of rice without their husband's knowledge (Abdullah and Zeidenstein, 1982). In Nepal, rural women have been found treating themselves to their favourite dishes by cooking secret meals in the woods when fetching firewood, etc. Even American housewives in the early 20th century were found to pad bills to get extra cash (Zelizer, 1994). Everywhere women complain about their double work burden. Consider what some landless Indian women had to say. I quote (cited in Sharma, 1980: 207):

> We women stay at home and do back-breaking work even if we are ill or pregnant. There is no sick leave for us. But we do not have any money of our own and when the men come home we have to cast our eyes down and bow our heads.

Here the overt appearance of compliance ("cast our eyes down") does not mean women lack a perception of their best interest. Rather, it reflects a survival strategy stemming from constraints on their ability to overtly pursue those interests ("we do not have any money of our own"). Compliance should not be read as implying complicity.

The policy emphasis here should thus be less on making women realise they deserve better, and more on providing options that would help them do better. Women's noted resistance to inequality is often individual and covert. And there are inherent limitations to the effectiveness of covert resistance. To be effective agents of change often requires that women overtly challenge the formal structures that disempower them.

This returns us centrally to the question: how do we enhance women's bargaining power in different arenas—the family, the community and the state?

Enhancing Women's Bargaining Power

As I have discussed at length, both in a theoretical paper and in other work, the determinants of women's bargaining power could vary by context and could include their command over economic resources, support from external agents such as the State and NGOs, and enabling social norms and social perceptions (Agarwal, 1997; 2001). But at least two factors appear especially important for all three arenas and for different contexts: external agent support and women's group strength. For illustration, again consider community forestry.

Community forestry experience indicates that pressure from external agents such as NGOs, donors and key individuals can prove significant in changing the initial rules of entry at the state level. For example, several states in India have now made their membership rules more gender inclusive, say by instituting that one man and one woman should be members of the GB, rather than only one person per household. Here village women did not need to bargain explicitly for change. External agent support and the larger women's movement gave village women implicit bargaining power *vis-à-vis* the state (Agarwal, 2001).

However, bargaining with the community, for ensuring that women have more voice in CFG forums, is more difficult. Here again external agent support can help to some extent. For instance, some NGOs have used their bargaining power on women's behalf to insist that meetings would be held only if men invited the women. Women on being so invited, often turn up in strength. Not all regions, however, have external agents committed to gender equity. A larger and sustained impact needs women's own input.

Ground experience suggests that for women to have more voice in mixed forums and for them to challenge restrictive social norms, they would need, for a start: (i) a critical mass of vocal women and (ii) a sense of group identity.

In many villages the women I interviewed stressed: "without a good majority of women present it is impossible to express opinions." The importance of a critical mass has also been noted in the western context. A study of Scandinavian women politicians found that as women became a significant percentage (say 30% or more) in Parliament or local councils, there was less stereotyping and open exclusion by men, a less aggressive tone in discussions, a greater accommodation of family obligations in scheduling meetings, and more weight given to women's policy concerns (Dahlerup, 1988).

However, in South Asia, an additional step appears necessary, namely building women's self-confidence in public interactions and increasing their sense of group identity. One way by which this is being attempted in India is by women's credit and SHGs (self-help groups). Such groups are found to enhance women's self-confidence and collective identity. They also tend to improve male perceptions about women's capabilities and weaken restrictive social norms. The following responses from women I interviewed are fairly typical:

> Initially men objected to our going to meetings. But our women's group helped men understand better. When we women became united in the women's group, men saw we were doing good work. That also helped.

These factors also help in bargaining within the family. Again I quote from my interviews with rural women in India:

> There were one or two men who objected to their wives attending our meetings.... But when our women's association came to their aid, the men let their wives go.

> My husband feels I contribute financially, take up employment, obtain credit for the home. This increases his respect for me.

In fact, these experiences are common to many women's groups across South Asia, namely that women's collective strength and visible contributions, along with external agent support, can change at least some norms and perceptions. Of course dilemmas persist. Many separate women's groups remain unintegrated into mixed groups, and unable to change the gender dynamics of the latter. Also certain norms, such as the gender division of domestic work, and gender inequalities in property, are more difficult to alter. To have an impact on them, a deeper structural change would be needed.

Concluding Remarks

Gender inequality takes both material and ideological forms. A critical neglected dimension of the material form is embedded in who commands public and private property, especially land. Critical hidden dimension of the ideological form are social norms and perceptions. The interactive effects of these gender disadvantages can lead to new inequality creation.

Of course which type of property is central, or the specific nature of norms and perceptions, can vary by country and culture. But the fact of their importance everywhere is indisputable, as is the need to enhance women's bargaining power through collective action, for mitigating such inequalities. In academic terms, understanding how such collective action among women and among progressive groups can emerge and sustain is, I believe, a challenge both for gender economics and for the social sciences more generally. In political terms, there is a challenge here for forging new strategic alliances.

This returns us full circle to Malcolm Adiseshiah. Forging Alliances was a project he undertook with great success for almost 50 years, first at UNESCO and then in India. And in a globalising world, today perhaps more than at any other time, it is a project that needs to be carried forward with renewed vigour.

References

Abdullah, Tahrunnesa and Sondra Zeidenstein (1982). *Village Women of Bangladesh: Prospects for Change.* Oxford: Pergamon Press.

Agarwal, Bina (1994). *A Field of One's Own: Gender and Land Rights in South Asia.* Cambridge: Cambridge University Press.

———. (1997). "`Bargaining' and Gender Relations: Within and Beyond the Household", *Feminist Economics* 3(1): 1-50

———. (1998). "Widows versus Daughters or Widows as Daughters? Property, Land and Economic Security in Rural India", *Modern Asian Studies* 32 (1): 1-48.

———. (2000). "Conceptualizing Environmental Collective Action: Why Gender Matters", *Cambridge Journal of Economics* 24(3): 283-310.

———. (2001). "Participatory Exclusions, Community Forestry and Gender: An Analysis and Conceptual Framework", *World Development* 29(10):1623-48.

———. (2002). "Gender Inequality, Cooperation and Environmental Sustainability", Paper presented at a workshop on *Inequality, Collective Action and Environmental Sustainability.* Working Paper 02-10-058. New Mexico: Santa Fe Institute.

———. (2003). "Gender and Land Rights Revisited: Exploring New Prospects via the State, the Family and the Market", *Journal of Agrarian Change* 3(1&2): 184-224.

Agarwal, Bina and Pradeep Panda (2003). "Home and the World: Revisiting Violence", *Indian Express,* August 7. p.9.

Alaka and Chetna (1987). "When Women get Land: A Report from Bodhgaya", *Manushi* 40: 25-6.

Britt, Charla (1993). *Out of the Wood? Local Institutions and Community Forest Management in Two Central Himalayan Villages.* Ithaca: Cornell University. Monograph.

Brown, Jennifer (2003). "Protecting Women's Land Rights through RLCL Implementing Regulations". *mimeo.* Seattle, Washington DC: Rural Development Institute.

Caldwell, John H., P.H. Reddy and Pat Caldwell (1988). *The Causes of Demographic Change: Experimental Research in South India.* Wisconsin: The University of Wisconsin Press.

Croll, Elizabeth (1978). *Feminism and Socialism in China.* London: Routledge and Kegan Paul

———. (2000). *Endangered Daughters: Discrimination and Development in Asia.* London and New York: Routledge.

Deere, Carmen, Diana Deere and Magdalena de Leon (2001). *Empowering Women: Land and Property Rights in Latin America*. Pittsburg: Pittsburg University Press.

Dahlerup, Drude (1988). "From a Small to a Large Majority: Women in Scandinavian Politics", *Scandinavian Political Studies* 11(4): 275-98.

Duraisamy, P. (1992). "Gender, Intrafamily Allocations of Resources and Child Schooling South India", *Economic Growth Center Discussion Paper* No. 667. New Haven, CT: Yale University.

Duaraisamy, P. and R. Malathy (1991). "Impact of Public Programs on Fertility and Gender Specific Investment in Human Capital of Children in Rural India: Cross Sectional and Time Series Analyses", in T. Schultz (ed.), *Population Economics*. Vol. 7. Greenwich, CT: JAI Press. pp.157-87.

Dwyer, Daisy and Judith. Bruce (eds.) (1989). *A Home Divided: Women and Income Control in the Third World*. Stanford: Stanford University Press.

Elson, Diane (1995). "Gender Awareness in Modelling Structural Adjustment", *World Development* 23 (11): 1851-68.

England, Paula and Barbara Kilbourne (1990). "Markets, Marriages and other Mates: The Problem of Power", in R. Friedman and A. F. Robertson (eds.), *Beyond the Market: Rethinking Economy and Society*. New York: Aldine de Gruyter.

Hinton, William (1972). *Fanshen: A Documentary of Revolution in a Chinese Village*. Harmondsworth, Middlesex: Penguin Books Ltd

Kandiyoti, Deniz (2003). "The Cry for Land: Agrarian Reform, Gender and Land rights in Uzbekistan," *Journal of Agrarian Change* 3 (1&2): 225-56.

Li, Zongmin (1999). "Changing Land and Housing Use by Rural Women in Northern China", in I. Tinker and G. Summerfield (eds.), *Women's Rights to House and land: China, Laos, Vietnam*. Boulder and London: Lynne Rienner Publishers.

————. (2003). "Women's Land Tenure Rights in Rural China: A Synthesis". M*imeo*. Beijing: Ford Foundation.

Quisumbing, Agnes R. and John A. Maluccio (2003). "Resources at Marriage and Intrahousehold Allocation: Evidence from Bangladesh, Ethiopia, Indonesia, and South Africa", *Oxford Bulletin of Economics and Statistics* 65 (3): 283-328.

Sarin, M. (1995). "Regenerating India's Forest: Reconciling Gender Equity and Joint Forest Management", *IDS Bulletin* 26 (1): 83-91.

Sen, Amartya K. (1990). "Gender and Cooperative Conflicts", in Irene Tinker (ed.), *Persistent Inequalities: Women and World Development*. New York: Oxford University Press. pp. 123-49

Sharma, Ursula (1980). *Women, Work and Property in North-West India*. London and New York: Tavistock Publications.

Thomas, Duncan (1990). "Intra-household Resource Allocation: An Inferential Approach", *Journal of Human Resources* 25 (4): 635-63.

Udry, Christopher, John Hoddinott, Harold Alderman, and Lawrence Haddad (1995). "Gender Differentials in Farm Productivity: Implications for Household Efficiency and Agricultural Policy", *Food Policy* 20 (5): 407-23.

Verdery, Katherine (1996). *What was Socialism, and What Comes Next?* New Jersey: Princeton University Press.

Walker, Cherryl (2003). "Piety in the Sky? Gender Policy and Land Reform in South Africa", *Journal of Agrarian Change* 3 (1): 113-48

Zelizer, Viviana (1994). The Creation of Domestic Currencies", *American Economic Review, Papers and Proceedings* 84 (2): 238-42.

2

JANDHYALA B.G. TILAK

State, Households and Markets in Education

As a student I learned a great deal from Dr Malcolm Adiseshiah's writings and speeches, his editorials in the Madras Institute of Development Studies (MIDS) Bulletin and mid-term and annual plan reviews. I listened to a lecture of his for the first time in the Department of Economics, Andhra University. My teacher Prof Sarveswara Rao was able to get stalwarts to deliver special lectures to his students and colleagues. It was my good fortune to participate in a seminar in MIDS, an occasion which brought me in contact with Dr Malcolm Adiseshiah. I benefited from his comments on a paper which I presented on resource requirements for education in the context of the 1986 National Policy on Education.

Later I was excited that he reviewed my book, *Economics of Inequality in Education,* in the MIDS Bulletin. His generous praise acted as a spur to me in my work. I was especially pleased that he chose to describe the book as "a treatise in the economics of education." In the Education For All Conference (1993), he referred extensively to my presentation, indeed the only one to do so. And when I thanked him, he graciously said, "I am an admirer of your research."

Even though my personal contact with him was limited, he encouraged me with his long, detailed and incisive comments on my work. This was particularly so of my book *Education for Development in Asia,* the draft of which I had sent him.

Dr Malcolm Adiseshiah invited me to deliver the keynote address to the annual meeting of the Heads of Social Science Departments of South Indian Universities. I discovered later that this was one of the last letters he had signed. He passed away 10 days before the meeting was scheduled to be held. When I heard of his passing away, I called MIDS to enquire whether the meeting was postponed to be told that Dr Malcolm Adiseshiah would not have wanted any meeting postponed least of all on his account. That was the essence of the work culture he established in MIDS and I understand in UNESCO.

My paper is in the area of education, a subject dear to Dr Adiseshiah. My initial readings on the economics of education began under the guidance of Prof Sarveswara Rao and included the seminal works of Dr Malcolm Adiseshiah.

I

As the title suggests, I wish to focus my paper on three closely related aspects of the financing of education in India: increasing reluctance of the state to spend on education, compulsion to pay for education by families, which in my view, is mistakenly termed 'willingness to pay' and the role of the market.

The literature on economics of education has considered only two domains, individual and social, in the context of investment decision-making in education (e.g., Majumdar 1983). But in my view there are three domains, namely, individual (household domain), market domain and public (social) domain. Investment decision-making in these three domains is influenced by three different sets of considerations, and therefore I argue that it may not be proper to combine the household and market domains into one category and call it individual or private domain, as many do. Decision-making in the public domain ought to be guided by several considerations. Principal among them are: the public good, merit good, basic need, human rights, nature of education, its basic role in promoting equity and nurturing social values. Public approach to education also ought to be guided by human development perspectives. The longterm interests of society figure prominently in the decision-making process in public domain. Individuals, on the other hand, have a relatively short-term perspective. They are concerned, apart from acquisition of individual values, mainly with the maximisation of their life-time earnings or at the most their horizon may extend to that of family earnings as a whole. Decisions in the market domain are guided by even shorter term considerations, in fact the single most important consideration is profit maximisation. Other considerations such as philanthropy and charity were once important factors but they are virtually extinct now. Thus the distinction between the three domains is quite sharp, and hence they need to be separately analysed, recognising, however, at the same time, the interrelationship between them.

II

First, let us examine state spending on education, focusing on some important characteristics and a few long-term trends.

The state spends on education, in many traditional and modern societies, out of the general revenues, as education is regarded as:

(i) a public good, producing a huge quantum of externalities—social, economic, technological, political and cultural,

(ii) a social merit good, whose consumption is good for the individual as well as for society, even if the individual is not aware of it and hence, reluctant to consume it, and

(iii) as a human right and human development (and also as a freedom in itself, *á la* Amartya Sen).

Besides, education is favoured by the state as it promotes equality of opportunity. Imperfect capital markets reinforce the case for the state's role in this sphere, as does the fact that education is subject to scale economics. Education is also favoured as it is considered a pious responsibility of the state.

The pattern of spending on education during the post-independence period in India does not indicate that these concerns have been clearly recognised. During this period, there has been a significant increase in expenditure on education: in absolute terms it increased about 900 times from ₹ 55 crore in 1947 to ₹ 75,000 crore in 1999-2000. But in real prices it increased at a rate of growth of 6 per cent during the five decades (1950-51 to 1999-2000). The real rate of growth of per capita expenditure on education was 3.8 per cent; and in per pupil terms, it was just 2.4 per cent per annum.

The decadal trends in growth in public expenditure on education are indeed interesting to note. During the 1950s, a good beginning was made in the growth in expenditure on education; the decade of the 1960s was the most favourable period, as in many developing and developed countries. This might have been the effect of 'the human investment revolution in economic thought' initiated by Schultz (1961). The global disenchantment with education, partly attributable to the growth of educated unemployment on the empirical scene, and the emergence of screening and credentialism theses on the role of education on the theoretical front (e.g., Arrow, 1973; Spence, 1973) caused a setback for the growth of expenditure on education during the 1970s in the third world. India also has had a similar experience.

The 1980s marked the revival of faith in education. Its role in poverty reduction was recognised. 'Human resource (led) development' (Behrman, 1990) became a favoured theme by the mid-1980s, and education was regarded as an important component of human resource development. Expenditure on education increased during the 1980s at a reasonably high rate, particularly as compared with the preceding decade. Though there were severe cuts in allocations during the first half of the 1990s, following the introduction of economic reforms, especially stabilisation and structural adjustment policies (Tilak, 1996b), the rate of growth rose to some extent. This was partly due to the global recognition of education as not only a means of development, but as development itself, as theorised by human development specialists (e.g., Amartya Sen and Mahbubul Haq). But on the whole, during the last 50 years, the rate of growth in per student expenditure on education was a bare 2.4 per cent per annum, less than the Hindu rate of economic growth (Table 2.1).

Table 2.1

Annual Real Rate of Growth in Public Expenditure on Education in India

(Per cent)

	Total	*Per capita*	*Per Pupil*
1950s	10.17	8.12	2.56
1960s	4.78	2.44	4.03
1970s	4.37	2.20	0.98
1980s	7.47	5.19	3.28
1990-91/1999-2000	8.99	6.94	6.84
1950-51/1999-2000	6.03	3.75	2.44

Source: Based on *Analysis of Budgeted Expenditure on Education, Selected Educational Statistics and Education in India* (various years). New Delhi: Ministry of Human, Resource Development, Department of Education.

What have been the trends in the relative priority accorded to education after independence?

Share of Public Expenditure on Education in GNP (Gross National Product)

On the recommendation of the Education Commission (1966), the Government of India fixed in the 'National Policy on Education 1968' a target of investing 6 per cent of the national income in education from the public exchequer by 1986. Over the years, this proportion has increased remarkably from 0.6 per cent of GNP at the inception of planning (1951-52) to about 4 per cent by the end of the century, even though the growth has not been smooth. This may seem to be a remarkable increase (Figure 2.1). However, it needs to be underlined that the current ratio is much below:

(i) the requirements of the education system to provide reasonable levels of quality education to all the students presently enrolled,

(ii) the requirements of the system to provide universal elementary education of eight years for every child in the age-group 6-14, as universalisation of elementary education in a comprehensive sense includes universal provision of resources, universal enrolment and universal retention, and consequent growth in secondary and higher education (estimated to be about 8-10%),

(iii) the recommendations of the Education Commission (1966), the resolve made in the 'National Policy on Education 1968', reiterated in the 'National Policy on Education 1986', the revised Policy (1992) and the promises made by successive Prime Ministers repeatedly even from the ramparts of the Red Fort to invest six per cent of GNP in education, and

(iv) the proportion of GNP invested in education in many other developing, leave alone developed, countries of the world, including those in Africa.

Figure 2.1

Share of Public Expenditure on Education in GNP (%) (1951-52 to 2001-02)

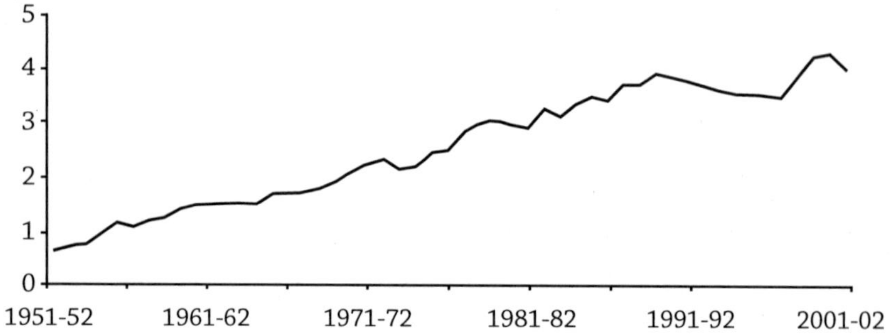

Source: Based on *Selected Educational Statistics 2001-02*. New Delhi: Government of India, Ministry of Human Resource Development, Department of Education.

It would be a stupendous task to reach a level of six per cent of GNP before the end of the Tenth Five Year Plan, i.e., by 2007, as promised by the Government of India recently, from the current level of about four per cent. The goal, originally set to be achieved about two decades ago, is being repeatedly postponed and may get further deferred, though it has little sanctity in view of the increasing needs of the education system.

Share of Expenditure on Education in the Total Budget

Perhaps a more important gauge of what is actually happening is revealed by the priority given to education in the budget. Considering the union and the state budgets together, government expenditure on education formed about 14 per cent of the total in 1970-71. Ever since, the ratio has tended to decline. It has been around 11 per cent in recent years. Even though the share of education in the union budget oscillated frequently, on the whole, it has increased from 1.6 per cent in 1967-68 to nearly 4 per cent by the end of the 1990s, and in the state budgets, it has been around 20 per cent. The total appears to be stabilising around 10 per cent—declining from 14 per cent in the early 1970s/1980s (Figure 2.2).

Figure 2.2

Expenditure on Education as % of Total Government Expenditure (1967-68 to 2000-01)

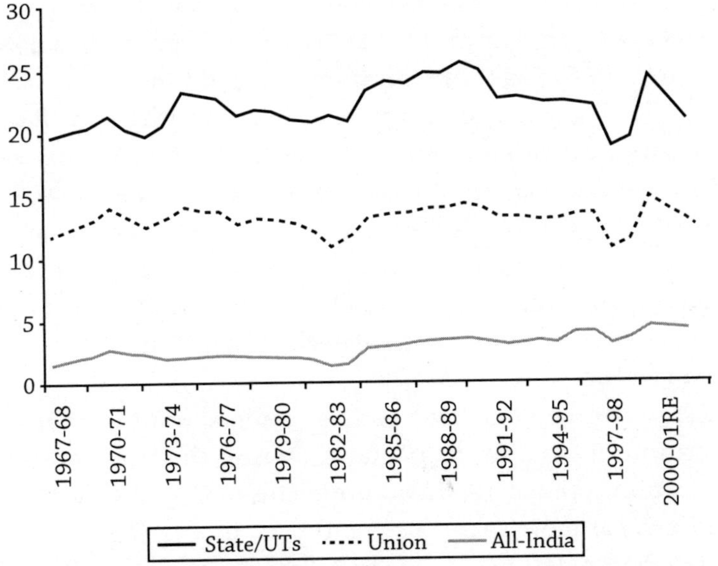

Source: *Based on Analysis of Budgeted Expenditure on Education*. New Delhi: Ministry of Human Resource Development, Department of Education.

With respect to the share of education in total government expenditure, India fares very poorly in comparison not only with advanced countries, but also some of the poorer ones. India has been spending only 11 per cent on education out of total government (union and state) expenditure, compared to more than 15 per cent in many advanced countries (1995-1997). The corresponding figure was above 20 per cent in several rich and poor, and small and big countries (UNDP, 2003).

In terms of these two indicators of the relative priority accorded to education, *viz.*, the share in GNP and the share in total government expenditure, India fared better during the 1980s. But after economic reforms were introduced in the beginning of the 1990s, the shift has been away from the education sector. Public finances for education began to be affected by severe squeezes.

Expenditure on Education in Five Year Plans

Five Year Plans are an important instrument of development strategy adopted by independent India. The Plan outlays set new directions for further development, and hence they assume importance, though they are small in size compared to huge non-plan expenditures in the case of education. Expenditure on education in the Five Year Plans has shown a rapid rise since the First Five Year Plan. But its relative importance has declined, from 7.9 per cent in the First Five Year Plan, to 2.7 per cent in the Sixth Five Year Plan. It was only during the Seventh Five Year Plan, and later in the Eighth and the Ninth Five Year Plans that this declining trend was reversed. The share in the Ninth Five Year Plan was quite high, above 6 per cent; but it was still much less than the proportion allocated in the First Plan (Figure 2.3).

There are three important phases in the allocation of resources to education in the Five Year Plans. During the first three Plans, the allocation to education as a proportion of total Five Year Plan expenditure was more than 5 per cent. Even though it declined in the Second Plan, the decline was immediately checked in the Third Plan. This phase represents the enthusiasm of the government immediately after independence to allocate higher outlays for education; the average expenditure during the three Plans was 6.9 per cent. The second phase, consisting of the Fourth, Fifth and the Sixth Plans, was characterised by a consistent decline in the relative share of education (to an average of 3.7%). This is indeed surprising as this is the period that followed the famous Kothari Commission Report on 'Education and Development' that emphasised, *inter alia,* the need for expansion of education for development. The '1968 National Policy on Education' for the first time accepted the 'investment' nature of education. But all these have had little effect on allocation of public resources to education. The Seventh, Eighth and Ninth Five Year Plans form the third phase when efforts were made to check the declining trend and to substantially increase the allocation to education. This phase of the post-1986 policy period reflects the positive effect of the policy, with the average of the three Plans increasing to 4.9 per cent. Whether

Figure 2.3

Expenditure on Education in Five Year Plans (% of Total)

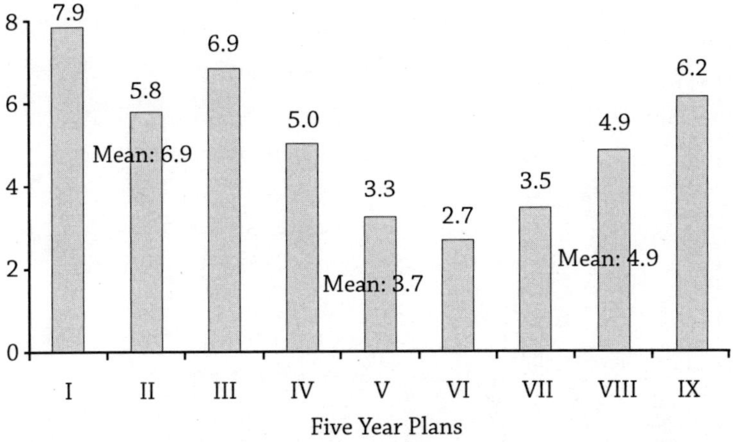

Source: Based on *Analysis of Annual Plan, Education Sector*. New Delhi: Government of India, Planning Commission, Education Division (various years).

the beginning of the century and the Tenth Five Year Plan mark a continuation of the third phase or a new phase is yet to be seen.

The relative allocations to all levels—elementary, secondary and higher education—as a proportion of total plan expenditures[1] have experienced a decline. However, there has been some attempt to increase expenditure on elementary education after the 'National Policy on Education (1986)' was formulated. The share of elementary education in plan expenditure has decreased, on the whole, from 4.3 per cent to 3.2 per cent from the First to the Ninth plan. It was at the lowest in the Fifth and Sixth Plans at a ratio of 0.8 per cent. The decline was less pronounced in the case of secondary education. For higher education, the share which was a meagre 0.7 per cent in the First Plan actually went down to 0.3 per cent in the Eight Plan (Figure 2.4) !

Figure 2.4

Share of Elementary, Secondary and Higher Education in the Total Five Year Plan Expenditure (%)

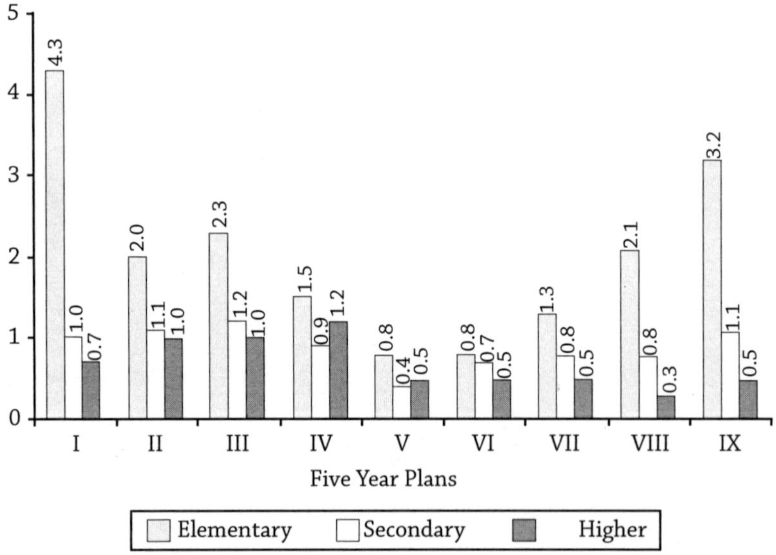

Source: Based on *Analysis of Annual Plan, Education Sector*. New Delhi: Government of India, Planning Commission, Education Division (various years).

National and more importantly international pressures have helped boost the tardy growth in the allocations to elementary education in recent years. International aid also came in handy. In fact, much of the growth in the allocation to elementary education is contributed by external aid and hence, it can be described as 'aid-led growth' (Tilak, 1999a). But secondary, and more so higher education, has suffered very severely. One notices a significant decline in public expenditures on higher education during the 1990s. Public expenditure on higher education per student declined in real terms by 27 per cent between 1990-91 and 1996-97; it has marginally increased in later years, according to revised/budget estimates, but the increase may not be sustained. The decline might continue.

A steep decline is noticeable in public expenditure on various items in higher education, such as scholarships—an important measure to promote equity. As a proportion of the total expenditure on higher education of the union government, the amount spent on scholarships that was always small declined further, from about 0.5 per cent to 0.25 per cent between 1990-91 and 2000-01. In absolute terms also one finds a similar decline in real prices.

To sum up, the state's reluctance and unwillingness to invest in education is attested by several indicators:

- real growth in total per capita and per student expenditure,
- trends in relative share of expenditure on education in the budget and in Five Year Plan outlays,
- the relative shares of various levels of education in total Five Year Plan expenditures, and
- public expenditure on higher education.

Even as a proportion of GNP, expenditure on education has not shown significant increases. It is rather reluctantly increasing at a snail's pace; currently it is below the six per cent norm, which was the target set for achievement nearly two decades ago.

The state's unwillingness to invest in education is also clear from the policy statements occasionally made, particularly with respect to, but not necessarily confined to, higher education. For example, following the recommendations of the committees set up by the University Grants Commission (UGC, 1993) and the All India Council for Technical Education (AICTE, 1994) (Dr Justice Punnayya Committee and Dr Swaminadhan Committee respectively), institutions of higher education were required to raise at least 20 per cent of the required resources through fees and other sources, implying that government subsidies would be restricted to less than or about 80 per cent of the requirements. Secondly, the Ministry of Finance (1997) in its paper on "Government Subsides in India", has stated that subsidies to higher education would be gradually reduced to about 50 per cent. Thirdly, when reformulating the student loan programme in the early 1990s, the government argued that loan programmes would be reorganised so that with the recovery of loans, higher education would eventually become self-financing. In case of school education, it has preferred expansion of low cost and low quality alternative systems of primary education and literacy to the formal school system. Also revealing is the preference for recruitment of untrained, under-qualified and poorly remunerated teachers to those who are fully qualified and reasonably well paid. Lastly, and tellingly, there is the encouragement and support given to private educational institutions with the almost stated objective of saving public resources. It is difficult not to infer from these the increasing unwillingness of the state to allocate budgetary resources to education.

The question is: Why is the government unwilling to spend on education?

First, there is the general belief that public expenditure has no significant impact upon the development of education, and that its effects on literacy, enrolment rates and achievement levels in school are not pronounced (World Bank, 2003).

But this is not necessarily true. As I have tried to show elsewhere (Tilak, 1999b), government expenditure on education per capita is the second most important factor (after number of teachers) for the development of education. As budget expenditure on education per capita increases, the rate of attendance of children in schools tends to increase systematically and significantly. The coefficient of correlation is as high as 0.8 (Figure 2.5). Similar strong relationships are found with expenditure on education and other indicators of educational development, including the aggregate index of education.

Secondly, the government's reluctance to spend on education is ascribed to the underdevelopment of the economy. One of the most widely held beliefs is that economically poor societies obviously cannot spend much on education and so must be the case in India.

Statistical evidence does not support such a presumption.

(i) There exists no statistically clear relationship between the level of economic development of states (state domestic product [SDP] per capita) and their level of spending on education as per cent of SDP. For instance, economically poor states like Bihar and Assam spend a higher proportion of their income on education, and relatively more prosperous ones like Haryana and Maharashtra allocate smaller proportions (Table 2.1).

Figure 2.5

Public Spending on Education and School Attendance in Major Indian States

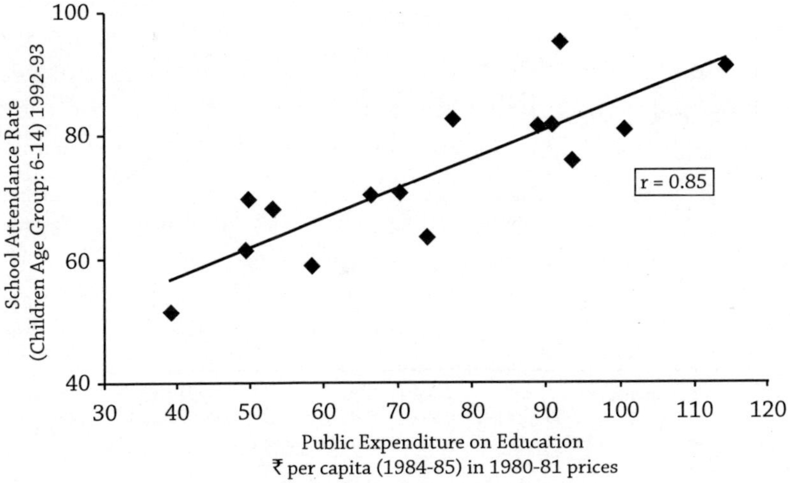

Source: Tilak (1999b).

(ii) That the levels of SDP vary and hence proportions of SDP do not mean much, may not be tenable, as the weak relationship between economic development and education expenditure holds true with respect to absolute levels of expenditures as well. In other words, this relationship is not confined to the relative proportion allocated to education and SDP per capita. It holds true with respect to SDP per capita and the expenditure on education per capita, and many other appropriate indicators as well. The relationship between SDP per capita and expenditure on education per capita is not significant and systematic. For example, among the 18 major states in India, Himachal Pradesh ranks 8th with respect to SDP per capita in 1997-98, but ranks at the top in its spending on education in 1998-99; so is the case of Tripura which ranks 12th in SDP per capita but spends the second largest amount on education; and the evidence of Kerala is well known: spending the third largest amount on education, it ranks 10th with respect to SDP per capita. The richer states like Punjab and Haryana (ranking respectively 2nd and 3rd in SDP per capita) rank poorly (7th and 8th respectively) with respect to

Table 2.2

SDP per capita and Expenditure on Education

SDP per capita, 1997-98	Education as Per cent of SDP (1998-99): High	Medium	Low	Very Low
High	Nil	Nil	Tamil Nadu Punjab Gujarat	Haryana Maharashtra
Medium	Himachal Pradesh	Nil	Karnataka West Bengal	Andhra Pradesh
Low	Tripura	Rajasthan Kerala	Nil	Nil
Very Low	Bihar Assam	Orrisa Uttar Pradesh	Nil	Madhya Pradesh

Source: Based on *Analysis of Budgeted Expenditure on Education and Selected Educational Statistics*. New Delhi: Ministry of Human Resource Development, Department of Education; and *Economic Survey*. Ministry of Finance, Government of India (relevant years).

spending on education per capita. West Bengal figures almost at the bottom (16th among the major states) with respect to spending on education, but ranks 6th with respect to SDP per capita. These are not exceptions; on the contrary, they seem to represent the general rule.

(iii) There also does not exist any significant systematic relationship between the rate of growth of national income per capita and the rate of growth of expenditure on education per capita in real terms. The simple coefficient of correlation between the two is 0.2, when estimated on the all India time series data from 1950-51 and 2000-01 (Figure 2.6).

But an increase in GNP per capita might lead to an increase in expenditure on education per capita. Government expenditure on education per capita was consistently more elastic to GNP per capita during the first four decades after independence, though the coefficient gradually declined in value over the years. The coefficient of elasticity was 5.4 in the 1950s, which declined to less than unity (0.8) by the 1990s (1990-91 to 1996-97).[2] The economic reforms introduced in the beginning of the 1990s seem to have affected the relationship considerably.

Figure 2.6

Real Growth in GNP Per Capita and Expenditure on Education Per Capita

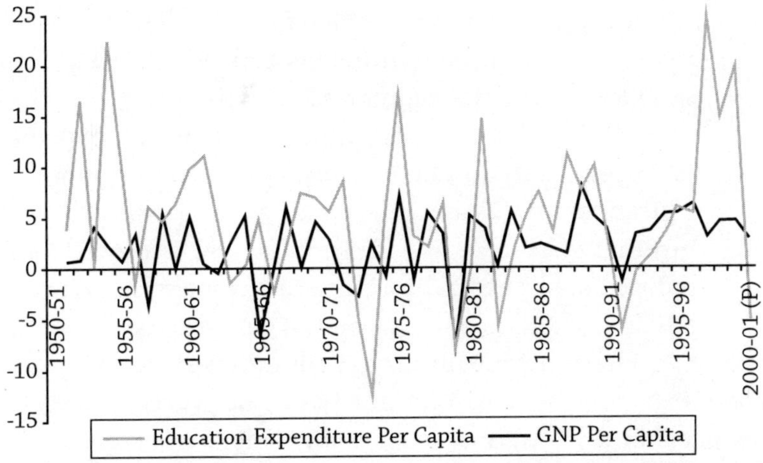

Source: Based on *Analysis of Budgeted Expenditure on Education, and Selected Educational Statistics*. New Delhi: Ministry of Human Resource Development, Department of Education (relevant years); and *Economic Survey*. Ministry of Finance, Government of India.

All this makes it clear that both at the national and state levels' economic conditions (as reflected in growth of GNP and the like) do not have a determining effect on allocation to education. Earlier, I have attempted to show that allocations for education by the Finance Commission and the Planning Commission to various states are also not systematically influenced by any meaningful criteria (Tilak, 1989). Allocations by the Planning Commission might be expected to favour educationally backward states in order to reduce regional disparities. This is, after all, one of the objectives of the plans. Awards of Finance Commissions, on the other hand, might be expected to tilt towards educationally advanced states, since these are mainly meant for maintenance of the system; and larger and more developed educational systems would require more resources. Yet, neither set of allocations can be explained with reference to stock or flow indicators on education development or by other economic factors.

Logically, the conclusion is that low levels of state expenditure on education are not due to economic constraints. Nor are they influenced by the level of educational development and corresponding needs. The explanation for the government's unwillingness to invest in education would perhaps lie in misconceptions such as that:

- education is not an imperative for economic development, indeed that economic miracles can be achieved without significant educational progress,
- even if education is important for development, higher levels of expenditure do not necessarily improve a population's educational status and
- internal efficiency in education can be improved through reduced public expenditure and cost recovery measures.

In addition, there is the occasional remark that the state is reluctant to increase expenditure on education since the quality of education is poor, teachers do not teach, no worthwhile learning takes place in schools, and colleges and universities perform only a baby-sitting role, etc. It is arguable that these are quite likely the consequence of under-funding. They cannot constitute a case for withdrawal of public resources. A 'conspiracy theory' is also advanced suggesting that elite governments do not want the masses to be educated and are therefore reluctant to invest in it. The most likely explanation for the state's unwilliingness to invest in education lies in the lack of 'political will' to accord due priority to education (Drèze and Sen, 2002).

III

Let us turn to households' willingness to pay for education.

'Willingness to pay' has gained ground in the context of growing budgetary cuts on education. It is strongly urged by many that this willingness should be tapped to the maximum so that the burden on the exchequer is reduced. Household spending on education is justified on three grounds:

(i) governments lack adequate resources to finance education and therefore households have to contribute at least partly towards the cost,
(ii) household expenditure through fees will improve the system's efficiency and

(iii) household spending reflects willingness and ability to pay for education and this should be tapped in full.

These grounds are resisted by counter arguments resting on the following:

(i) household expenditures, more appropriately payment of fees and other user charges, militate against the letter and spirit of free and compulsory education as enshrined, for example, in the Constitution of India and the Convention of the Rights of Children (1948),

(ii) such expenditures perpetuate inequities since they tend to vary directly with household incomes,

(iii) high levels of expenditure may compel the poor not to opt for schooling and hence the demand for education will be distorted,

(iv) household expenditures are actually a reflection of the state's inability and inefficiency in providing education and

(v) household expenditure on education is inconsistent with the nature and philosophy of education and reduces it to a 'commodity' that can be bought.

However, household expenditures on education in India are substantial and they have increased over the years. According to the 'National Accounts Statistics', household expenditure (private final consumption expenditure) on education in India was of the order of ₹ 15.7 thousand crore in 1996-97. This is indeed sizeable, forming more than 1 per cent of GDP (gross domestic product). It increased nearly 100 times in 36 years from ₹ 159 crore in 1960-61 to ₹ 15.7 thousand crore in 1996-97! In real terms, the growth has been 7 times between the same periods and in per capita terms the real increase has been 3.3 times.

The overall rate of growth in household expenditure on education per capita in real prices was 3.4 per cent per annum during 1950-51 to 1996-97, but the growth has not been smooth over the decades. While the first two decades after the inception of planning, i.e., the 1950s and the 1960s registered a reasonably high rate of growth, the economic problems of the 1970s in terms of high inflation, adversely affected total household budgets and allocations to education.

Accordingly the rate of growth was as low as 1.2 per cent per annum in the 1970s. Though in the 1980s there was some reversal in the trend, the situation in the 1990s was not favourable to education. During 1990-91 to 1996-97, the real rate of growth has been only 2 per cent per annum (Table 2.3).

Table 2.3

Rate of Growth in Household Expenditure on Education

	Total	*Per capita*
1950s	7.1	5.1
1960s	9.1	6.8
1970s	3.5	1.2
1980s	4.8	2.6
1990s*	3.9	2.0
1950-51-1996-97	5.6	3.4

Note: *: 1990-91-1996-97.

Source: Based on *National Accounts Statistics*. (various years) New Delhi: Department of Statistics, Planning Commission. *Secondary Source*: Tilak (2000).

Analyses of the 42nd and the 52nd rounds of the National Sample Survey data that refer respectively to 1986-87 and 1995-96 (Tilak, 1996a; 2002b) and the National Council of Applied Economic Research (NCAER) surveys on human development (Tilak, 2002a) highlight certain interesting features relating to household expenditure on education. We shall take note of a few of them.

Households incur huge expenditure on education of their children. According to the National Sample Survey (1995-96), on average a household has to spend ₹ 500 per child per annum on primary education. For upper primary education, the expenditure increases to about ₹ 900; it further increases to ₹ 1577 in secondary schools and to ₹ 2923 in higher education. These figures refer to 1995-96. A quick comparison with the earlier set of estimates shows that there has been a steep increase in the levels of household expenditures between 1986-87 and 1995-96. The expenditure on primary education per student in 1986-87 varied between ₹ 84 in government schools in rural areas and ₹ 569 in private schools in urban areas (Table 2.4).

Table 2.4

Average Annual Household Expenditure (₹) per Student (Age Group: 5-24), 1995-96

	Rural	*Urban*	*Total*
Primary	297	1149	501
Middle	640	1529	915
Secondary	1180	2219	1577
Higher	2294	3304	2923
All	570	1686	904

Source: National Sample Survey Organisation. Secondary Source: Tilak (2000).

Household expenditure on education is highly elastic to income levels. Rich households spend more than low-income households on education. According to the 52nd round of the National Sample Survey, average household expenditure of the top expenditure quintile on education is about six times that of the bottom expenditure quintile.

The 'wealth effect', defined simply as a ratio between the expenditure of high and low income households minus one, is more pronounced in private schools than in government schools. Further, more interestingly, the wealth effect is quite pronounced in primary education and declines with the level of education (Figure 2.7). In a sense, the present system of financing seems to be more equitable in higher education than primary education. This pattern may significantly change with the rapid growth in high fee charging private colleges. Consequently, the wealth effect could become equally, if not more pronounced in higher education.

Figure 2.7

Household Expenditure on Education: Wealth Effect in Education

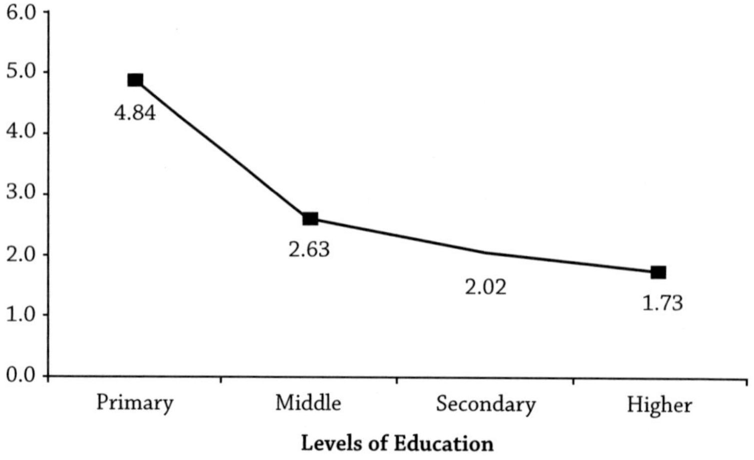

Source: Based on *National Sample Survey*. *Secondary Source*: Tilak (2000).

As a proportion of household income, poor households spend consistently more than the rich. Bottom income households have to spend, according to the NCAER survey (Tilak, 2002a), 6.9 per cent of their total income on education and this proportion declines consistently with increasing levels of household income, as one would expect. It is only 0.6 per cent of household income that top income households have to spend on the education of children. This holds for all groups in the population—caste groups including Scheduled Castes, Scheduled Tribes and others, religious groups including Hindus, Muslims and Christians, boys and girls, and among different land owning groups. Further, it is found to hold in all states with almost no exception. The poor households have to spend a larger proportion of their meagre incomes on education than richer households.

The coefficient of elasticity of household expenditure on education to total income (in fact, expenditure) of the households between 1950-51 to 1996-97 is positive, and greater than 1; it is 1.5. These are based on 'National Accounts Statistics'. It means that household expenditures on education are elastic to household income. A 1 per cent increase in total household income would result in a 1.5 per cent increase in household expenditures on education. When the figures are considered in per capita terms, the coefficient of elasticity is much higher at 2.1. If household income per capita increases by 1 per cent, household expenditure on education per capita increases by 2.1 per cent. This suggests that household expenditures on education change considerably and positively to changes in household income (or expenditure) levels.

In terms of the coefficient of elasticity of household expenditures on education per capita to total household expenditure per capita, the 1950s were a good decade (with the coefficient being 3.0), the decade of the 1960s being the best period, with the highest coefficient of elasticity (5.9); 1970s the worst period (the coefficient was 0.24) and 1990s not much better than the 1970s (the value of the coefficient was 0.78); during the decade of the 1980s, it was marginally better (1.0). The spiraling inflation and other economic problems of the 1970s seem to have weakened the relationship between household income (or total expenditure) and expenditure on education over the decades. More basic needs like food and other items might have been given higher priority than education and accordingly increase in incomes might not have caused increase in expenditures on education to any noticeable extent. The relationship did not improve much during later periods.

The values of the coefficients of elasticity of household expenditures on education to household income (or expenditure) are higher than the coefficients of elasticity of government expenditures on education to total government expenditure. This means that households respond to education needs more favourably than governments. A one per cent increase in household incomes would result in a more than proportionate increase in expenditure on education, which is much higher than the response of government expenditure to a similar one per cent increase in income (or total expenditure) of the government.

Average household expenditure on education per student in a state shows some relationship to the SDP per capita. Economically prosperous states/union territories like Delhi, Chandigarh, Punjab and Haryana figure at the top of the list in household expenditure on education per student, with backward states like Madhya Pradesh, Assam and Bihar at the bottom (Figure 2.8). For example, households in economically advanced states spend more than the households in economically poor states. The simple coefficient of correlation between SDP per capita and household expenditure on education in 1995-96 was 0.6. Household expenditure is also inversely related to poverty level in the state, the coefficient of correlation being –0.45.

Quite strikingly, according to the 1995-96 *National Sample Survey*, there are no significant differences in household expenditures on education by gender, i.e., between girls and boys (Table 2.5). In fact, except for a small difference at the primary level, the differences favour girls in other levels of education. This is particularly true in rural areas and for India as a whole. In urban areas, the differences are against girls in all levels of education but are marginal. Perhaps the importance of girls' education is being increasingly recognised by the households; and accordingly they do not discriminate against girls in spending on their education—a welcome feature.

Why are households 'willing' to spend on education? In general, employment and economic returns, including not only employment related earnings but also factors like dowry, may exercise considerable influence on investment decisions by households in education. This is particularly true with respect to higher education. But why do households spend even on elementary education that is (expected to be) provided free by the state? Households are found to be spending considerable amounts on their children's primary education. As noted earlier, according to the National Sample Survey (1995-96) estimates, on average a household has to spend ₹ 500 per year per child on acquiring primary education, and about ₹ 900 on upper primary education. Even poor households (bottom quintile) spend nearly ₹ 200 on primary education per annum per child. Households from even lower socio-economic backgrounds—scheduled castes (SCs), scheduled tribes (STs), households whose primary occupation is not high in the occupational hierarchy—all spend considerable amounts on acquiring education, specifically primary education. About 30 per

Table 2.5

Household Expenditure on Education per Student, by Gender, 1995-96

	Boys	Girls	All
Primary	507	494	501
Middle	904	933	915
Secondary	1552	1619	1577
Higher	2879	2995	2923
All	919	882	904

Source: National Sample Survey. Secondary Source: Tilak (2000).

Figure 2.8

Household Expenditure on Education per Student, by States (₹), 1995-96

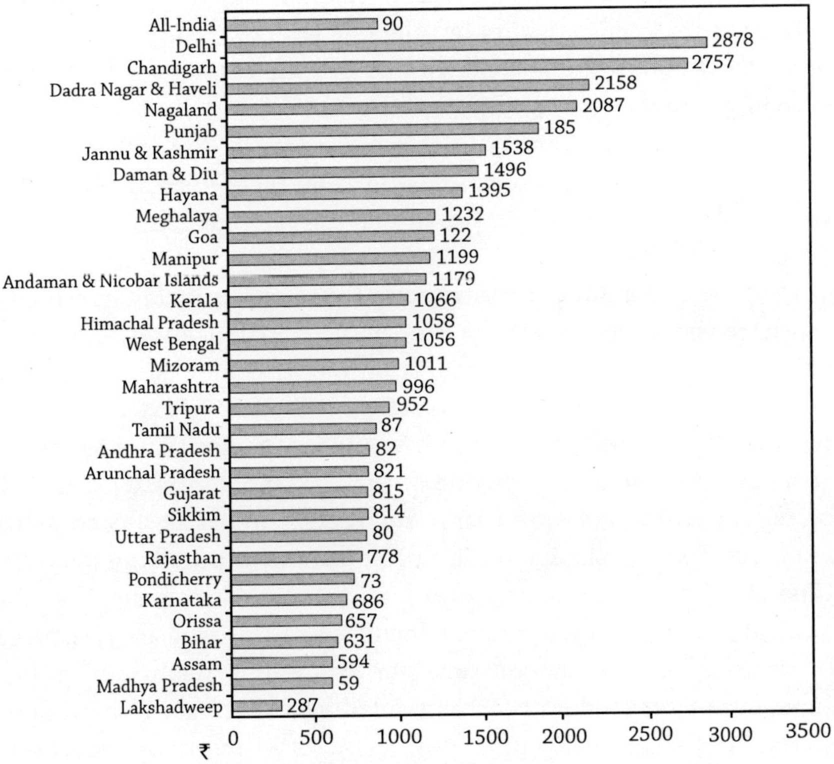

Source: National Sample Survey. Secondary Source: Tilak (2000).

cent of the expenditure on primary education goes in the form of fees—tuition and other fees, one-fourth on uniforms, another one-fourth on books and stationery, and a sizeable amount on private coaching—all of which are expected to be provided by the state. Apart from free education, learning/instructional materials like textbooks, stationery and other incentives such as uniforms and noon meals are received free only by a small fraction of the students.

In addition to the expectation of attaining a higher social status, households may also spend on education to ensure that their children others in the race for ranks. Rich households tend to 'buy' quality education for their children, which is not affordable by the poor households. This means that the households perceive perhaps rightly that public resources are not adequate to ensure 'good quality' education for their children. 'Good' quality may be defined at the bottom as reasonable quality or tolerable level of quality. Households tend to equate, in the absence of any other information, high costs with high quality.

What I wish to argue is, it is not necessarily the willingness of the households, but the compulsion they feel which makes them spend on education. Households may feel compelled to invest in education, if public efforts, as reflected in the quantity and quality of physical and human infrastructure (teachers) available in schools, are perceived to be inadequate. Under such circumstances, even poor households would spend on education out of compulsion. Therefore the poorer the quality of infrastructure and other facilities in public schools, *ceteris paribus,* the higher would be the level of expenditure of households on education. The quality of school infrastructure can be measured in terms of a large number of indicators, such as its availability within the habitation or at least within walking distance, type of school buildings, quality and number of teachers, etc. The quantity and quality of school facilities can as well be measured in terms of public expenditure per student. A decline in public expenditure per student is accompanied by an increase in household expenditure on education. If the facilities in public schools were better, then families would perhaps not feel the need for incurring expenditure. Therefore I argue that it is wrong to suggest that families are willing to spend on education; they are in fact compelled to do so. The 'willingness to pay' is also measured in terms of the amount of fees paid to the schools and other expenditures incurred by households. This may reflect the ability to pay to some extent; in some cases, it may not even represent the true ability to pay (as the expenditures might have been incurred by borrowing and even mortgaging their small fixed assets or their own future earnings), but this does not necessarily reflect 'willingness to pay.'[3]

IV

Now about markets in education.

The private sector in education is not a new phenomenon in India. Role of private sector in education is favoured essentially to meet `excess' and also 'differentiated' demand for education. Excess demand refers to the demand unmet by the public sector institutions. Differentiated demand refers to demand for a particular type and quality of education (e.g., religious education, English medium education, high quality education, etc.), different from what is provided in public institutions. I have argued elsewhere (Tilak, 1994) that, in India, differentiated demand might explain growth in private education at school level, whereas excess demand may be the main factor for growth in private higher education. The private sector is also favoured by the government, as it can tap the untapped resources available in the society for the development of education and correspondingly the government can reduce its expenditures.

Many other claims that are made in this context, such as that the private sector will contribute to increase in access, quality and equity in education, etc., are, to my mind, to a great extent untenable and even false. In an international comparative analysis, I have tried to explore many of these and related myths on private education (Tilak, 1991).

The private sector founded several schools and colleges in India before and immediately after independence. The motives of the private sector of the 1950s and the 1960s were to a considerable extent, philanthropy, charity and education development to meet excess and to some extent, differentiated demand. Many of the institutions established during this period willingly subjected themselves to state control and regulation in all respects and even accepted state financing with all its conditions. Profit was not the main consideration. Hence, they cannot be equated to the private institutions that have sprung up in the last quarter century, and more particularly after marketisation of education became the buzzword. That the earlier kind of private institutions—state-aided private institutions that can be aptly described as pseudo private institutions, led to distortions in allocation of public resources is a different matter (Tilak, 1994).

Private institutions born in the era of marketisation are solely guided by the market principle, *viz.*, profit maximisation. They are also self-financing and tend to defy or at least resist state regulation of any kind, necessitating judicial intervention very often. Student fees, charged not necessarily in proportion to costs, is often the only source of funds for such institutions. Investment by the private management is very limited and, if any, is confined to capital investments in the initial years, which are also recovered in a short period.

The growth of this modern private sector in education is a response to the lack of a clear government policy on the role of the state and markets in education. The historic judgment of the Supreme Court in 1992 that practically banned capitation fee colleges, stating that capitation fee is "patently unreasonable, unfair and unjust", was followed by another historic judgment in 1993 that paved the way for the growth of the very same capitation fee colleges, under the name of self-financing colleges. Elaborate mechanisms were developed by the state that helped in the proliferation of self-financing fee colleges. For instance, in Andhra Pradesh, such colleges have increased in number from almost nil in the early 1980s to 450 by 1996-97 (Table 2.6). Today such colleges offer not only engineering and management education, but also arts and sciences and outnumber public institutions, by several times. In fact, in absolute numbers, and also as a proportion of the total, government colleges turn out to be negligible. For example, in Andhra Pradesh, there were 95 private self-financing engineering colleges, compared to 11 government colleges; similarly there were 303 self-financing medical colleges, compared to 25 government colleges (2000-01) (Figure 2.7). The casualty is not just equity, which is well known, but also quality of higher education. Gresham's law of money seems to operate in education: private (bad) colleges drive away public (good) colleges out of circulation.

Table 2.6

Growth of Colleges in Andhra Pradesh

	Government	*Private*			*Total*
		Aided	*Unaided*	*Total*	
1969-70	40	80	0	80	120
1979-80	64	147	1	148	212
1984-85	133	181	9	190	323
1989-90	147	182	33	215	362
1993-94	156	182	88	270	426
1996-97	167	187	450	637	804

Source: *Performance Budget of Andhra Pradesh, 1997-98*. Hyderabad: Government of Andhra Pradesh.

Figure 2.9

Growth of Private Sector in Higher Education in Andhra Pradesh

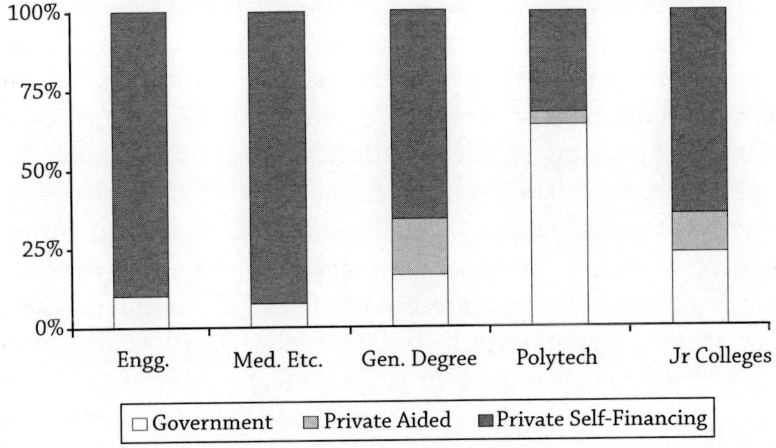

Source: *Performance Budget of Andhra Pradesh, 2001-02*. Hyderabad: Government of Andhra Pradesh.

The Private Universities Bill, introduced in Rajya Sabha in August 1995, with a view to providing for the establishment of self-financing universities is still pending in Parliament. It is widely felt that the Bill was not processed and passed in the Parliament, not because the government was not keen on privatisation of higher education in India, not because the private sector was not interested in the Bill, but probably because the latter was not happy with several clauses in the Bill. For example, the Bill requires formation of a permanent endowment fund of ₹ 10 crore, provision of free-ships to 30 per cent of the students, and for government monitoring and regulation of the system.

Though the Private Universities Bill has not yet been passed by Parliament, and the recommendations of the Ambani-Birla Committee report (Prime Minister's Council, 2000) were *per se* not accepted, several initiatives taken by the government suggest that higher education is getting rapidly privatised. Perhaps there is no need for the bill. For example, a few private institutions of higher education have been virtually given the status of universities, by recognising them as 'deemed universities.'[4] Universities (e.g., the Guru Gobindsingh Indraprashta University in Delhi) are created that consist of only affiliating private self-financing colleges. A few other private institutions (e.g., International Business Schools, IITs, etc.) are allowed to operate almost as universities or their equivalent offering degree/diploma programmes. All this is in addition to allowing rapid growth of private self-financing institutions at college level, and conversion of government-aided private institutions into private self-financing (unaided) institutions in several states.

The private sector found it convenient to remind the state governments that education is, according to the Constitution, a concurrent subject, and that state governments could themselves enact legislation for private universities.[5] Consequently, quite a few state governments have enacted such bills, and private universities have sprung up in large numbers, almost in no time, without necessarily obtaining any approval of the University Grants Commission (UGC) or other concerned authority.

Currently we have a variety of private educational institutions, private universities, private institutions deemed to be universities, and self-financing (capitation fee) colleges, in addition to hundreds and even thousands of unrecognised ones, such as teaching shops, `parallel colleges' and coaching centres—all working within the market framework with the sole objective of profit maximisation. Such institutions are rapidly increasing in number. State-aided private schools and colleges operate within a different framework. But their growth has come to a standstill, if it has not declined.

These trends of privatisation are already producing serious effects on various dimensions of the educational system and society at large. These include effects on quantity, quality and equity in education, research, supply of teachers and 'balanced' development of higher education, as I have described elsewhere (Tilak, 1999c).

Since there exists 'excess demand' for higher education, it is possible to argue that demand for higher education in India is rather inelastic to changes in fees. But the coefficient of elasticity may not be zero; it is not in fact less than unity or inelastic for all levels/types of higher education. For example, it is already noted that steep increases in fees at post-graduate and research levels in the Indian Institutes of Technology have been counterproductive, leading to a decline in enrolments by more than 37 per cent in the mid 1990s.

One of the most important problems is of ensuring equity in higher education. While the government can, to a great extent, make sure that protective discrimination policies are followed in government and government-aided private institutions, resistance to such policies is much higher in private institutions. The overall fee elasticity of demand for education may not be high but it could certainly be so for economically weaker sections. In other words, with privatisation, even if the size of total enrolments does not change, the composition might change in favour of better-off sections with the poor getting completely marginalised.

The government's inability to control the quality of education in private institutions is also being increasingly felt. Even strong proponents of private higher education systems somewhat paradoxically argue that the state should take responsibility for regulating quality in private education. But given the social and politico-economic milieu, the government seems to feel severely handicapped in maintaining quality in these institutions. Generally, once recognition is granted to a private institution (and that is not found to be very difficult), the government cannot enforce any of its conditions. This is true to some extent even for state-aided private colleges. State grants are not usually stopped or delayed for any reason. Massive erosion of quality in private colleges might push down the quality of higher education as a whole.

Further, conflicts between national manpower needs and short-term market signals that influence private higher education institutions can be serious, and in the long run might produce serious manpower imbalances—both shortages and gluts. This is evident from the estimates and corresponding recommendations made by professional public bodies like the All India Council for Technical Education (AICTE) and the Medical Council of India (MCI) with regard to the required number of colleges and manpower which are least taken note of by private colleges, operating in collusion with the government.

All these problems are with respect to 'recognised' private institutions. Emergence of 'fake' national and foreign universities and ghost institutions imparting 'education' and awarding obviously fake degrees is also a problem that is coming to surface. As these institutions are not even 'recognised', the role of the government is practically nil. Occasionally, the UGC or the Association of Indian Universities makes public announcements listing fake universities and ghost institutions, to warn students and parents to be cautious.

In case of school education, even such an arrangement does not exist, though it is well known that there are a large number of private institutions that the government does not recognise. In fact, they cannot be recognised. Many of them were opened under the Registration of Shops Act relating to shops and commercial establishments (Deshpande, 1991). Unfortunately, no quantitative information is available on such institutions, though it is known that they are booming. Such institutions range from teaching shops to new centres offering computer literacy and training, management institutions, institutions of fashion design and what not. They are run completely on a commercial basis, and public educational bodies have no control over them.

The most important apprehensions, which are proving true, relate to vulgar commercialisation of education and playing on the anxieties of "gullible parents", charging exorbitant fees formally and informally, starting from application fee to examination fees, fee for grade-sheet and fee for attestation by the universities. The unparalleled greed of private enterprise in education in India has been unravelled. The "carnal lust" (Neave, 1996: 20) is visible to the naked eye. Education is being viewed by private enterprise as a very lucrative investment to make huge and quick profits. Students who pay exorbitant fees obviously cannot be involved with consideration for national interests such as public service, service in rural areas, service of the poor, etc. The sole objective of these students, whether it is actually realised or not, is to emigrate to greener pastures. No wonder, the products of the carnal lust cannot be expected to be otherwise. This would be the most harmful effect of marketisation of education on the society.

The many legal battles being fought in the high courts and the Supreme Court and the detailed instructions that the courts issue frequently to public bodies suggest a serious malaise with private educational institutions in the country that have little concern for equity, efficiency, norms of educational excellence, and most importantly cherished national goals and ideals. Yet they are increasing in number, as there exists a nexus between them and the seekers of profit, and seekers of political power and influence. The casualty is education. As Kothari (1986: 596) noted, with the growth of these institutions, "the objective of equal opportunities for education would be jeopardised in a big way. The overall effect would be to convert education into a force for reinforcing the existing stratification of the society."

All this indicates that markets are highly imperfect and incomplete in India, like in many other developing countries (Stiglitz, 2002), and fail to perform any normative role in the development of education, and hence any significant reliance on them would be counterproductive.

Let me conclude. I have focused on three closely related aspects of financing of education in India, *viz.*, the unwillingness of the government to spend on education, compulsion on households to spend on education and exploitative markets in education. The government is increasingly unwilling to spend on education; households have little choice but to spend huge amounts even on elementary education that the state is expected to provide free. And markets are taking advantage of the situation.

The unwillingness of the government is related to attitudes and policies towards education. The two other phenomena, *viz.*, increase in household expenditure on education and the rapid growth of private sector in education are direct outcomes of government policies and attitudes. They are also mutually related to each other. Rather than perceiving increase in household expenditure as a negative reflection on its inadequacy, and feeling guilty and ashamed of the same, governments are actively encouraging this trend. There is a formidable constellation at work: absence of a coherent long-term policy on education, and lack of clarity regarding the respective domains of households and markets. This has enabled the private sector to hold the state and households to ransom.

The best answer is provision of good quality education by the state to all its citizens, financed out of tax and non-tax revenues. I have examined earlier (Tilak, 1997) alternative methods of financing education, and concluded that, of all, State financing remains unequalled. It is not households but the government that should feel socially, economically, educationally and ethically compelled to invest in education. After all, this is the practice in most civilised societies of the world.

Notes

1. This, namely, the share of a given level of education in total five year plan expenditure, may be a more reliable indicator of the relative priority accorded to a given level of education than the share of a given level of education in the total expenditure on education in a five year plan. The later, which is used extensively, implicitly places one level of education against another level, and causes an avoidable fragmented look at education development.

2. The corresponding coefficient was 2.3 in the 1960s, 3.2 in the 1970s and 2.0 in the 1980s.
3. The hollowness of the concept of 'willingness to pay' becomes clearer in the context of health care, where also the concept is used almost synonymously. A person will be ready to incur large expenditures, as he/she knows that the alternative could be fatal. Can this be described as 'willingness to pay'?
4. In the last couple of years, there has been a big jump in the number of deemed universities, mostly private, which led the UGC to feel the need to review their working.
5. Interestingly, the concurrency clause was conveniently not remembered by any state government, when the bill to make elementary education a fundamental right was pending before Parliament for more than five years, before it was finally passed in December 2002 as the 86th Amendment.

References

AICTE (1994). *Report of the High Power Committee for Mobilization of Additional Resources for Technical Education* (Dr Swaminadhan Committee Report). New Delhi, All India Council for Technical Education.

Arrow, Kenneth J. (1973). "Higher Education as a Filter", *Journal of Public Economics* 2(3): 193-216, July.

Behrman, J.R. (1990). *Human Resource Led Development? Review of Issues and Evidence.* New Delhi: ILO-ARTEP.

Deshpande, J.V. (1991). "Boom in Teaching Shops", *Economic and Political Weekly* 26(30): 1787, July 27.

Drèze, Jean and Amartya Sen (2002). *India: Development and Participation.* Delhi: Oxford University Press.

Education (Kothari) Commission (1966). *Education and Development.* New Delhi: Government of India, Ministry of Education.

Kothari V.N. (1986). "Private Unaided Engineering and Medical Colleges: Consequences of Misguided Policy", *Economic and Political Weekly* 21(14): 593-96, 5 April.

Majumdar, Tapas (1983). *Investment in Education and Social Choice.* Cambridge: Cambridge University Press.

Neave, Guy (1996). "Higher Education in Transition: Twenty Five Years On", *Higher Education Management* 8(3): 15-24, November.

Prime Minister's Council on Trade and Industry (2000). *A Policy Framework for Reforms in Education* (Mukesh Ambani-Kumaramanglalam Birla Report). A Report submitted by special subject group on Policy Framework for Private Investment in Education, Health and Rural Development. New Delhi: Government of India. *http://www.nic.in/pmcouncils/reports/education*

Schultz, Theodore W. (1961). "Investment in Human Capital", *American Economic Review* 51(1): 1-17, March.

Spence, A.M. (1973). "Job-market Signalling", *Quarterly Journal of Economics* 87(3): 355-74, August.

Stiglitz, Joseph (2002). *Globalization and its Discontents.* London: Allen Lane/Penguin.

Tilak, Jandhyala B.G. (1989). "Center-State Relations in Financing Education in India", *Comparative Educational Review* 33(4): 450-80, November.

———. (1991). "Privatization of Higher Education Prospects", *Quarterly Review of Education* (Unesco) 21(2): 227-39.

———. (1994). "South Asian Perspectives (on Alternative Policies for the Finance, Control, and Delivery of Basic Education)", *International Journal of Educational Research* 21(8): 791-98.

———. (1996a). "How Free is 'Free' Primary Education in India?", *Economic and Political Weekly* 31 (5 & 6): 275-82; 355-66, 3 & 10 February.

———. (1996b). "Higher Education Under Structural Adjustment", *Journal of Indian School of Political Economy* 8 (2): 266-93, April-June.

———. (1997). "Lessons from Cost Recovery in Education", in C. Colclough (ed.), *Marketising Education and Health in Developing Countries: Miracle or Mirage?* Oxford: Clarendon Press. pp. 63-89.

———. (1999a). "National Human Development Initiative: Education in the Union Budget", *Economic and Political Weekly* 34(10-11): 614-20, 6 March.

———. (1999b). "Investment in Human Capital in India: An Inter-State Analysis of Stock and Flow of Human Capital", *Journal of Indian School of Political Economy* 11: 39-75, January-March.

———. (1999c). "Emerging Trends and Evolving Public Policies on Privatisation of Higher Education in India, in P.G. Altbach (ed.), *Private Prometheus: Private Higher Education and Development in the 21st Century*. Westport: Greenwood Publishing. pp.113-35

———. (2000). *Household Expenditure on Education in India: A Preliminary Examination of the 52nd Round of the National Sample Survey*. New Delhi: National Institute of Educational Planning and Administration.

———. (2002a). "Determinants of Household Expenditure on Education in Rural India", *Working Paper* No. 88. New Delhi: National Council of Applied Economic Research.

———. (2002b). "Education Poverty in India", *Review of Development and Change* 7(1): 1-44, January-June.

UGC (1993). *UGC Funding of Institutions of Higher Education: Report of Justice Dr. K. Punnayya Committee*, 1991-92. New Delhi: University Grants Commission.

UNDP (2003). *Human Development Report*. New York: Oxford University Press.

World Bank (2003). *World Development Report*. New York: Oxford University Press.

3

DIPANKAR GUPTA

Whither the Indian Village?

Culture and Agriculture in Rural India

Country-Town Nexus

There is a certain resistance in accepting the fact that the Indian village is undergoing major changes, not just economically but culturally as well. The reluctance in coming to terms with this reality arises largely from the widely prevalent belief among intellectuals that the Indian village is timeless and unchanging and that the Indian villager likes nothing more than living in a rural setting. These notions need to be revised, not just for the sake of factual accuracy but also because of the imperatives of the planning and developmental process. If the village is really the mainstay of India's economy, then that would require a certain set of policy prescriptions that would centralise agriculture. But if, on the other hand, the agrarian character of the village is fast changing, then that should certainly inspire a significant shift in perspective, especially when thinking in developmental terms.

It is not as if these changes have not been noticed by others. In fact, this paper will refer to such studies and, hopefully, build on them. There are two points that need to be noted in this connection. The first is that while there is the acknowledgement that rural India is changing in factual terms, yet at the conceptual level the village and the villagers remain resolutely in the past.[1] This is probably because of the hangover of earlier scholarship, as well as popular conceptions regarding India, that depict Indian society to be essentially rural. So the theoretical cum analytical frameworks remain largely unchanged, while at the level of facts, there is a clear recognition that things are not what they used to be.

The second feature that needs to be recognised in terms of contemporary rural dynamics is that it is not urbanisation that is always the critical factor that is impacting the village from the outside. The village landholding structure is such that there are few jobs available in the fields that can engage the rural population on a sustained, albeit, suboptimal, basis. It is true that the availability of urban jobs has made a difference, it is also true that there are more electrified villages in India, many more motorised vehicles, and better roads connecting country to town than was the case a few decades ago. Yet, it is not as if the village is transforming internally on account of urban inputs, but rather because it is expelling people outside because of sheer inertia of the agrarian economy that hardly allows for any optimism. In this sense then, it is not that the village is changing in one direction towards urbanisation, but rather the impetus for change is taking place in the village itself. The town is not coming to the country, as much as the country is reaching out to the town, leaving behind a host of untidy rural debris.

It is better then to look at the relationship between country and town not only in terms of how the urban world is changing rural life, but also enquiring into the modalities by which villagers are leaving their agrarian pasts for an uncertain non-agrarian present. It would not be quite right to liken their contemporary situation as 'urban', but it is not agrarian either though they continue to live, in the main, in what are still called 'villages'. To live in the village and be alienated from agriculture surely demands a new analytical optic, but for that it needs to be admitted that rural India cannot be comprehended under earlier rubrics. The uprooting of village life from within and the linkages with towns and cities bring to light a country-town nexus within which those who are deracinated at home are structurally compelled to function.

Village Under Duress

The Indian village is not what it used to be, and even further from what it has been for long imagined to be. There are unambiguous statistics that point to the falling rates of growth in agriculture and to the increasing exodus from country to town. On top of this, we have the phenomenon of non-farm employment whose scale has increased tremendously over the years. It is estimated today that about 24 per cent of villagers are engaged in non-agricultural occupations. This is not a small number, and in all likelihood, it is probably a conservative estimate.

While these gross statistics do suggest a whittling down of the importance of agriculture as the mainstay of Indian society, there is in addition a general undermining of values and practices that have their origins in the villages and are imbrued with the so-called 'rural ethos'. There was a time, not too long ago, when a Jat farmer in Uttar Pradesh or Punjab, would proudly proclaim that farming was the noblest of all occupations. Today this swagger is missing amongst them. They want an urban foothold, and would even consider taking up occupations in towns and cities that they would deign to perform in their own villages.

The profundity of changes in rural India is not fully captured by census figures or by statistical surveys. Useful though they are, it is necessary to comprehend the depth of disenchantment that prevails in the villages through in-depth field investigations. This disenchantment is on a variety of fronts. Indian agriculture has always lurched from crisis to crisis. If the monsoons are good then there are floods, if they are bad then there are droughts, if the production of mangoes is excellent then there is a glut and prices fall, if the onion crops fail then that too brings tears. The artisanal nature of agriculture has always kept farmers on tenterhooks, not knowing quite how to manage their economy, except to play it by (y)ear.

Even in green revolution areas, where there has been a spectacular increase in mechanisation and chemical inputs, the dependence on the vagaries of the weather and on the insufficiency, and irregularity, of electrical supply and other infrastructural inputs can throw the best agricultural calculations out of gear. It is not surprising then that whenever the occasion arises, villagers are more than willing to up and leave for a future outside the mud walls of their homes and in fields as distant from agriculture as industrial labour. The village is shrinking as a sociological reality, though it still exists as space. Nowhere else does one find the level of hopeless disenchantment as one does in the rural regions of India. In urban slums, there is squalour, there is filth and crime, but there is hope and the excitement that tomorrow might be quite different from today.

Rarely would a villager today want to be a farmer if given an opportunity elsewhere. Indeed, there are few rural institutions that have not been mauled severely from within. The joint family is disappearing, the rural caste hierarchy is losing its tenacity, and the much romanticised harmony of village life is now exposed for the sham it perhaps always was. If anything, it is perhaps Dr B.R. Ambedkar's analysis of the Indian village that strikes the truest of all. It was Ambedkar who said that the village was a cesspool of degradation, corruption and worse. That village India was able to carry on in spite of all this in the past was because there was little option for most people, rich or poor, outside the confines of the rural space.

If rural India has lost its centrality in the minds of most villagers in contemporary India today it is not, as we mentioned earlier, only because an urban world has opened up their horisons, but also because the village economy itself has lost its sustaining power. Consequently, the country side has witnessed a kind of cultural implosion that has shaken many of the verities of the past. With the abolition of landlordism and the introduction of adult franchise (the two must necessarily go hand in hand), old social relations that dominated the country side are today in a highly emaciated form, when not actually dead. Roughly 85 per cent of landholdings are below 5 acres and about 63 per cent are below even three acres. What land reforms and land redistribution could not do, demography and sub-division of holdings have done to land ownership. Where are the big landlords? There are some, but they are few and far between. But does this make the village an egalitarian utopia? Far from it!

Medium-sized owner cultivators contend against landless labourers, both economically and socially. While the rigidities of the caste systems no longer operate in their pristine form, caste prejudices and identities die hard. The stigma of tradition sits incubus like on social relations even if the prescriptions of tradition cannot be followed with equal facility these days. Other than the lack of economic opportunities, it is the nature of social relations in rural

India that drive many poorer castes and classes out of the village. Clearly, the poorer one is, the greater the temptation to up and leave the village before the sun finally sets on one.

Where landholdings are so fragmented, there is little scope for agricultural regeneration. Planners would be happy if agricultural production could be sustained year after year, and elated if there is a modest increase of even one per cent. Last year, there was in fact a negative growth rate. In small plots there is always a preponderance of family labour, and the Chayanovian logic of balancing drudgery and needs usually operates in such cases. But for that to happen without emotional philippics, the needs horison must curve within the village perimeter. Only then is the family farm a precious gift to be harvested in perpetuity. But now needs have escalated and the family farm is no longer what it was earlier cut out to be. It cannot support the ambition to be where the bright lights are. Nor can family farms provide employment to the landless youth in the villages. Therefore no matter which way one looks at it, as owner cultivators or as landless labourers, the village is no longer a site where futures can be planned.

Pre-conceptions and Conceptions of Village India

That India's villages were changing was noticed in the late 1950s. Several studies, the most renowned being McKim Marriot's edited volume, *Village India* (1955), indicated that India's villages were not little republics. A select group of distinguished anthropologists commented on the fact that the great culture of Hinduism interacts with the little cultures of the villages, and in that process both are transformed. Scarlett Epstein's work which was a longitudinal time study of two villages also demonstrated the growing relationship between town and country. Even so, till the late 1960s and early 1970s, the importance of farming was overwhelmingly visible, as also the incidence of hired labour even though mechanisation had made some inroads into agriculture (Epstein, 1973: 86, 99, 192). There is not much evidence by way of non-farm occupations except for the number of cafes that have sprung up in the villages she studied (Epstein, 1973: 117). She also found that the poor in these villages have suffered a definite fall in their standards of living (Epstein, 1973: 165), though the rich peasants have certainly grown richer with opening up of the jaggery market (Epstein, 1973: 171). But otherwise the villages were not terribly influenced by the world outside: their shops buy from without but sell wholly within, and even their university graduates were not expected to "exert much influence over village affairs" (Epstein, 1973: 240). In spite of changes noticed by Epstein, it appears that the villages she examined over forty years ago still looked up to agriculture as the mainstay of their economic life. This is notwithstanding the fact that a large number of poorer farmers had become distinctly worse off in the 15 years interim between her first study and the second one.

The village has often been essentialised as an idyllic locale where community ties bind the population together. These villages were little republics, timeless and unchanging—obdurate too in their stasis, but engagingly so. In such conceptions, the Indian village knows no evil, and is counterposed to the harsh and immoral life of the cities. This is where the native 'authentically' lives. Charles Metcalfe and James Mill were among the early popularisers of this view. Even Marx, who tirelessly championed dialectical movement, fell prey to this 'village republic' conception of rural India. Dynasties may come and go, great wars may be fought by ambitious monarchs and potentates, but the steady hum of village life is scarcely ever disturbed (see Cohn, 1987: 213). According to Ronald Inden, colonial administrators saw the village as the atom of Indian civilisation, no less (Inden, 1990: 131). Much of this can be found in Gandhi's exhortation to revive the Indian village to its earlier authentic existence. He, of course, recognised many of the shortcomings of rural life, but nursed the political goal of returning the village to its pristine ways.

Gandhi was not however unchallenged in the years leading up to the national movement. Peasant leaders like Swami Sahajanand Saraswati brought forth the harshness of village life where the landlords plundered poor peasants and lived off the fat of the land (see Rasul, 1974). The much-written about *jajmani* system was clearly a much-romanticised phenomenon (see Wiser, 1936; Beidelman, 1959). Even if the perfectly orchestrated organic division of labour based on caste did not quite exist, nevertheless, M.N. Srinivas (1987: 59) argued, "the power wielded by the dominant caste was real." Members of the dominant caste were the chief patrons of the village (see Beteille, 1980: 110-15), though they had to encounter factional rivalries within (see Dumont, 1970: 163-4). What remained largely undisputed was that everyday life, politics, economics and rituals included, pivoted around the dispensations of the dominant caste. Social anthropology was clearly cured of any romantic naiveté primarily because leaders in the field insisted on the field view and not the book view. The fact that the village community, howsoever defined, did not mean egalitarianism comes through quite clearly in the works of several scholars, foremost among them is perhaps M.N. Srinivas. Even so, the concept of the dominant caste does not illumine village India today like it used to a few decades ago. Bose (1991), Bandopadhayay and von Eschen (1991), Harriss (1982), Sahay (2001), Chakravarti (2001) and a host of other authors discussed tensions between agrarian classes, bringing out the severe asymmetry of rural social relations. So for some time now, village India has ceased to be a quiet, idyllic rural haven in academic writings.

Traditionally, caste and village called out to each other in synergy. If the village was said to be tranquil, it was argued that caste ideology was responsible for it. This is how the much-vaunted *jajmani* system. was understood. Each caste had its specific locus and all castes agreed in the hierarchy of purity where the Brahman sat on top. What most scholars failed to notice was that the hierarchy on the ground was not an outcome of ideological acquiescence, but an outcome of an unequal distribution of wealth and power in a closed agrarian economy. In fact, every caste values itself and its ritual practices very highly, and no caste actually believes that it is essentially impure. Origin myths of castes clearly demonstrate this. In every instance, these origin tales recall a mythic past when a supposedly 'low caste' actually held a very high status in the distant past. Loss of status took place in such cases because of chicanery, deceit, reversals in war, and sometimes also because the gods were idiosyncratic. But on no account did the members of the so-called lower caste participate willingly in their own subjugation. Nor is it that ideas of grandeur crop up once a caste has economic and political power. In fact, these ideas are always there, except that they cannot be extraverted when conditions are not propitious as in a closed village economy under the sway of a dominant caste. As this aspect of unconditional dominance is rapidly becoming a thing of the past in Indian villages, the assertion of caste identities is becoming much more strident and out in the open. This is also why caste politics has so much purchase in contemporary India (see Gupta, 2000 for details).

Caste Identity and Caste System

The gradual diminution of status of the dominant castes and of the earlier village oligarchs who controlled the agrarian economy of the village has brought about a number of changes at the cultural level too. One instance is the stridency with which backward castes and SCs (scheduled castes) express their political views and preferences. In Uttar Pradesh, the impact of the Bahujan Samaj Party has been written about quite extensively and does not need repetition here (see Jaffrelot, 2003). The reason for the rise of SC political assertion in recent times is primarily because the propertied classes in rural India can no longer exercise economic domination over the landless peasants. As they cannot employ the landless any more because of the shrinking size of their own landholdings, the power of landowners as patrons and as political leaders has also diminished over time.

Apart from the political side of SC mobilisation in recent years, what needs also to be mentioned is the symbolic defiance of the hitherto subaltern castes towards those who, till less than a generation ago, were their unchallenged social superiors. In Punjab, the once low caste Chamars now identify themselves as Adi-Dharmis (Jodhka, 2002: 1816). Without formally giving up Sikhism, they have established their own Gurudwaras and do not go to those that are controlled by Jat Sikhs. In order to mark their distance further from Jats, the Adi-Dharmis display a portrait or statue of Guru Ravi Das in their Gurudwaras. Most Adi-Dharmis have given up wearing the Sikh turban and are clean-shaven though their parents adorned the Sikh visage till not so long ago. In Talhan village in Jalandhar district, the Ramgarhias (carpenters by caste occupation) have also been drawn into the Adi-Dharmi fold. The Jat Sikhs do not approve of the ascendance of the Adi-Dharmis but there is little they can do about it. In fact in Talhan, every third Adi-Dharmi household has a family member living abroad. I found three beauty salons in the Adi-Dharmi hamlet of Talhan village. All these are signs of prosperity and a clear indication that the Adi-Dharmis can do without Jat patronage. Even in districts where the Adi-Dharmis are not as assertive as in Jalandhar, such as in Taran Taran, they, nevertheless, refuse to do menial work, nor will they work in fields owned by Jats as agricultural labourers. The Mashabi Sikhs, who were traditionally scavengers, have now begun to be employed as agricultural labourers, when the occasion presents itself, but the Adi-Dharmis refuse to be engaged in that kind of work anymore as they consider it humiliating to bow before Jat landowners. The Mashabi Sikhs still do not have the economic capabilities to oppose Jats frontally. Though many of them have their own Gurudwaras, as they feel slighted in those run by Jats, yet they have not made a defiant, symbolic break with Jat culture and orthodoxy as the Adi-Dharmis have.

This story is a familiar one and is played out in different parts of India by different castes. In Uttar Pradesh (UP), the Jatavs refuse to be agricultural labourers so the Valmikis have taken their place. Even so, the Valmikis are not as supine either any longer. During my visit to Behrichi village in Saharnapur district of UP, I found that a large number of Valmikis had left the village in search of jobs outside to the utter disapproval of the land-owning Tyagis of that region. The Tyagis, like the Jat Sikhs of Punjab, cannot complain enough against what they consider the upstart effrontery of those whom they consider to be of low caste. The Tyagis never let SCs enter their Shiv Temple, and this is an age-old phenomenon. In recent years, however, the SCs have built their own temple dedicated to Ravidas and play recorded hymns *(bhajans)* which are often lifted from popular Hindi films. In Maharashtra, the literate and culturally advanced Mahars have for a long time now given up their traditional occupation and have moved over to cities and town where they are employed in a variety of services. This process has a much longer history in Tamil

Nadu, with the Chakaliyar (Arunthodiar), the Pariyar (Adi-Dravida), and the Pallar (Devendrakula Vellala) showing scant respect today to local dominant castes. In recent years, the Arunthodiars have raised their levels of defiance by setting up Ambedkar statues which the landed Gouders find objectionable. The Arunthodiars (or Chakaliyars) are also very mobile and clearly prefer non-farming jobs to working on Gouder fields.

Caste identity has resurfaced at every level now. It is no longer the case that the property less castes in the village could only speak of their origin tales in hushed tones. Now every caste proudly digs into deep pockets of heritage in order to claim an elevated status, frontally denying the station that tradition had accorded to them. Thus while the caste system has collapsed, caste identities are to be seen everywhere in a highly exaggerated form. This has given rise to the optical illusion that the caste system is enjoying a fresh lease of life. In fact, because caste as a system is dying in rural India that caste identities can now afford to come up. In the reign of the closed village economy ruled by the oligarchs of the dominant caste, there was little scope for poorer castes to express their sense of self-worth through origin myths without being subjected to persecution from the superior communities. Now that the pressure of the upper class, landed castes has been lifted in the economic domain, the ex-untouchable castes have the space and the opportunity to proudly extravert their origin myths and their sense of identity without fearing reprisals. There are still some pockets where landed castes can be quite domineering, but the writing is already on the wall and the trend is irrevocably set against them.

Farmers' Movement

Rural agitations today are no longer between agricultural labourer and landlord as used to be the case as late as the 1970s. During this period, there were a large number of organisations with political allegiance to left-wing national parties that were active in rural India campaigning for the landless labourer and poor sharecropper. Such mobilisations are things of the past and except for certain pockets in Bihar and Andhra Pradesh, they do not exist anywhere else. Even in these areas, such as Bihar, it is not clear to what extent the Naxalite brigades are actually Maoist in their orientation and to what extent they are now extortionate groups feeding off a poorly organised state machinery. The simple reason why such organisations have lost their initial focus is because agricultural labour is no longer a critical issue that involves masses of rural Indians. As most holdings are run on family labour, the need for wage labour is intermittent during peak seasons. This has reduced the scope for left-wing organisations to be active on their own terms.

By the 1980s, it was clear that landless labourers had no viable future in the economy of the village. The increasing incidence of family farms made hired labour less critical for agricultural production than before. Where there was substantial agricultural prosperity in the years following the Green Revolution, such as Punjab and Haryana, labour could be hired from among migrants who came from East India in search of employment. Agricultural prosperity among capitalist farmers almost always meant a scarcity of local labour. This is primarily because even in large farms, the amount of labour required per acre decreased substantially owing to mechanisation. Increased prosperity of the region also meant greater opportunities outside the farm which is where the local labour set off for in search of employment. This left the field open for migrants from East India who were happy to get some employment even though they were far from home.

In this context, it must also be kept in mind that in many parts of India, particularly in Punjab and West UP, those who worked earlier as agrestic labour are no longer willing to work in the same capacity. As we mentioned earlier, Harijans and Adi-Dharmis of UP and Punjab respectively have more or less set their minds against labouring on others' fields. Cumulatively, this led to the diminution of the agricultural labourer's presence in rural India. By the time 1980s came around, agricultural labourer movements that involved huge rural unions and supra-local organisers became more or less a thing of the past. Now was the turn of Mahendra Singh Tikait and Nanjudaswamy to lead agitations espousing the interests of owner cultivators. In these mobilisations, it was clearly stated that anyone who did not own land was not really a farmer. There was no room now for agricultural labourers in these movements which the Bharatiya Kisan Union (BKU) of UP and Haryana articulated most cogently.

Even as the owner cultivators were getting restive, a new configuration was taking place in rural politics. In the past when agricultural labourers mattered most in rural uprisings, the target was always the local landlord, *jotedar* or *thanedar*. With the shift to owner-cultivator brand of agitation the enemy was no longer local, but supra-local, even the government of India. Not surprisingly, BKU and Kshetkari Sangathan were constantly moving into cities to impress upon the public, and upon recalcitrant politicians, the authenticity of their demands. Thus while they were still agriculturalists, in the main, already the link between town and country was being strongly established (see Gupta, 1997). Concurrently, there was the demand among the same category of owner-cultivators for reservations in urban jobs and in educational institutions. The Mandal Recommendations of 1990 were timed just right to coincide with the urban aspirations of cultivating castes such as Yadavas, Gujars, and Jats. An urban job was clearly a prise catch for communities that for generations prided themselves in being farmers first and last. There is a play on a famous couplet in West UP that captures this sentiment rather nicely. The famous Urdu poet, Ghagh, had once eulogised rural life when he wrote: "*Uttam kheti, madhyam baan; nishidh chakri, bhikh nidam*." Translated it means that agriculture is the best, followed by business, salaried jobs and beggary. Today, the villagers have recast the ditty along the following lines: "*Uttam chakri, madhyma baan; nikrisht krishi, bhik mahan*." In this case, a politician who begs for vote is on top, followed by a salaried job, and at the bottom of the heap is the agriculturist.

The Marginalised World of the Owner-Cultivator

Though it is difficult to say where the process of cultural alienation from the village began, it can nevertheless be maintained that the relative stagnation of the rural economy has contributed significantly to it. This can be gauged not just from the growth rates between industry and agriculture, but also in terms of the quite remarkable shift that is taking place in the number of agricultural workers of all descriptions.

The belief that India is overwhelmingly an agricultural society obviously is in need of further finessing. The sectoral distribution of Rural Net Domestic Product for agriculture is down to 54.41 per cent from 72.37 per cent in 1970-71 (Chadha, 2003: 58). As Parthasarathy *et al.* (1998: 140) argue, workforce changes in India did not match the production structure of its economy. The National Sample Survey (NSS) points out that the number of rural people working in urban India has doubled between 1987-88 and 1993-94. Also the annual GDP growth in agriculture in value added terms has declined from 3.5 per cent in the 1980s to 2.8 per cent in the 1990s. Thereafter, the figure dipped even more dismally to 1.3 per cent in 1999-2000 and unbelievably to a negative growth rate of minus 2 per cent in 2000-01 (Mujumdar, 2002: 3983). Further, trends show that urban households earn more than their counterparts in villages and that the disparity is growing. In a 1975-76 survey, urban households earned on an average 1.82 times more than rural households, but today the figure stands closer to 2.1 per cent (Pradhan *et al.*, 2000: 2531). Though there is a noticeable increase in inequality in urban India, poverty levels are on the whole much lower than in the countryside (Vaidyanathan, 2001: 1814).

Just because a majority of Indians live in villages, it would be rather hasty to conclude from this that India's national culture is determined by the village. Most of the political debates in the country do not have a rural character at all. This is rather surprising given the fact that a large number of politicians in the Parliament and legislatures have rural origins. Occasionally a Mahender Singh Tikait or a Nanjudaswamy will stir things up in the villages, but in the main, political ideologies that inform most of the national parties do not have a strong rural component. The usual concessions are made in terms of subsidies or minimum price for agricultural produce, but the kernel of political ideologies do not reflect any major pre-occupation with the village. Even Laloo Yadav and Maulayam Singh Yadav demonstrate little by way of rural concerns. Playing the arithmetic of caste does not necessarily mean committing oneself to the chemistry of the village.

Yet, because it is also a question of arithmetic, politicians often vie against each other in coming through as champions of the beleaguered owner-cultivators. There is very little concern shown today with respect to agricultural labourers in political discourses nationwide. But even here there is a strong element of political gamesmanship at work. In the name of protecting the poor farmer, political parties have in general opposed the institution of tax on agricultural incomes. Yet, as many owner-cultivators have told me repeatedly, this tax concession makes no difference to them as their incomes would be below the taxable amount anyway. These farmers argue that the exemption on agricultural tax is to help the rich entrepreneurial farmers and those in cities who want to escape the burden of taxation by diversifying into agricultural production, or in animal husbandry, or poultry farming, and so forth. At the same time, politicians are alive to the fact that the opening up of agricultural imports would ruin the owner-cultivators who are in substantial numbers. As this would lead to political and economic stability, they are obviously cautious about it. Even so, there are peasant activists like Sharad Joshi of Shetkari Sangathan who welcome an open market for he believes that the peasants in Maharashtra would do very well if they could take their produce abroad. Mr Joshi's calculations need to be looked into closely, for he is obviously not keeping his books very carefully. To imagine that the Indian farmer could compete against the west where agriculture as industry is quite difficult to conceive. Indeed this is precisely the reason why India constantly opposes moves in international forums to let the market dynamics control Indian agriculture.

While the owner-cultivators are protected politically, their futures are left unplanned. In 2000, the National Agricultural Policy formally recognised that agriculture has become "a relatively unrewarding profession," and that efforts to revive it have to be multi-pronged in character. Horticulture, floriculture, the cultivation of aromatic and medicinal plants, over and above animal husbandry and fisheries are some of the alternatives they have presented to straight agriculture. While these recommendations sound good on paper, there are vast infrastructural deficits that have to be overcome.

To begin with, the conditions of owner-cultivators do not in general favour heavy investments in chancy cash crops. The suicide rate of farmers in Andhra Pradesh and Punjab is most alarming. In search for a better economic future, they had taken loans to upgrade their agricultural production which they could not repay. According to reports, the overwhelming number of suicides among farmers is on account of their inability to pay back loans. Further, this happens with those agriculturists who are ambitious and want to move on, but are suddenly pulled up because the empirical structures are far too unyielding which makes their attempts to take off lack throttle and thrust. The village also lacks other kinds of basic facilities like transportation systems, cold storages, modern silos and a sound marketing framework.

Without this kind of infrastructural back up, the hope that the production of non-food crops will revive the village is not very realistic. Regardless of how feasible this strategy will eventually be, there is no gainsaying the fact that agricultural production of food is far from being either romanticised or valorised for its own sake any longer. Though the majority of Indians live in villages, the village leaves little impress upon the national culture today.

Rural Non-Farm Employment

Perhaps the most telling aspect of the transformations that are being wrought on rural culture can be gauged from the extent of rural non-farm employment (RNFE). Till 1983, there were 12 states where the RNFE was below 20 per cent. These states included Punjab, Maharashtra and Gujarat. This left only five states where the RNFE was more than 20 per cent. In 1999-2000, roughly 20 years later the situation has changed dramatically. Now 12 states have RNFE figures above 20 per cent and only five are below 20 per cent. In the 50th round of the NSS held in 1993-94, the data suggest that about 32.9 per cent of rural households were outside agriculture. By the 57th round in 2000-02 the percentage has gone up to 35.2 per cent. In fact in Kerela, Haryana and Punjab, over 50 per cent of rural households are non-agricultural in the 57th round of the NSS. Further, in Jammu and Kashmir, West Bengal, Himachal Pradesh and Bihar (yes, Bihar), about 40 per cent of households are non-agricultural. These figures are indeed staggering!

It is however difficult to see any pattern beyond this except to say that RNFE is widely prevalent across the country and is not exactly in proportion to rural prosperity, or the lack of it. This is because Maharashtra and Gujarat have RNFE below 20 per cent in the 1999-2000 survey. These states rank below even Orissa, Rajasthan and Uttar Pradesh. But in Punjab, the RNFE climbed from a modest 17.4 per cent in 1983 to 27.1 per cent in 1999-2000. In Haryana, likewise, the figure went up from 22.3 per cent in 1983 to over 30 per cent in 1999-2000. Himachal Pradesh showed a dramatic increase for the figure doubled in these years from 12.4 per cent to 25.2 per cent (Chadha, 2003: 55). We can approach the same scenario from another angle of vision. If one takes into account the number of male workers engaged in agriculture, one again finds a significant drop in numbers from 77.5 per cent in 1983 to 71.4 per cent in 1999-2000. In other words, about 30 per cent of male workers in rural India are not working in the primary sector any more (Chadha, 2003: 12; Simmons and Supri, 1995: 136). Chadha estimates that the services sector attracts a majority of those who are engaged in RNFE. According to him in 12 of the 17 states in the country, the service sector plays a much "weightier" role than manufacturing when it comes to RNFE (Chadha, 2003: 16). At any rate the rural non-farm sector contributes as much as 45.59 per cent of rural net domestic product (Chadha, 2003: 58).

But what accounts for the growing incidence of RNFE? True, as we mentioned earlier, the scope for agricultural employment has fallen rapidly, but along side that there has been a re-focussing of aspirations as well. It is argued that the growth in agricultural production creates many types of post-harvesting activities that relate to trade where a high degree of non-farm employment takes place. Though this argument can be sustained up to a point by demonstrating the extent of RNFE in Punjab and Haryana, it is difficult to explain how the figure is so low in this regard in Maharashtra and rather high in Assam (Chadha, 2003: 55).

It has also been argued that RNFE is an instance of 'distress employment'. Unlike many other historical instances when the fall in rural employment is accompanied by high rate of agricultural growth, RNFE has continuously increased in India in spite of stagnant rates of agricultural growth. Thus the rural unemployed go out searching for jobs and are willing to do whatever comes their way (see Parthasarathy *et al.*, 1998: 141). Simmons and Supri (1995: 145) show from their research an inverse relationship between land ownership and RNFE. 88 per cent of their sample who were engaged in RNFE had less than 10 acres of land and hence, the deduction that there is a distress aspect in RNFE (Simmons and Supri, 1995: 149). There is little doubt that the poorer one is, the greater the pressure to seek off-farm employment. Yet, it must also be mentioned that owning around 10 acres of land in India does not really signify a poor farmer who is in distress.

Our field studies indicate that in Punjab and West UP villages, all castes are active in rural non-farm employment. Adi-Dharmis and Jats in Jalandhar own stores, run STD booths, sell grocery, sweets and snacks and stitch footballs for multinational companies. Surprisingly, in village Khara in Taran Taran district, we also found Jats who work as tailors (see also Abbi and Singh, 1997). But it also needs to be mentioned that in UP villages, the non-landowning caste is more active in RNFE than the landowning communities. In Behirchi in Saharnapur district and Baijalpur in Ballia district, both in UP, the Tyagis and Thakurs respectively are not as active in non-farm occupations as the other poorer castes are. In fact, in Baijalpur in Ballia, very few Thakurs are involved in non-farm occupations, other than joining the army or buying truck and taxis for commercial purposes.

Thus while there are indications that villages in East India are less dynamic than those in Northwest India in shedding some of their values and prejudices, what is common in all instances is the general disenchantment with village life. The ambition to leave the village for a better life outside it, or to stay in the village but not to work on land, is too pronounced to be overlooked. It is also true that while RNFE attracts people from diverse castes, their location in the structure of employment outside the farm depends a lot on where they come from, and to the kinds of household they belong. What is also common is that the SCs are not without ambition, and in terms of RNFE they show a much greater degree of aggressiveness. In every village the SCs resent the treatment of the hitherto dominant castes, and have in many instances given up performing those menial tasks that they traditionally performed and which they believed, rightly so, to be humiliating in character.

Quite clearly, at an all-India level there is no pattern as such, though traditional and landowning castes in regions such as UP are less prone to step out of agriculture than their counterparts in places like Punjab. But these are caste-specific predispositions, and they cannot be generalised across the country. Nevertheless, what our findings show is that the recourse to non-farm employment varies, not just with respect to one's economic position, but also with caste-related attitudes and prejudices.

In an interesting case study by Ruthven and Kumar (2002), it is the availability of off-farm employment that drives the local villagers to seek jobs outside the village. This exodus of locals from the village obviously draws in a sisable number of migrants who are willing to work for less. And yet, because wages outside agriculture are better, it is those who live in the vicinity who can take advantage of it first. Yet, the study conducted by Parthasarathy *et al.* (1998: 149) suggests that the degree of urbanisation in a district has little impact on RNFE. Certainly, if agricultural income had been plentiful perhaps such labouring jobs in urban areas would have been less attractive, but the jury is still out on whether or not it is distress employment, or pure urbanisation, that drives up the figures of RNFE (see Basu and Kashyap, 2002: A-180-1).

The availability of jobs outside agriculture is certainly an important factor for RNFE, almost axiomatically so. What one would really like to know is the nature of these jobs and their provenance. Pravin Visaria details the contribution of public utilities investments that have spurred RNFE (Visaria, 1995: 404). Indeed, Ruthven and Kumar's (2002) study of a UP village provides empirical micro-level data that substantiates this position. Men are the main takers of jobs that arise from investments in public utilities and construction.

In addition, as Visaria (1995: 404) pointed out, villages which have gas, electricity and water are places where there is a greater incidence of RNFE. Statistically, where land productivity is high, RNFE is also high (Basu and Kashyap, 1992: A-181), but this cannot be posited as a general condition either. In some cases it is distress RNFE, in other cases, the incidence of RNFE is driven up by better wages (Basu and Kashyap, 1992: A-187). When this happens it helps to increase the bargaining power of farm labourers. What, however, remains incontrovertible is that there is a growing increase in the number of those who work in non-agricultural operations in the village.

Finally, it is not as if all the non-farm employment is in the villages. Indeed, the number of people working in off-farm jobs outside the village must not be ignored. This is a factor that the census enumerators have not quite grasped and hence, the census figures are probably not very reliable. In an earlier work I had pointed out, with data from West UP, that a large number of landless villagers work in towns and cities in the day, but return at night—or even during the weekend (see Gupta, 1997). It is, therefore, safe to conclude that RNFE can well be a local phenomenon that is often encouraged by supra-local factors. Further, RNFE is also an indicator of other changes that are occurring in the culture of the village, some of which we have already mentioned.

Is the Indian Village Vanishing?

In terms of the many diacritics of village life, a lot seems to be changing in rural culture. Old taboos against holding certain kinds of jobs are disappearing, the caste system does not operate, though there is a strong assertion of caste pride and caste identity. Untouchability is not practiced widely, though there are pockets of upper caste intransigence. On the economic front, even prosperous landowners seek a future outside the village or in non-farm enterprises. We did not find too many instances of satisfied farmers. Most of them have grievances against the government for not providing them with better amenities.

The most striking feature of all, of course, is the growing incidence of rural non-farm employment across the board. The importance of this cannot be exaggerated. It is not possible to convincingly demonstrate that there are linkages between agriculture and RNFE, other than saying that better off farmers are investing their money and their ambitions outside agriculture. The poor in rural India do not see a future in the village either, but for them the recourse is primarily in terms of manual labour and long distance migration.

Predictably, wealthy landed people often have considerable political leverage in villages and form a vested interest group. While many of them draw their wealth and esteem from the village, they either live in cities, or they recreate an affluent urban ambience in their rural setting. In stark contrast to the poorer villagers with urban aspirations, when the rural rich engage with the outside world, they do so from a position of relative strength. Yet, they too see their future outside the village, or in interacting with the town in enterprises that require rural and urban inputs.

It is against this background that the culture surrounding agriculture must be understood. This culture is not a stable one. History has not left behind a consistent legacy, nor does rural culture have a temporal overhang that is safely cantilevered on present commitments. Agriculture is an economic residue that generously accommodates non-achievers resigned to a life of sad satisfaction. The villager is as bloodless as the rural economy is lifeless. From rich to poor, the trend is to leave the village, and if that entails going abroad, then so be it.

All this may sound a trifle alarming, but this is what India's villages are telling us—whether or not we are inclined to listen to these rustic murmurs.

Note

1. Rural life was portrayed in a variety of ways in the past. For example, *Do Bigha Sameen,* a 1950s classic gave a moving account of a poor peasant eking out a living in the harsh environs of a metropolis as a rickshaw puller so that his family could survive back in the village. The film begins with a song in praise of the rain gods, but when the monsoon fails, the protagonist of the film has no other option but to seek work in the cities in order to pay back the loans he had taken. Shyam Benegal, ideologically committed to a radical revision of a placid village commune, directed films that brings to the fore the colours of rural violence. It is usually the landlords or their henchmen who are the perpetrators of such violence. If in movies such as *Mirch Masala* or *Nishant*, Benegal gives a vivid picture of exploitation in rural India, other films such as Manoj Kumar's *Upkaar* glorifies the village, the agriculturalists, and the rural way of

life in general. The village is presented largely as a homogeneous community where the moral economy thrives. The agriculturalist is the salt of the earth in more ways than one, and mother India yields food in the villages for her millions. The hit song, *Is Desh ki Dharti* exemplifies this sentiment.

The city is where the undesirables live with their crass and immoral ways. The city is the home of the black marketer, the cheat, the swindler. Villagers do not drink, smoke or play the fool in nightclubs like city people do. *Khottey Sikke* and *Adalat* are two other films which put forward a similar message. *Lagaan*, the latest mega hit, also showed the village as a community, where everybody pulled as one against the extortionate demands of the British administrators in colonial times. In this case, even the native upper caste was presented with sympathy.

The opposition between town and country, or between India and Bharat (Manoj Kumar was called Bharat in one of his movies), is a fairly recurrent theme when Indian cinema deals with the village. In Bimal Roy's other great classic *Devdas*, the hero Devdas lives in idyllic enchantment with his lover in the villages. When Devdas is forbidden from marrying the woman he loves he takes off for the city of Calcutta and it is there that he gives himself up to alcohol with dogged determination. In Mehboob Khan's *Mother India*, the heroine looks for her husband who has run off to the city and consequently can hardly keep track of his disintegrated character (see Dwyer and Patel, 2002: 63-4). Today, the bucolic characters of the Indian village rarely attract viewers any more. It is hard to recall a film made in the late 1990s that extols the Indian village, or glorifies it at the expense of the city. In fact, these counter positions no longer seem to resonate.

References

Abbi, B.L. and Kesar Singh (1997). *Post Green Revolution Rural Punjab: A Profile of Economic and Socio-Cultural Change*. Chandigarh: Centre fro Research in Rural and Industrial Development.

Bandopadhayay, Suraj and Donald Von Eschen (1991). "Agricultural Failure: Caste, Class and Power in Rural West Bengal", in Dipankar Gupta (ed.), *Social Stratification*. Delhi: Oxford University Press.

Basu, D.N. and S.P. Kashyap (1992). "Rural Non-Agricultural Employment in India: Role of Development Process and Rural–Urban Employment Linkages", in *Economic and Political Weekly* 27 (Review of Agriculture): A-178-A-189.

Beidelman, T.O. (1959). *A Comparative Study of the Jajmani System*. New York: Locust Valley.

Beteille, Andre (1980). "The Indian Village: Past and Present," in E.J. Hobsbawm *et al.* (eds.), *Peasants In History: Essays in Honour of Daniel Thorner*. Calcutta: Oxford Univeristy Press.

Bose, Pradip K. (1991). "Mobility and Coflict: Social Roots of Caste Violence in Bihar", in Dipankar Gupta (ed.), *Social Stratification*. Delhi: Oxford University Press.

Chadha, G.K. (2003). "Rural Non-Farm Sector in Indian Economy: Growth, Challenges and Future Direction" (Mimeo), Paper presented in the joint JNU-IFPRI Workshop on *The Dragon and the Elephant: A Comparative Study of Economic and Agricultural Reforms in China and India*, March 25-26 held at India Habitat Centre, New Delhi.

Chakravarti, Anand (2001). *Social Power and Everyday Class Relations: Agrarian Transformation in North Bihar*. New Delhi: Sage.

Cohn, Bernard (1987). *An Anthropologist Among Historians*. Delhi: Oxford University Press.

Djurfeldt, Goran and Staffan Lindberg (1975). *Behind Poverty: The Social Formation of a Tamil Village*. London: Curson Press.

Dumont, Louis (1970). *Homo Hierarchicus: The Caste System and its Implications*. London: George, Weidenfeld and Nicolson.

Dwyer, Rachel and Divia Patel (2002). *Cinema India: The Visual Culture of Hindi Film.* Delhi: Oxford University Press.

Epstein, Scarlett (1973). *South India: Yesterday, Today and Tomorrow.* London: Macmillan

Fertiliser Association of India (1988). *Report of the High Powered Committee on Fertiliser Consumer Prices.* New Delhi.

Harriss, John (1982). *Capitalism and Peasant Farming: Agrarian Structure and Ideology in North Tamilnadu.* Delhi: Oxford University Press.

Gupta, Dipankar (1997). *Rivalry and Brotherhood: Politics in the life of Farmers of North India.* Delhi: Oxford University Press.

———. (2000). *Interrogating Caste: Understanding Hierarchy and Difference in Indian Society.* New Delhi: Penguin.

Inden, Ronald (1991). *Imagining India.* Oxford: Basil Blackwell.

Jaffrelot, Christophe (2003). *The Silent Revolution: The Rise of the Low Castes in North Indian Politics.* Delhi: Permanent Black.

Harriss, John (1982). *Capitalism and Peasant Farming: Agrarian Structure and Ideology in Northern Tamilnadu.* Delhi: Oxford University Press.

Jodhka, Surinder (2002). "Caste amd Untouchability in Rural Punjab", *Economic and Political Weekly* 37: 1813-23.

Marriot, McKim (1955). *Village India: Studies in the Little Community.* Chicago: Chicago University Press.

Mujumdar, N.A. (2002). "Rural Development: New Perspectives", *Economic and Political Weekly* 37: 3983-87.

Parthasarathy, G., Shammem and B. Sambi Reddy (1998). "Determinants of Rural Non-Agricultural Employment: The Indian Case", in *Indian Journal of Agricultural Economics* 53: 139-54.

Pradhan, Basanta, P.K. Roy, M.R. Saluja and Shanta Venkatram (2000). "Rural-Urban Disparities: Income Distribution, Expenditure Pattern and Social Sector", *Economic and Political Weekly* 35: 2527-39.

Rasul., M.A. (1974). *A History of the All India Kisan Sabha.* Calcutta: National Book Agency.

Ruthven, Orlanda and Sushil Kumar (2002). "Moving Mud, Shifting Soil: Change and Development in Wage Labour Livelihoods in Uttar Pradesh, India" (Mimeo), *Working Paper 176.* London: Overseas Development Institute.

Sahay, Gaurang Ranjan (2001). *Village Studies in India: A case of Bihar.* Jaipur/New Delhi: Rawat.

Simmons, Colin and Salinder Supri (1995). "Participation in Rural Non-Farm Activity in India: A Case Study of Cultivating Households in Jalandhar District, Punjab", *International Journal of Punjab Studies* 2: 133-53).

Srinivas, M.N. (1987). *The Dominant Caste and Other Essays.* Delhi: Oxford University Press.

Vaidyanathan, A. (2001). Poverty and Development Policy, *Economic and Political Weekly* 36: 1807-14.

Visaria, Pravin (1995). "Rural Non-Farm Employment in India: Trends and Issues for Research", *Indian Journal of Agricultural Economics* 50: 398-409.

Wiser, W.H. (1936). *The Hindu Jajmani System: A Socio-Economic System Interrelating Members of Hindu Community.* Lucknow: Lucknow Publishing House.

4

AMITA BAVISKAR

Cultural Politics of Environment and Development

The Indian Experience

A City Story

Let me begin by recounting an incident that happened 10 years ago, an incident that has a central bearing on the subject of my paper, the cultural politics of environment and development in India. On the morning of 30 January 1995, Delhi was waking up to another chilly winter day. Imagine the well-to-do colony of Ashok Vihar in north Delhi, posh houses shrouded in grey mist, early risers setting off on morning walks, some with their pet dogs—Pomeranians and Alsatians, straining at the leash. As one of these morning walkers entered the neighbourhood 'park', the only open area in the locality, he saw a young man, poorly clad, walking away with an empty bottle in hand. Outraged, he caught hold of the man and called out to his neighbours. Someone phoned the police. A group of enraged house-owners and two police constables descended on the youth and, within minutes, beat him to death.

The young man was 18 year old Dilip, a visitor to Delhi, who had come to watch the Republic Day parade in the capital. He was staying with his uncle in a *jhuggi* (shanty house) along the railway tracks bordering Ashok Vihar. His uncle worked as a labourer in the Wazirpur industrial estate nearby. Like all other planned industrial areas in Delhi, Wazirpur too has no provision for workers' housing. The *jhuggi* cluster with more than 10,000 households shared three public toilets, each one with eight latrines, effectively one toilet between more than 2,000 persons. For most residents, then, any large open space, under cover of dark, became a place to defecate. Their use of the 'park' brought the industrial workers and their families up against the more affluent residents of the area who paid to have a wall constructed between the dirty, unsightly *jhuggis* and their own homes. The wall was soon breached to allow the traffic of domestic workers who lived in the *jhuggis* but worked to clean the homes and cars of the rich, and to offer access to the delinquent defecators.

Dilip's death was thus the culmination of a long-standing battle over a contested space that, to one set of residents, embodied their sense of gracious urban living, a place of trees and grass devoted to leisure and recreation, and that to another set of residents, was the only available space that could be used as a toilet. If he had known this history of simmering conflict, Dilip would probably have been more wary and would have run away when challenged, and perhaps he would still be alive. The violence did not end there. When a group of people from the *jhuggis* gathered to protest against this killing, the police opened fire and killed four more people (PUDR, 1995).[1]

This incident made a profound impression on me. During my research in central India, the site of struggles over displacement due to dams and forestry projects, as well as the more gradual but no less compelling processes of impoverishment due to insecure land tenure, I had witnessed only too often state violence that tried to crush the aspirations of poor people striving to craft basic subsistence and dignity (Baviskar, 2001). Now I was watching a similar contestation over space unfold in my own backyard. I had previously analysed struggles over the environment in rural India; now my attention was directed towards how, in an urban context, the varied meanings at stake in struggles over the environment were negotiated. This concern has been strengthened over the last five years by two sets of processes, each an extraordinarily powerful attempt to remake the urban landscape of Delhi. Through a series of judicial orders, the Supreme Court of India initiated the closure of all polluting and non-conforming industries in the city, throwing out of work an estimated two million people employed in and around 98,000 industrial units.

1. I have narrated this incident in Baviskar (2003a).

For the first time since Independence, perhaps for the first time since the British sacked Shahjehanabad in 1857, workers who had come to the city to earn a living are leaving Delhi, retracing their steps and returning home. At the same time, the Delhi High Court has ordered the removal and relocation of all *jhuggi* squatter settlements on public lands, an order that has already resulted in large-scale demolitions and that may ultimately affect the homes of more than three million people. Both these processes, which were set in motion through public interest litigation by environmentalists and consumer rights groups, indicate that upper-class concerns around health and safety, aesthetics and order, and the desire to live in a 'world-class' city, have come to significantly shape the disposition of urban spaces. In a city of 12 million people, the enormity of these changes is mind-boggling. Already, before our eyes, we have seen the cityscape transformed, new malls and multiplexes, flyovers and wider roads, the Metro, and shops, shops everywhere. And yet, the darker side of this development, the demolitions and displacement, remains invisible to all except those who endure it. The resounding media silence about how workers are losing livelihoods and homes is perhaps not all that remarkable; as P. Sainath (2006) points out, there are more important things like fashion shows to report.

I dwell on these events because, to my mind, they pose a challenge both intellectual and political. On one hand, there are striking resonances between these conflicts over urban resources —land, water, air—and conflicts over rural resources—land, water, pastures and forests. Both pit different classes of people against each other; both involve powerful state institutions that are markedly biased; and both sets of conflicts contain invocations of a transcendental public interest: a 'clean and green city' in one case, and 'national development', 'economic growth', and 'biodiversity conservation' in the other. On the other hand, the urban question raises some perplexing issues, which don't come up in the case of rural conflicts over environment and development, or at least not with the same intensity. One, if clean air and green areas are environmental goods, and indeed no one would dispute that they are, then the protagonists in this case are bourgeois environmentalists who use all the weapons at their command to make the city liveable. This is rather different from what has now come to be an accepted position in debates about rural resource management, that it is those who directly depend on these resources for their subsistence who are best placed to conserve them. It seems as if the connection between ecology and equity, and the related issue of which cause and whose efforts to support, is harder to establish in the urban case. Also, there is the problem of 'environment' and 'natural resources'. What exactly is the environment? In the rural case, it seems to be self-evident that we are referring to land, water, animals and plants and other elements of the bio-physical world. In the urban case, we often fall back on an idea of nature derived from rurality—green areas, clean air and water. But the urban environment, that apparently unnatural, artefactual space of concrete and steel, cement and tar, is in its own way merely nature transformed. And when workers describe their environmental concerns, they rarely mention clean air or parks as a priority; most often, they speak of space, just the sheer ability to have a secure foothold in the city, a place to live. They, and this is especially true of women, also talk about toilets and taps. Shelter, sanitation and water—these are the environmental goods that are most meaningful for the urban poor. There is thus a lack of consensus on what defines an urban environmental issue, and who speaks for the urban environment. Into this discursive gap have disappeared the environmental concerns of an urban underclass that makes cities possible.

Why have we, as scholars and researchers on environment and development, neglected the urban question? Despite a strong secular trend towards urbanisation, why have we concentrated single-mindedly on the rural? As the ecological footprint of urban India grows larger and deeper by the day, rural-urban resource flows acquire greater importance, as does the traffic of migration. Why have we ignored the fact that "the relation of country and city is not only an objective problem and history, but has been and still is for many millions of people a direct and intense preoccupation and experience" (Williams, 1973: 3)? In my own case, I suspect that it has something to do with growing up as an urban, upper middle class nature-lover, and presuming that environmentalism means mainly caring about trees and birds. But in order to address these questions more substantively, I now present before you a short, spotty and highly idiosyncratic survey of what we have done in the last thirty or so years in terms of engaging with the cultural politics of environment and development. By tracing the trajectory of Indian environmental questions in the social sciences, I intend to show that scholarship has been inspired and shaped by popular mobilisations on the ground. In turn, academic research has lent greater legitimacy to the positions espoused by progressive environmental movements. This has been both its strength and its limitation. Such a survey also enables me to pay homage to some of the stalwarts in this field whose work has inspired and influenced me over the years. While I did not have the privilege of personally knowing Dr Malcolm Adiseshiah, the institution that he founded and the scholarship that it fostered have been major resources for me. Prof Vaidyanathan's early writings on agriculture and irrigation had an environmental sensibility that was rare among economists (and still is). To him and to Prof Nirmal Sengupta, for his work on tribal identity and social movements (rather unusual subjects for an economist!), and both of them together for their critical perspectives on large dams, I owe a large intellectual debt. To the Madras Institute of Development Studies (MIDS) as a whole must go the credit of showing us the importance of paying attention to the region as a unit of analysis. In our preoccupation with the village and the nation, we ignore all too often the regional specificities of landscape, history and culture. In correcting this and other oversights, MIDS leads the way.

Social Movements and the Social Sciences

It would not be an exaggeration to say that, in the social sciences of the 1970s, there was no environmental question; there was only the agrarian question. Political economists concerned about poverty, inequality and social change concentrated on areas of irrigated agriculture and how social relations had been transformed by the Green Revolution. Sociologists studied caste and class in villages and, if the subtitle of many books of that time is an indication, usually found both 'continuity and change'. It took two landmark intellectual contributions in the early 1980s—one by a bureaucrat and the other by a journalist—to open up the field. Vohra (1980) drew attention to the massive degradation of the rural environment due to intensive agriculture, ill-planned irrigation and deforestation. In 1982, Anil Agarwal published *The State of India's Environment: A Citizen's Report*, a monumental work drawing on the work of researchers and activists all over the country (CSE, 1982). If Vohra's alarm-call was directed towards the government, Agarwal's encyclopaedia alerted an urban, educated audience. Both were, to some extent, influenced by the emerging environmental movement in the west, but a more proximate cause, especially for Agarwal, was that remarkable movement happening in the Himalaya—Chipko. Of course, there is more than one story to tell about the rise of environmentalism in India—others will emphasise the key importance of the Kerala Sastra Sahitya Parishad and its campaign to save Silent Valley. Still others will recall the campaign against eucalyptus plantations in Karnataka and the Mitti Bachao Andolan in Madhya Pradesh. But I will focus on Chipko here because it was this movement that inspired Ramachandra Guha's (1989) pioneering study of forest policy and peasant resistance, *The Unquiet Woods*.

Guha has been a guru not only to me, but to an entire generation of social scientists. The principles and propositions that his work delineated were to define the field of environment and development for many of us. Like other subaltern historians, Guha wrote about peasant resistance but, unlike them, he focused on forests and not agricultural land. Guha emphasised that forests were not abstract objects of value, but had their own specificities—mixed deciduous stands of oak and rhododendron were decidedly different from pine monocultures. By focusing on the Garhwal and Kumaon hills—not on the Indo-Gangetic heartland or the Cauvery delta, or for that matter Bengal—the region that continues to claim hegemonic status in the social sciences as representing all of India if not the entire postcolonial world, Guha brought attention to the 'marginal' areas of the country which continue to sustain millions of people. Also introduced was the concept of moral economy (Scott, 1976), now firmly yoked to the notion of environmental sustainability. These concepts and concerns were to become the hallmark of engagements with environment and development in India.

If Chipko (and Silent Valley) marked the advent of an environmental sensibility among upper class urban Indians and introduced a generation to the notion that 'red' and 'green' issues were inseparable, its gains were reaped in the decade of the 1990s with the Narmada Bachao Andolan. The academic challenge to big dams began in a small way with Vijay Paranjpye's (1990) critique of the benefit-cost analysis of the Sardar Sarovar and Narmada Sagar projects. That study showed quite clearly that major decisions were being made on the basis of scant data and dubious assumptions; that the social and environmental impacts of the projects were largely a matter of ignorance and indifference to planners. From examining the project on its own terms, the critique widened to consider the class and region-specific implications of benefits and costs. Is it fair to displace some of the most impoverished citizens of the country in order to benefit those who are already well off? Why are the voices of those adversely affected by the dam excluded from the development debate, forcing them to take to the streets? Besides issues of equity and political representation, the anti-dam movement also spurred scholars to examine the actual performance of large dams, leading to the realisation that many of them had failed to deliver the benefits that they promised (for a survey, see Singh *et al.*, 2000, also Manthan Adhyayan Kendra, 2005). In turn, this led to a closer consideration of alternatives to large dams, in the form of technological choices for irrigation and power generation, and modes of watershed management that were based on more decentralised, local and regional scale planning. As these wide-ranging issues came into prominence because of the anti-dam movement, there was also a meta-critique that emerged. This meta-critique challenged dominant conceptions of citizenship and development. Drawing on the experience of the millions who had been displaced and impoverished by development projects since Independence, it asked what the dominant model of capital-intensive development had done for the poor. If it benefited the nation, weren't the poor a part of the nation too? The lives of hill Adivasis in the Narmada valley testified that there were many ways of relating to nature besides building large dams, and dams submerged this great cultural diversity and autonomy (Baviskar, 2004).

More than any other movement, the Narmada Andolan forced us to deal with questions of citizenship and cultural pluralism in the politics of development and environment. The overwhelming opposition that the Andolan and the critique of large dams encountered was revealing. It showed that there were not only crass political and economic interests promoting large dams, which of course there were—huge contracts promise huge kickbacks and commissions, but there was an equally influential factor at work—the power of development as an ideology. The engineers who invoked Bhakra's success and quoted Nehru on 'the temples of modern India' without a sense of irony were not evil men out to swindle the poor. For the most part, they were well-intentioned, patriotic Indians whose dreams of a better world demanded large dams.[2] They imagined that dams would bring progress and prosperity to all Indians, an amorphous mass that got hazy around the edges where the displaced multitudes lurked. The same power of development as an ideology resonating with nationalist desires informed the Supreme Court's judgment on the Sardar Sarovar case that "dams are good for the nation". The reversals suffered by the Andolan due to the effective counter-mobilisation of regional sentiments in Gujarat and nationalist ambitions at the Centre remind us of the importance of ideas and ideologies that exceed materialist concerns.

As Guha (1989) has pointed out in his subsequent writings, there is a distinctively Indian quality to the critique of development fostered by the Chipko and Narmada movements. In espousing an environmental ethic that challenges the ideology of industrial development and the class inequalities that sustain it, these movements embody an engagement with European modernity without being defined or encompassed within its terms. By adopting the discipline of *satyagraha* and struggling for *swaraj* for ordinary

---

2. For a brilliant exposition of the cultural politics around the construction of the Aswan Dam in Egypt, see Mitchell (2002).

Indians, Chipko and Narmada revived the possibility of imagining alternate utopias. In the project of what Dipesh Chakrabarty (2000) calls "provincialising Europe", perhaps the true inheritors of Gandhi's legacy are the people who sing of Uttarakhand as paradise, the Himalaya as a flower, or those who praise the Narmada as a generous girl bestowing the gift of life on all whom she meets. Re-signified by the context of political struggle, these localised imaginings of sacred landscapes are far removed from monolithic Hindu nationalism and inspire actions in defence of places which have been made meaningful through labour and love.

Achievements and Exclusions

Drawing upon these movements, we have developed a distinctive cultural politics of environment and development and I now want to evaluate the conceptual gains from this process. I have discussed elsewhere why I find the term 'cultural politics' more apt than 'political ecology' for this field (Baviskar, 2003b), so I will leave that aside for the moment, and focus on its distinctive attributes. First, the field of environment and development in India emphasises holism and inter-connectedness. This may be unsurprising, given that any discussion of ecological processes must necessarily do so. But there is also a careful distancing from ecological theories such as homeostasis, and awareness about the dangers of uncritically importing organic metaphors from ecology. The tendency towards holism leads to frequent trespassing across disciplinary boundaries, creating a productive hybridity that is an antidote to the compartmentalised approaches of the past. Second, we now treat the environment not simply as a set of 'factors of production' but as material and symbolic resources, sustaining livelihoods but also life in the larger sense, including a life of the imagination that strives to understand the mundane but also to transcend it through individual and collective projects both secular and spiritual (Kumar, 2003). Third, we respect much more the notion of ecological as well as social limits to growth. For generations of Marxists brought up on technological optimism, social relations were the primary constraints on equality and prosperity, for the productive forces of industrialism created the potential of plenty for all. Later, for a post-materialist generation of scholars, especially those influenced by science studies and the social construction of everything, 'objective' ecological constraints were not relevant; what mattered was the discursive production of things. This focus on perceptions, on how authoritative versions of truth were produced, led to a form of pluralism that emphasised how nature was capable of being appropriated in an infinite variety of ways. What got lost was an appreciation of the biophysical properties of nature, all the elements one cannot get around—that the 'social construction of forests or dams' cannot be independent of the specific properties of forests or rivers in particular locales. It is this respect for the biophysical, for ecological as much as social limits, that is central to the cultural politics of environment and development. Fourth, this approach reintroduces a focused view of the operations of power. The post-structuralist notion of power as diffuse and immanent, while no doubt adding nuance, was not very helpful in addressing social inequality or ecological degradation, or the question that Lenin asked so precisely: What is to be done? This is the question to which the cultural politics of environment and development addresses itself.

This, then, is the critical gap that cultural politics spans. It offers a critique of knowledge, especially that which claims the authority of common sense, challenging the self-evident verities of developmentalism and, now, globalisation. At the same time, it remains alert to the power relations that produce hegemonic forms of knowledge as well as the entire set of social practices through which inequality is reproduced. It has tended to concentrate on the workings of state institutions such as forest and irrigation bureaucracies, as well as on the micro-practices of politics within the household and village. These sites of conflict have been more readily available for analysis, often because they have been highlighted by social movements. Research on participatory development fostered by international development organisations has also helped to direct attention to common property resources, perhaps even at the expense of private property—an area for reform that's been off the public policy agenda for a while.

In deriving inspiration from social movements and the many collective struggles taking place across the country, our scholarship has been enriched in manifold ways. At the same time, it has made us less attentive to more low-key issues, the quotidian workings of power that, by their very ordinariness, deflect and disarm our scrutiny. I will discuss only three issues here: markets, middle classes, and mobilisation across sites and scales, all of which to my mind need to be incorporated more thoroughly into our analyses. Consider the gradual processes of commoditisation and privatisation that have made incursions everywhere. Spectacular struggles against a Gwalior Rayon factory or a Coke bottling plant extracting and polluting water get noticed. But the gradual infiltration of packaged water and private water treatment solutions like Aquaguard in the lives and homes of the well-to-do represents no less of a challenge, signalling as it does that the rich have abdicated their power to intervene on the issue of water quality as a common good. The environmental implications of the increasing segregation of what used to be common property resources—water, space, sanitation, transport, biodiversity, where the rich are able to buy their way out of scarcity while the poor are condemned to sub-standard and scant resources—simply haven't received enough attention. Could this be because there has been no major social mobilisation around these issues? Or take the question of the labour market and how it naturalises the predicament of poor workers. I quote from an interview with S.P. Marwah, an IAS officer and ex-Labour Commissioner for Delhi, the most senior official responsible for safeguarding the rights of workers in the city:

> *Marwah:* The main issue of concern before the Delhi government is population—unchecked immigration in the city. This is the basic cause of all problems... It also results in environmental problems... The Supreme Court acted on public interest litigation and acted to clean the air. Delhi is the fourth most polluted city in the world.
>
> *Interviewer:* Has it improved?
>
> *Marwah:* Oh yes. Recently kids were asked if they could see the sky and stars and they responded that they could see the stars now. It was bad [before], you could not see the sky, only black clouds.
>
> *Interviewer:* But what about the workers?

> *Marwah:* They were given compensation.
>
> *Interviewer :* But what about the unorganised labour?
>
> *Marwah:* Some must have gone back to their villages and others took up [other] jobs in the city. Water finds its own way. In practice, no workers were laid off or dislocated. There are large-scale development activities... Overall, it seems everyone welcomes the efforts and is happy. Who would want to see dirt and no development?

Indifference about the devastating effect of displacement for the poor is summed up in the Labour Commissioner's remark, "water finds its own way", naturalising their trauma as the simple ebb and flow of footloose and fancy-free nomads. The mass of workers displaced by the closing of factories and demolition of squatter settlements in Delhi work in what is euphemistically called 'the informal sector'. There is nothing informal about the systematic exploitation that they experience; a better term to use is 'unorganised' because it is that which defines their conditions of work and limits the possibility of collective resistance and transformation. The loosening of labour laws, however imperfectly applied in the past, and the 'freeing' of the market has only worsened their lot. Their vulnerability renders workers invisible to all but a few scholars of labour relations or those whose long-term attention to a region gives them the temporal vantage for tracking demographic and livelihood changes. But why do migrant workers have few allies among those studying environment and development? It strikes me that we prefer social groups from whom we can expect the task of sustainable management of natural resources—seeking ecology and equity simultaneously. Those who wind up on the pavements of Delhi and Chennai looking for work have few resources besides their own labour-power and ingenuity. Do we find them less interesting because, in the ultimate analysis, we are concerned more with safeguarding resources rather than promoting the welfare of those whose lives are marked by extreme deprivation?

In looking back at our analyses of the cultural politics of environment and development with the benefit of hindsight, it is apparent that we have neglected a critical section of the population, *viz.*, the middle class, especially that fraction which can be described as the intelligentsia. The middle class has a matter-of-fact hegemonic presence in the life of our nation; its domination has a patina of `naturalness' that renders it difficult to challenge. Support and mediation by this "reference public", to use Lipsky's term (1968), has sometimes been a crucial resource for grassroots movements. But, for the larger part, the intelligentsia's pursuit of the 'public interest' has generally secured its own interests and ensured its own reproduction (Deshpande, 1997). Impatient with and disdainful of the messiness of political engagement, the intelligentsia takes recourse to avenues of influence that are more amenable to its power, including the short-cut of approaching the higher judiciary. Revealing a fascination for charismatic authority that verges on the fascist, it acclaims and applauds vigilante judicial action that infringes on legislative and executive jurisdiction. The Indian experience shows that the bourgeoisie does not safeguard the public sphere, or uphold civil society in a democracy. In fact, as projects of development and conservation make evident, it often works to systematically exclude the poor from citizenship. Access to a public sphere of political debate and action is usually predicated on access to private resources. For instance, the urban spatialised form of a public sphere, 'the republic of the streets' (Joyce, 2003) created by unruly, recalcitrant vendors and itinerant crowds, is marked by great inequality—while the bourgeois citizen can stroll along confidently, others must keep an eye out so that they are not caught in a municipal raid. The poor struggle against the denial of resources, environmental and political, by protesting when they can but, more often, by simply enduring great hardship. Chatterjee (2004) uses the term "political society" to describe the parallel road to power adopted by those denied access to civil society, but I think what is most striking and poignant about such efforts is that they strive for inclusion within civil society, not seek to carve out a domain outside it. It is the role of the intelligentsia in maintaining unequal access to resources that we must examine more closely. The cultural politics of environment and development demand that we make the connections between poverty and the unbridled consumerism of a privileged class, its sense that it can have it all, aspirations that can never be met without sacrificing someone or something. In other words, we need to 'study up'.

Finally, we need to pay far closer attention to how the cultural politics of environment and development mobilises groups across scales and sites. How, for instance, does the anti-dam campaign bring together disparate entities—caste Hindu peasants and Adivasis in the Narmada valley, environmental and human rights organisations in India and abroad, disillusioned engineers and disaffected bureaucrats, unions of public sector employees, metropolitan *causeratti* and many others to pursue a common cause? This is another taken-for-granted aspect of contemporary movements that scholars shy away from addressing except in general or celebratory terms (Keck and Sikkink, 1998; Khagram *et al.*, 2002; Khagram, 2004). Accusations about being anti-national and anxieties around authenticity have led many activists and scholars to downplay the importance of solidarities across class, region and nation, and the hybridity that marks all creative politics. To contend with global actors, institutions, ideas and processes, we need counter-flows of transnational support. We need to acknowledge and encourage these coalitions even as we remain alert to the consequences of the compromises of power. For instance, a globalised discourse on indigeneity compelled Adivasis to perform acts of 'strategic essentialism' so that they were represented as ecologically noble savages. Perhaps the predicament of displaced workers in Delhi has not attracted the sympathy and support of the intelligentsia because, unlike Adivasis or distant peasants, they seem to be so totally devoid of ecological virtue. The urban poor are a proximate presence defying projects of improvement—they come uninvited to cities, have too many children, live in squalor and, the biggest threat of all, they don't know their place. The barely disguised disgust and unease that mark social relations across class in the urban context convey the depth of this cleavage. When we do not study alliances closely and critically, we also miss the opportunity to understand the absence of alliances that make progressive political projects possible.[3] Markets, middle-classes and multiple scales of action—I urge that we attend to these. And to the intimate connections between the country and the city, places articulated by the above three, places of injustice and suffering but also always places of hope.

I would like to close with the following lines written by Raymond Williams (1973: 5-6), the great cultural critic, in his classic work, *The Country and the City:*

> H.G. Wells once said, coming out of a political meeting where they had been discussing social change, that this great towering city [London] was a measure of the obstacle, of how much must be moved if there was to be any change. I have known this feeling, looking up at great buildings that are the centres of power, but I find I do not say 'There is your city, your great bourgeois monument, your towering structure of this still precarious civilisation' or I do not only say that; I say also 'This is what men have built, often so magnificently, and is not then everything possible?' Indeed this sense of possibility, of meeting and movement, is a permanent element of my sense of cities: as permanent a feeling as those other feelings, when I look down from the mountain at the great coloured patchwork of fields that generations of my own people have cleared...; or the known living places, the isolated farms, the cluster of cottages by castle or church, the line of river and wood and footpath and lane; lines received and lines made. So that while country and city have this profound importance, in their differing ways, my feelings are held, before any argument starts.

---

3. However, there is always the possibility of unintended outcomes. The revolt by Delhi's Residents Welfare Associations against the privatisation of water supply and the hike in water rates has gleaned lessons from South Africa and Bolivia. Used to getting subsidised water, middle class citizens have opposed privatisation, but perhaps their initiative might also ensure that water remains affordable for the poor.

References

Baviskar, Amita (2001). 'Written on the Body, Written on the Land: Violence and Environmental Struggles in Central India', in Nancy Peluso and Michael Watts (eds.), *Violent Environments*. Ithaca, NY: Cornell University Press.

———. (2003a). 'Between Violence and Desire: Space, Power and Identity in the Making of Metropolitan Delhi' in *International. Social Science Journal*. 175: 89-98.

———. (2003b). Tor a Cultural Politics of Natural Resources' in *Economic and Political Weekly*. 38 (48): 5051-5055.

———. (2004). *In the Belly of the River: Tribal Conflicts over Development in the Narmada Valley*. Delhi: Oxford University Press. (second edition).

Chakrabarty, Dipesh (2000). *Provincializing Europe: Postcolonial Thought and Historical Difference*. Princeton, NJ: Princeton University Press.

Chatterjee, Partha (2004). *The Politics of the Governed: Reflections on Popular Politics in Most of the World*. New York: Columbia University Press.

CSE (Centre for Science and Environment) (1982). *The State of India's Environment: A Citizen's Report*. New Delhi: CSE.

Deshpande, Satish (1997). 'From Development to Adjustment: Economic Ideologies, the Middle Class and 50 Years of Independence' in *Review of Development and Change*. 2 (2): 294-318.

Guha, Ramachandra (1989). *The Unquiet Woods: Ecological Change and Peasant Resistance in the Himalaya*. Delhi: Oxford University Press.

and Juan Martinez-Alier (1998). *Varieties of Environmentalism: Essays North and South*. Delhi: Oxford University Press.

Joyce, Patrick (2003). *The Rule of Freedom: Liberalism and the Modern City*. London: Verso.

Keck, Margaret and Kathryn Sikkink (1998). *Activists beyond Borders: Advocacy Networks in International Politics*. Ithaca, NY: Cornell University Press.

Khagram, Sanjeev, James Riker and Kathryn Sikkink (eds.) (2002). *Restructuring World Politics: Transnational Social Movements, Networks, and Norms*. Minneapolis: University of Minnesota Press.

Khagram, Sanjeev (2004). *Dams and Development: Transnational Struggles for Water and Power*. Ithaca, NY: Cornell University Press.

Kumar, Nita (2003). 'The Ganga at Banaras' in Amita Baviskar (ed.) *Waterlines: The Penguin Book of River Writings*. New Delhi: Penguin India.

Lipsky, Michael (1968). 'Protest as a Political Resource' in *American Political Science Review*. 62 (4).

Manthan Adhyayan Kendra (2005). *Unravelling Bhakra: Assessing the Temple of Resurgent India*. Badwani, MP: Manthan Adhyayan Kendra.

Mitchell, Timothy (2002). *Rule of Experts: Egypt, Techno-Politics, Modernity*. Berkeley: University of California Press.

Paranjpye, Vijay (1990). *High Dams on the Narmada: A Holistic Analysis of the River Valley Projects*. New Delhi: Indian National Trust for Art and Cultural Heritage.

PUDR (People's Union for Democratic Rights) (1995). *A Tale of Two Cities: Custodial Death and Police Firing in Ashok Vihar*. April.

Sainath, P. (2006). "Where India Shining Meets Great Depression", in *The Hindu*, April 01. Available at: *www.thehindu.com/todays-paper/tp-opinion/where-india-shining-meets-greats-depression/article3140861.ece*. Accessed on October 15, 2014.

Scott, James (1976). *The Moral Economy of the Peasant: Rebellion and Subsistence in Southeast Asia*. New Haven, CT: Yale University Press.

Singh, Shekhar, Raman Mehta, Vishaish Uppal, Asmita Kabra, Bansuri Taneja, Prabhakar Rao. (2000). *Environmental and Social Impacts of Large Dams – The Indian Experience*. Report prepared for the World Commission on Dams. New Delhi: Indian Institute of Public Administration.

Vohra, B.B. (1980). *A Land and Water Policy for India*. Sardar Patel Memorial Lecture. Delhi: Ministry of Environment, Government of India.

Williams, Raymond (1973). *The Country and the City*. New York: Oxford University Press.

5

SHARMILA REGE

Dalit Studies as Pedagogical Practice

Claiming More Than Just a Little Place in the Academia

My paper is in the area of inequalities in higher education: a subject with which Dr Adiseshiah remained passionately engaged. Following the exemplary path set by Madaras Institute of Development Studies (MIDS) in mapping the region, as a unit of analysis, the focus of my paper, will be western India. As for the theme of my paper, Dalit studies, I have neither formal training in nor sustained experience of doing Dalit studies. Yet, I dare to speak on the theme because the contours of the field are being imagined and contested, raising issues of engaged scholarship in ways that are relatively free of the usual gatekeeping practices of established disciplines.

In order to speak about Dalit studies, I would abstract from my experience of being located in a university where the institutional presence of Dalit studies is limited to a newly constituted adhoc Board of Studies for Dalit Studies. While the university has several chairs in the name of Jotiba Phule, Dr Babasaheb Ambedkar and Anna Bhau Sathe, which organise annual lecture series and seminars, there are yet no interdisciplinary courses in Dalit studies. Only recently, some departments on campus have proposed optional courses at the postgraduate level on theory and practice of Dalit studies. A refresher course sponsored by the University Grants Commission (UGC) for social science teachers, initially planned as a course in Dalit studies, in the name of broader outreach, had to be renamed "Caste Studies in India: 1990s and After". This personal recounting, I hope amply demonstrates that the institutional possibilities of Dalit studies as an academic field with clearly mapped scope and boundaries are still being debated. It may serve here to recall that this process is not unique to Dalit studies. Academic and disciplinary formations, even the most traditional have been founded on boundaries that are products of history and not some *a priori* essence. The tension in the case of fields such as gender and Dalit studies lies in their overt expression of scholarship with commitment,[1] which the academy with its assumed axiological neutrality often misrecognises as violation of scientific objectivity.

In the recent past, there have been wide-ranging expressions of concern about the embracing of market values by the university under conditions of globalisation. Most of these declare the demise of the university following the retreat of the state, increasing force of market values, and the impact of globalisation. Within this current tendency that sees the university in terms of a model of decline, speaking of Dalit studies as situated optimism, a terrain to struggle for within the university may seem anomalous. Following more differentiated views of the university as an institution that marks major transformations within modernity,[2] I shall begin by foregrounding the social and cultural contradictions of colonial modernity as expressed in battles about the nature and function of knowledge.

Colonial and Nationalist Binaries: Erasing the Third Space of Dalit Intellection

Scholars have outlined the early battles over the function and nature of social science knowledge, articulated in the contestations between the colonialist and nationalist discourses of Indian society. Central to the colonial representation of India as distinct and disjunct from the West was caste, represented as the spirit of Hindu civilisation. While the classification and categorisation of 'Indian tradition' created norms for colonial rule, it also enhanced the status of *brahmans* as indigenous intellectuals over and above all political entities.[3] Nationalist knowledge of caste fell broadly within two camps: one that justified the system based either on traditional

1. I am using Bourdieu's conception of 'scholarship with commitment'; see Bourdieu (2003).
2. See for example Delanty (2005).
3. I am drawing my argument from Patel (2006).

arguments of divine intervention or modern idiom of eugenics, and the other that sought to reform it.[4] Whether based on the traditional or modern argument, caste was understood in terms of practices of purity/pollution and in terms of corruption in the 'original Varna order'. Colonial knowledge was structured on binaries that distinguished India from the West, Orient from the Occident, thus homogenising the Indian experience into a Hindu *brahmanical* one.[5] The nationalists imagined alternate knowledges within these binaries, reversing them to claim over the West, a civilisational superiority located in the Vedas. Thus, though the colonialists and nationalists contested the function of knowledge, for both, the nature of knowledge was essentially Hindu and *brahmanical*. The normalisation of knowledge as Hindu and *brahmanical* thus structured by the colonial and nationalist binaries has resonated in the ethnographic and indological perspectives that constituted the dominant social science of India. In the formation of social sciences in universities, an understanding of caste as an ideological system based on an irreconcilable opposition of the principles of purity and pollution came to dominate disciplinary knowledges. After the Second World War, social science discourse refashioned the binaries that emerged in the colonial period within the tradition/modernity thesis. Indigenous approaches suggested as alternatives to discursive dominance of the 'West', postulated exclusive nativism which collapsed the structural inequalities in Indian society.[6] For a generation and more of scholars in the Indian academia, caste was played out through the *dharmashastric* texts or in villages and rituals but not in cities, bureaucratic structures or social movements. Indigenous perspectives that sought to understand India through 'own' categories reproduced the models of the Hindu *dharmashastras* in modern sociological language as alternative discourses on caste. The linkages between the *brahman* male control over knowledge production in the university

4. For a complex and nuanced debate on caste in colonial Maharashtra see Bhagwat (1988) and Palshikar (1998).

5. See Cohn (1987). Also see Patel (2006).

6. Ibid.

departments and the canonical understanding of caste that emerged cannot be underestimated.

It may be recalled that Phule and Ambedkar in different ways, by weaving together the emancipatory non-Vedic materialist traditions and new western ideas had challenged the binaries of Western modernity/Indian tradition and private caste/public nation. Social scientists in search of alternative/'indigenous' perspectives rarely turned to the Dalit discourse—a third space that had interrogated the binaries constructed by colonial and nationalist discourses. Why did social scientists in search of alternative core concepts and constellation of concepts turn usually to Gandhi, Aurobindo and Nehru and rarely to Phule, Shahu or Ambedkar? How might this 'Dalit Phobia'[7] in the academia and its cognitive structures be explained?

It may be argued that the consensual models of caste that resonated in social science practices have fostered the divide between the theoretical *brahman* and the empirical *shudra*[8] producing knowledges that have erased the intellectuality of Dalits. Dalit intellectuality came to be erased by the dominant sanskritisation paradigm, which viewed Dalits as only capable of replication of elite structures. Marxists in the name of diversion from real politics, and Subalterns by situating elites within discourse and Dalits in insurgency denied the intellection of Dalits.[9] Feminist scholarship recognised Dalit women's intellectuality, at best as something 'new', emerging out of the exclusionary practices of mainstream feminism.[10] Thus, different theoretical trends in the social sciences with their focus on the Vedic, economistic class or an autonomous sphere of the pre-modern failed to engage seriously with Dalit intellectual discourse. This has resulted in the absence of a rational engagement with core analytical categories emerging from Hindu metaphysics, leading to a blurring of linkages between Hinduism and Hindutva.[11] Further,

7. Prasad (2006).
8. See Guru (2002).
9. See Menon (2006).
10. For an interrogation of the frameworks that see Dalit feminism as `new' see Rege (2006).
11. Nanda (2002).

an absence of engagement with contestations of the elite claims to name and represent the modern, resulting in the blurring of deep segmentations and tensions within 'our modernity'.[12] The unintended affirmation of the common sense of Hindu right wing movements by 'indigenist' scholarship and the vocal support of prominent social scientists to the anti-Mandal position and their inability to say anything beyond popular common sense[13] demonstrate the serious implications of these absences. Voices on premier campuses decrying reservations for OBC (other backward castes) in the name of merit, equality, nation, citizenship and even 'right' marital partners have laid bare, the tensions between new forms of modernities as they are being articulated in the academic sphere. Critical social science in India has paid little attention to the tensions between new forms of modernities in Indian society and lesser still to their expressions in battles about the nature and function of knowledge.

In this paper, I wish to draw attention to three moments of tension between Dalit and fractured modernities of the dominant public sphere and discuss its implications for the practice of social science of India. I shall briefly trace the first moment in the discourse of Phule, Dr Ambedkar and Shahu which mapped caste as political and then outline the strategies that excluded this discourse from the public sphere and from the formation of social sciences in postcolonial India. The second moment may be traced in the discourse of the Dalit Panthers and Dalit literature of the 1970s that foregrounded the experience of caste and mapped caste as feudal backwardness of Hinduism. I shall then outline the strategies that incorporated the cultural and economic radicalism of the moment in academic discourse, leaving relatively untouched the binaries that structured the core of disciplinary knowledges. I shall then sketch the present, moment in which Dalit studies has emerged drawing upon and rewriting the earlier two moments, establishing caste as a modern form of inequality reproduced not only in villages and rituals

12. See for example Chatterjee (1997).

13. For a precise clarification of the blind spots of sociology revealed by Mandal, see Deshpande (2003) and for the postmodern indigenist scholarship's affirmation of common sense of Hindutva, see Nanda (2002).

but also in global software firms and university classrooms. This moment is marked by the rendering of claims to the modern as being situated, local and partial as also by arguments against collapsing all appeals to caste into casteism.

The second section of this paper presents an outline of two projects undertaken with the explicit pedagogical intent of countering the absence of 'experience of caste' and erasure of Dalit intellectualism in the social science curricula. I shall share some of the 'on ground' experience of introducing Dalit *testimonios* and Ambedkarite music in a classroom and discuss pedagogical strategies designed to promote political and interpretative engagement with caste.

I

Interrogating Fractured Modernity: Excluding 'Enlightenment' from Social Science Discourse

In late 19th century western India, the middle class was[14] emerging as a social group of 'upper castes' using older resources of power and privilege and newer ideas of politics and society in constructing the modern. These 'fractured'[15] modes of speaking caste stitched new principles of individualism with endogamy and *varna-ashrama-dharma* with notions of universal division of labour. In the Marathi public sphere, modernity and nation were mobilised to make the public expression of caste and the woman's question illegitimate. The binaries of spiritual/material and public/private that structured colonial and nationalist knowledges not only delegitimised caste from the domain of the political, but also led to programmes for its amelioration under 'modern' *brahman* leadership. The binaries and their contingent logic of exclusion were challenged within the third space of Dalit discourse, which emerged in response to the opportunities of education opened up by the colonial rule. The Dalit discourse of this moment was constituted by the efforts to recover

14. Words like 'upper and lower' 'castes and untouchables' have been put within quotes the first time they appear in the text, to express distance from the ideology in which these linguistic practices emerge.

15. I borrow the conception of 'fractured modernity' from Joshi (2002).

space in the colonial public sphere for the language of caste on its own terms.[16]

Phule's critique of the caste system contested colonial representations and turned the nationalist imagination of a 'golden past' on its head by interpreting the avatars of Vishnu as different stages of Aryan conquest. The choice between rule of the *Aryabhats* (*brahmans*) and the British is rendered as a choice between two foreign rulers. In his letter to the Conference of Marathi Authors, Phule clearly contested the relegation of caste to the private for 'common good', arguing that those who are genuinely interested in common good must discover its basis and put it forth for debate. Both Phule and Ambedkar in varying ways underlined the historical character of caste-based exploitation, rejected the *Varna* order and suggested annihilation of caste as the only path to an egalitarian society. This language of speaking of caste on its own terms did not draw upon Sanskritic sources alone, but reviewed also the Buddhist, Jain, Bhakti, Prakrit and popular traditions. Phule argued that a society divided by caste could not constitute a nation and those who were claiming to represent the nation were actually its destroyers. Dr Ambedkar too in a similar vein outlined the lack of associated living in a caste-based society, arguing therefore that Hindus could not constitute a nation.[17] The legal terrain constituted by the efforts of Shahu Maharaj in the Kolhapur state (1900-1920)[18] posed a challenge to the discourse of reforming women and lower castes for 'their own good'. Those mobilising the nation, it was argued, were not only ignoring the hierarchical divisions in society but also maintaining them as a basis of power. Dalit modernity was thus fashioned by a sewing together of the emancipatory materialistic traditions that challenged *brahmanism* and new western ideas, seeking a rational reexamination of core values of Hindu metaphysics, heralding thereby an Indian Enlightenment. It was based not on an affirmation

16. For insightful analysis of the two competing sets of languages of caste, see Pandian (2002).

17. For details see Omvedt (1994).

18. I refer here to the efforts of Shahu Maharaj to reserve 50 per cent of all positions in the administration for Backward castes, his orders for compulsory primary education and a series of laws against cruelty against women and for promotion of intercaste and religious marriages.

of inherited values but was a project of giving new emancipatory meanings to modernity.[19] It is paradoxical that in the formation of social sciences in the Indian academia the very discourse of Enlightenment came to be excluded. How then may this exclusion be interpreted?

Baburao Bagul, the revolutionary Dalit writer has explained this in terms of the intelligentsia turning the "Indian liberation struggle into a lop-sided fight and reducing the other movements to a secondary status". The national movement, he argues, "was turned into a form of historical, mythological movement and ancestor worship."[20] Nationalist labeling of the Dalit discourse as anti-national, ideologically specific to certain castes or as emergent from the British policy of divide and rule resonated in the institutionalisation of social science practice in postcolonial India. Dalit discourse was rendered as cultural, particularistic and therefore the other of 'universalistic' social sciences.

Social scientists, who made caste the object of their scientific inquiry in the postcolonial academia, 'naturally' did not turn to the 'particularistic' Dalit discourse. In fact, as caste came to be equated to tradition in social science discourse fashioned by the tradition/modernity theses, the modern secular social scientist came to be imagined as one who publicly and politically disavowed caste. Thus, the elite, upper caste scholars who publicly disavowed caste could claim modernity while labeling the Dalit discourse as betrayal of the nation. The pleas for alternative, decolonised, indigenised and autonomous social sciences were limited by the absence of a rational examination of the *dharmashastras* and by the use of Hindu metaphysics as sociological texts and analytical categories.[21]

---

19. There has been considerable debate on Dalit modernist, anti-modernist and communitarian positions. See Dhareshwar (1993); Ilaiah (1998); Nigam (2000); Nanda (2001); Guru (2000); Pandian (2002) and Rege (2006).

20. See Bagul quoted in Dangle (1992).

21. Oomen (2001) has critiqued the curious equation between theological and sociological texts made by the sociologist D.P. Mukherji in his presidential address at the All India Sociological Conference in 1955. For this and other essays that propose understanding Indian society from non-*brahmanical* perspectives, see Dahiwale (2005).

Neo-*brahmanism* through the idiom of gossip, malicious propaganda and condescending attitude put claims of the upper castes to represent both the universal and indigenous social sciences beyond examination. Those who publicly disavowed caste could assume an Archimedean standpoint and thus claim to name, classify and represent modernity and its sciences. The paradox of the exclusion of discourse of Indian Enlightenment from the formation of social sciences in the name of national and universal surely calls for further inquiry into the micro-politics of our academia.

Interrogating the Opposition between Marx and Ambedkar: 'Including' Dalits in Social Science Discourse

The second moment is marked by the new social movements of the 1970s, particularly the feminist and Dalit movements. These movements interrogated the interpretations of the public sphere as a sphere of secular categories, split along the public/private and class/caste-gender axis. Efforts in this second moment to recover a language of caste on its own terms came from unconventional Marxists (Yuvak Kranti Dal, Satyashodhak Marxist party and the Shramik Mukti Dal in western India), the Dalit Panthers and the Dalit Literary Movement. Since the mid–1960s, reflections on the relationship between caste and class in Maharashtra had pointed to the limitations of mechanical application of Marxist categories to the Indian situation.[22] There were critiques of merely adding caste to class as the caste system came to be conceptualised as neither merely ideological nor a simple cluster of concrete and interacting *jatis*. The principles and practices that constitute the *jatis* (endogamy, rules of purity-pollution, occupational tasks that govern the hierarchy and exploitation) were seen as shaping and being shaped by changes in state formation, economic and social relations.[23] There were efforts to synthesise Marxist and Phule-Ambedkarite thought to underline the autonomy of *varna-jati* categories in determining the processes of material transformation. Shifts in signification and gendered

22. See for example Pandit (1979).

23. See Omvedt (1994).

relations were marked as constitutive of all social formations.[24] The formulation of the category *brahmani* and *abrahmani* introduced a new binary and came to be debated across Maharashtra, thus opening up for analysis the politics of representation as played out in India. The Dalit Panthers movement that gathered momentum in 1970s marked another defining moment in the politics of speaking caste on its own terms. The Panthers sought to universalise Dalit identity as proletarian experience, interrogating the separation between economic and cultural spheres and the assumed opposition between Marx and Ambedkar.[25] The Dalit literary movement foregrounded the experience of caste, underscoring the feudal backwardness of Hinduism. The organised left however continued to see the public and political expression of caste as backward ideology having a retarding effect on class struggle. The Shiv Sena and Jan Sangha protested violently against the radicalism of the Panthers labeling their critique of treatment of Dalits in independent India as a betrayal of the nation.[26]

These developments resonated in the social sciences as the number of doctoral thesis on Dalit communities, movements and

24. See Patil (1994). The word non-*brahmanical* as used in this text refers to an English translation of *abrahmani* and is different from *brahmaneter* literally meaning all except the brahmans and which has been translated as non-*brahman*. The concept abrahmani has been articulated in the voluminous work of comrade Sharad Patil, the founder of the Satyashodhak Communist Party and continues to be rigorously debated. Patil argues that the epistemological conflict in Indian Philosophy is between *brahmani* and *abrahmani* schools and that these categories have evolved from the history of social conflict in Indian Society. He argues that the Sankhya, Lokayata, Buddhist, Kauala, Shaiva, Tantra and in the modern period Phule, Periyar and Ambedkar schools of thought represent the abrahmani tradition. Recently scholars have mapped the possibilities of bringing *abrahmani* perspectives into the academy, especially in doing feminist history and understanding Indian society from non-*brahmanical* perspectives. See Bhagwat and Pardeshi (1998) as also Ilaiah (2001) and Dahiwale (2005).

25. See Omvedt (1995).

26. An article published in the socialist journal *Sadhana*, written by Raja Dhale, a founding member of the Panthers called for the 25th anniversary of independence to be observed as a Black day. The Panthers had argued that "A flag that could not guarantee dignity and equality to Dalits was likened to 'a piece of cloth to be stuffed up the arse of the savarna'". The Jan Sangh and Shiv Sena led protest marches, threatened to burn down the magazine, and called for punishment to Raja Dhale for disrespecting the national flag. Vidyut Bhagwat who attended the meeting held to discuss the controversial issue and the threats, observed that several senior socialist leaders attending the meeting had also expressed their displeasure and unease with the insult of the symbol of the nation.

literature showed a marked increase, and 'topics' on the same came to be 'included' atleast in some courses in sociology and political science curricula.[27] This period also saw the emergence of a generation of Dalit scholars in social science departments of the universities in Maharashtra. Many of these scholars trained at the Jawaharlal Nehru University or Dr Babasaheb Ambedkar Marathawada University had engaged in Dalit movements of the 1970s and early 1980s, and carried that political commitment into academic careers. We are yet to put together oral histories of Dalit intellectual and political journeys and understand systematically how their relationship to the academy was constructed. We need to understand the ways in which despite `inclusion' both at the level of practice and within the substantive areas of the disciplines, Dalits continued to be marginalised in the cognitive structures of the disciplines.

The epistemological challenges posed by the Dalit movement of the moment were disciplined through frameworks of the marginal man, 'his' relative deprivation, reference groups and social mobility. Dalits became an object of social science research leading to claims about the expansion of the subject matter to include the marginalised. However, this substantive inclusion did not interrogate the core of the disciplines, which continued to be maintained through the taken-for-granted binaries of humanities/social sciences, social/political, social world/knower, objectivism/subjectivism and macro/micro. This is best seen in the curricular practices of the moment that at one level channelised the challenge of 'experience of caste' foregrounded by Dalit literature and *testimonios* to optional courses in literature departments, while compulsory courses in social sciences continued to intellectualise rather than explain the structures of caste. The Dalit question was limited to optional courses on state policies and programmes for protection and mobilisation of SCs (scheduled castes) and STs (scheduled tribes) or at best to a module in a course on social movements. Barring notable exceptions, much of the research of the period can at best be described as advocacy

27. For an account of Dalits in the cognitive structures of sociology, see Kumar (2005) and Rodrigues (2003).

social science, which presumed that the proper relationship between the researcher (in here) and the Dalits (out there) was to 'represent' them. So surveys, interviews and other data of Dalit groups and communities were represented with a new sentimentalism, in what has been aptly called Hewlett Packard photo-real printer style. As the advertisement of the printer goes, Dalits were represented 'just as they are—only reality looks more real.'[28]

The inclusion of Dalits in the academia in the second moment was co-opted by liberal frameworks and displaced by the Marxist. While the former channelised findings of research into solutions or policy suggestions, the latter insisted that in the final analysis caste was indeed class. What I wish to emphasise is the hierarchies that structure the academy and the ways in which prevailing theoretical frameworks liberal, Marxist re/produced Dalits and Dalit intellection as the 'other' of the modern and secular. As was true of the new social movements of the period, in the academia too, all 'others' occupying the borderlands, like women's studies, peasant or environment studies did not necessarily address each other's issues. Thus in the second moment what emerged in the academia may in retrospect be named 'social science of Dalits', a space in *brahman galli* (*brahman* residential quarters). Its practices more often suggested an 'inclusion of Dalits' than reflexive reconstruction of theoretical frameworks, conceptual systems and epistemological positions.

Interrogating the Space in Brahman Galli: Reflexive Dalit Reconstruction of Social Science Discourse

The third moment, the present, is marked by the emergence of Dalit studies as a perspective/field in the Indian academia, the category 'Dalit' being understood as historically constructed through the revolutionary struggles of Dalits.[29] The varying narratives of the emergence of Dalit studies in different regions suggest the significance of the interface between the local Dalit movement, the national and international contexts for this process. In Andhra Pradesh, for

28. See Stanley (2000).

29. See Guru (2001).

instance, the Karamchedu massacre (1985), the formation of Dalit Mahasabha, the Dalit intellectual domain of *Dalitvadam* and the pro-Mandal agitations have been seen as significant for the emergence of Dalit studies.[30] At the national level, the 'rise of Dalits and the renewed debate on caste' or 'secular upsurge of caste'[31] in the 1990s became a significant force. This renewed debate was constituted by several forces like the birth centenary celebrations of Dr Ambedkar that gave new visibility to Ambedkar scholarship, the emergence of the Bahujan Samaj Party, implementation of the Mandal Report and the consequent violent opposition and debate in the media and academia. The 'emergence' of Dalit feminism and the challenge it posed to the construction of Dalits and women as consistent case was also a crucial force in the constitution of Dalit studies. Also significant was the international context, the addressal of caste at the U.N Conference against Racism at Durban, the mobilisation of the Dalit question by NGOs and its prioritisation by funders like the Ford Foundation.[32]

Questions of definition of Dalit studies came to be debated:[33] Is it a study of Dalits by Dalits? Is it a perspective to be included or at best integrated into existing disciplines or is it an academic field in the making? Dalit studies, as K. Satyanarayana has argued, "is not just a new body of knowledge about Dalits, that it is a new perspective to study Indian society and to redefine existing disciplines." Drawing from the Manifesto of the Dalit Panthers, Gail Omvedt too sees Dalit studies as not a little place in *brahman galli,* but a field of scholarship, where, from Dalit perspectives, the whole social system and history of society become the object of study. G. Aloysius in outlining the agenda of Dalit studies as not `merely interpreting reality but changing it', underlines Dalit studies as critical and inclusive social science. Criticality suggests that Dalit studies is not the

30. For a nuanced and critical review of the local, regional and international contexts of emergence of Dalit studies, see Satyanarayana (2005).

31. See Kothari (1994).

32. For the international context see Thorat and Kant (2003).

33. For the debates see Kumar and Kumar (2005).

indiscriminate valorisation of Dalitism while inclusiveness suggests that fundamental to Dalit studies are conceptualisations that in challenging fake universalism seek to be potentially and theoretically universal.[34] The intersectionality and overlap of structures of caste, class, gender, ethnicity and sexual orientation are seen as crucial for Dalit studies.[35] There have been exercises to delineate the subject matter of Dalit studies as also to take a stock of disciplinary methodologies from Dalit perspectives and trajectories through the contributions of individual scholars. The significance of reflexive exchange of experiences of institutionalisation with gender studies, Black and ethnic studies has also been outlined.[36]

Having traced the three moments in Dalit studies in India, I shall not undertake a review of the field of Dalit studies here[37] but conclude this discussion by underlining the distinctive character of the present moment. The present moment is distinctive in its critical recovery of the Dalit discourses that constituted the first two moments and in foregrounding them to interrogate the binary conceptualisations of modernity, democracy, community, secularism or subjectivity. Tensions between new forms of modernities in Indian society, played out in the debates of the 1990s—Mandal, Ayodhya, globalisation and quota within quotas—are crucial to the formation of this moment. The resurgence of caste and community within women's movement and feminism in the Dalit movement has promoted in this moment a greater historical sensitivity to intersectionality. The dangers of hasty opposition and fusion between Dalit rights and women's rights have been spelt out. This moment is marked by convincing arguments against appeal to caste being equated to casteism and by rendering of unmarked claims to represent and classify the modern as situated, local and partial.

34. See Aloysius (2005).

35. See Mani (2005).

36. See Kumar (2005).

37. I have attempted an extensive review of interface between debates in Dalit movements, feminist analysis of colonialism and new developments in the study of culture and society and its implications for Dalit studies in Rege (forthcoming).

A clear map of the third moment in terms of trends in Dalit theory, 'on ground' practices of research and teaching in Dalit studies and boundaries which decide who is in and out of the field may be difficult to draw. However in the present moment, Dalit studies as an epistemic community is visible in the funding categories of state and international funding bodies, formation of new centres in universities and research institutes, publishing houses, websites, special issues of journals, autonomous agendas and programmes of intellectual collectives and debates on list-serves. It may be clarified, lest my mapping of the moments has created a linear narrative that the three moments—Dalit exclusion, disciplinary co-optation and reflexive reconstruction—co-exist in the academic space generating tensions at the level of practice.

Reception of Dalit Studies in the Academia: Scripts of Denial, Accusation and Reflexive Reconstruction

Developments in Dalit studies have been received in the academia with scripts of denial, scripts of accusation and scripts of reflexivity. As practitioners of Dalit studies, I think we need to avoid the temptations of collapsing these responses into classifications of scholars as *brahmanical* and non-*brahmanical* or pro and anti-Dalit persons. Such classifications produce intellectual closures by equating responses to individual attitudes and thereby foreclosing thoroughgoing critiques of dominant epistemological positions that structure social sciences in the academy.

Scripts of denial usually begin with a listing of how Dalits have always been an object of research and thereby denying all claims of exclusion. Such scripts miss out the moral epistemology placed at the heart of Dalit studies which is foundationally concerned with material conditions that underpin the knowledge that the academy claims to produce. Scripts of accusation are often expressed in terms of a moral panic about identity politics in the academy resulting in a crisis of fragmentation, relativism, falling standards and retreat of good academic practices. Underpinning such calls is misrecognition of Dalit studies within the academy as a 'thing'—that is identitarian. It may serve to recall that every discipline has its internal divisions which may be expressed in binaries of structuralist/interactionist, realist/idealist, postmodernist/essentialist, communitarian/modernist and so on. Dalit studies too is a broad field inhabited by a diverse set of people who agree and disagree on several issues and may debate the possibilities and limitations of identitarian perspectives for Dalit studies. Following Bourdieu[38] what I want to underline is that the scripts of accusation show a high co-relation between the types of cultural capital at the disposal of the scholar and the practices they defend as good social science. Further, it is possible to see these scripts of accusation against Dalit studies as examples of what Dorothy Smith following Marx theorises as the "ideological three step"[39] which is a means of caricaturing and then dismissing views we disapprove of.

Scripts of reflexive reconstruction do not reduce the claims of Dalit studies to 'benign introspection' or a 'turn inwards that assumes away power', or a 'topic' for social sciences.[40] The claims of Dalit studies are seen as objective since their implications are general and not limited to the subjective experiences of the group in question. The epistemic privilege is not a sentimental gesture but a way to push towards greater social objectivity and therefore to be evaluated, as any social and historical explanation should be.

For many teachers like me located in universities, an issue of concern is the translation of this reflexivity into curricular and pedagogical practices. For instance, how do we operationalise truth-seeking principles of Phule-Ambedkarite pedagogies in our classrooms? What do the new terms for democratisation of knowledge set by Dalit studies suggest for feminists teaching women's studies in the academy? How do we address in our classrooms the disjuncture between academic knowledge systems and social practices of caste made apparent by Dalit scholarship? I shall in the next section address some of these questions through the presentation

38. See Bourdieu (1990).

39. See Smith (1974).

40. My conception of reflexivity draws upon the work of Liz Stanley; for Stanley's conception of analytical reflexivity, see Stanley (2000).

of on-going research on the uses of *testimonios* and of empirically researched histories from below of Dalit collective struggles.

II

Dalit Studies as Pedagogical Practice: Seeking Political and Interpretative Engagement with Caste

Over the last two decades, women's studies in India has raised important questions about the invisibility, distortion and marginalisation of gender as category of analysis in the mainstream disciplines and their practices of cannonisation. Despite the feminist critiques of mainstream social sciences, the classical frameworks of caste have cast their shadow on women's studies too. Post-Mandal violence by upper caste, elite students posed a direct challenge to the assumption that caste identities in urban India were personal and private matters. The burden of caste in our universities and classrooms, as in other institutions, has always weighed more heavily on the Dalit and *bahujan* students. Elite, upper caste girl students protesting against Mandal had, through their placards, displayed their anxiety at finding educated husbands, thus expressing publicly their commitment to caste endogamy. Dalit scholarship drew attention to the new modes of reproduction of caste inequalities whether through the idiom of citizenship or merit. The conceptualisation of *brahmanical* patriarchy and the historical delineation of its emergence in a social formation of graded hierarchies was veritably a theoretical 'discovery' of the last decade.[41]

Another important challenge came with the emergence of the Dalit feminist assertions and critiques of the Dalit and women's movements both at the regional and national levels. The writings and manifestos of different Dalit women's groups underlined that the 1970s unmarked feminism had infact been in theory and praxis *brahmanical* feminism. Dalit feminist critiques of the 1990s thus posed challenges to feminist canons, curricular protocols and

---

41. For incisive theorisation on *brahmanical* patriarchy, see Chakravarti (1993). For a brilliant and by far the best feminist engagement with the caste question in India, see Chakravarti (2003). See also Geetha (2001).

alliances with *brahmanical* power and privilege. Except a few notable exceptions, women's studies scholars did not seriously engage with Dalit feminist critiques. Reflections on caste in the curricular protocols of women's studies are quite rare.

In the post-Mandal period, as feminists forming alliances with democratic *Dalitbahujan* groups and cultural movements like the Vidhrohi Sanskritic Chalval, one of the first realisations was about the gross ignorance of histories and cultures that have been violently marginalised and the manufacture of ignorance in which the practice of women's studies is complicit. For some of us involved in developing undergraduate and postgraduate courses, curricular transformation and pedagogical strategies were the immediate sites for engagement. Consequently, projects with explicit pedagogical functions were undertaken. The first involved interviews and workshops with social science teachers to map the reproduction of 'gender and caste inequalities' in the undergraduate and postgraduate curricula of seven universities in Maharashtra. Such an exercise made apparent among other things, the absence of writings on/by Phule, Ambedkar and selections from Dalit literature and life narratives in the course readings. While the relevance of the former was seen as limited to optional courses on political thinkers in Maharashtra, optional courses in Marathi literature departments were seen as the rightful location for the latter. Discussions on Dalit movement in Maharashtra both in courses in sociology and political science are filled with details of factionalism in the Republican Party, the decline and degeneration of the Dalit movement and gratuitous conclusions about deification of Dr Ambedkar by the Dalit masses.

Discussions in the workshops around these issues and on conceptual challenges and pedagogical strategies suggested the need for putting together interdisciplinary teaching/learning materials to promote political and interpretative engagement with issues of caste and perspectives from Dalit collective struggles. In this section, I shall outline two such efforts. One such effort sought to counter the absence of 'experience of caste' and the hegemony of White/*brahmanical* feminisms as default frames of reference in theory courses. This project sought to translate into English eight testimonios of Dalit women in Maharashtra and histories of anti-race feminisms into Marathi. The second sought to counter the erasure of Dalit intellectualism in comprehending Dalit collective action. This project aimed at building an empirically researched history from below of the events in the Ambedkarite calendar. It documented the booklet, music and cassette cultures of the Ambedkarite counterpublics, tracing historical linkages with the *Satyashodhak* and non-*brahman* modes of publicity.[42]

Introducing Dalit Women's *Testimonios* in the Curricula: Countering Unmarked Feminisms as Default Frames of Reference

Dalit *testimonios* as historical narratives of experience counter the conveniently more popular readings of caste derived from `talking with *brahmans*' and views from 'top to down' that structure the social science curricula. However, reading Dalit 'autobiographies' minus the political ideology and practices of the Dalit movement does stand the risk of making a spectacle of Dalit suffering and pain for non-Dalit readers.[43] In Maharashtra, since the early 1960s, issues related to the consumption of Dalit literature of protest and revolt had come to be debated. Several Dalit scholars argued against Dalits writing autobiographies and compared the process to 'digging out stench from hateful waste bins of the past'. Others, in defending the importance of the genre, outlined the specific characteristics of Dalit life narratives and their significance for the community. Important questions are related to the origins of the genre of Dalit life narratives, its political significance as well as limitations and the challenges it poses to the genre of bourgeois autobiography. Can the Dalit life narrative be called an *atma charitra* (autobiography)? Is it better described as Dalit *atmakathan/svakathan* (defined as narratives of Dalit self and community)? Are Dalit life narratives a moral source

42. The first project has culminated in the book *Writing Caste/Writing Gender: Narrating Dalit Women's Testimonios* and a series of 12 articles in Marathi on African-American Feminisms in the *Satyashodhak Sanghatak*. The second project is being translated into a book *Caste, Identity and Public Sphere: Documenting Ambedkarite Counterpublics*.

43. For a critical debate on this issue see Anand (2003).

for political movement or reminders of a hateful past? The entire debate on whether the hateful past should be written and brought into the present suggests the complex relationship between official forgetting, memory, and identity. Dalit life narratives, it came to be argued, are in fact testimonios, which forge a right to speak both for and beyond the individual and contest explicitly or implicitly the 'official forgetting' of histories of caste oppression, struggles and resistance. Dalit life narratives thus historically created the genre of testimonios in which the individual self seeks affirmation in a collective mode. Yet as has been pointed out, we need to remember that by bringing into public domain details of life, they also challenge the communitarian control on self.[44] This dialectics of self and community assumes further significance in Dalit women's *testimonios* as they challenge the communitarian notions of singular Dalit community.

Introducing the *testimonios* in the curricula is a complex and difficult process as distinct from efforts to 'caste-sensitise' curricula. Constructing oppostional Dalit feminist pedagogies, a complex and difficult process, is distinct from efforts to 'caste-sensitise' women's studies curricula or curricula in any discipline or academic field. The absence of caste cannot as if be easily resolved by adding Dalit women to the curricula, thus making Dalit women bear the excessive burden of caste in the curricula. Two models of 'including' Dalit women in the curricula that are commonly practised can be best described as the "feminist as tourist" and "feminist as explorer models".[45] While the first model prescribes, 'add Dalit women and stir', the other suggests 'add Dalit women as separate and equal'. The feminist as tourist model operates a paradigm that assumes unmarked feminism as 'original' and makes brief forays into the 'problems' of Dalit women through a single module or example. The picture briefly then is one of monolithic images of Dalit who have the problems, and unmarked feminism which has the theory and historical agency. The feminist as explorer model operates through pedagogical strategies

44. See Guru (2003).

45. I borrow these models from, Talpade (2003).

that may be misconstrued as sensitive because entire courses seem to be dedicated to Dalit women. The explorer model constructs separate courses on Dalit women's writings largely falling into a framework of cultural relativism. Therefore in such courses, it appears as if women from different cultures write differently, so we are treating them separately but equally. All questions of power, agency and common criteria for evaluation are thus silenced in such curricular models. Oppostional Dalit feminist pedagogies reject uncritical classical anthropological gaze at Dalit women and suggest that Dalit women's analytical gaze be thrown back at theories and praxis that does not state caste on its own terms. Such curricular models propose that Dalit women's testimonios be read historically and relationally in the Dalit articulations of the woman's question and the articulations of caste in the writings and associations of upper caste women in late 19th and early 20th centuries. The pedagogical project therefore sought to put together materials drawn from printed and oral modes of publicity to engage readers of the *testimonios* in a complex relational understanding of social location, experience and history.

I have discussed elsewhere in detail the recovered articulations of the woman's question in the *Satyashodhak* counterpublics of the Phuleites as well as of the emergence of a distinctly non-*brahman* discourse on rights for women in the Kolhapur state in the first two decades of the 20th century.[46] I shall skip these details and argue that the developments after the 1920s in the non-*brahman* movement saw considerable reordering along the lines of caste and, as compared to the *Satyashodhaks*, the non-*brahman* publics became a conservative force. The efforts of early Ambedkarite publics to recover a space for the language of caste that challenged not only the place occupied by the *brahmans* but the ideology and practice of the caste system radicalised once again the imagination to reconceptualise gender codes and society.

In the early decades of the 20th century, all three national women's organisations of the time (All India Women's Conference [AIWC], National Conference of Indian Women and Women's Indian

---

46. For details, see Rege (2006).

Association), even those who had earlier supported reservations for women, opposed all reservations and denied the right of political representation to the 'depressed classes'. The AIWC in 1932 passed a resolution against communal hedges and argued that the practice of untouchability was a disgrace to Hindu religion and stated that this had been brought into notice by Gandhi's fast. Most of the women's organisations of the period thus addressed the issue through programmes of the '*Harijan* campaign'. In the Ambedkarite public sphere, the organisation of independent meetings and conferences of women marked this period a consequence of Dr Ambedkar's practice of organising a women's conference along with every general meeting that was called. The only but very significant historical account of these articulations of women's question and voices in the Ambedkar movement that we have available is Moon and Pawar's documentation of oral narratives of women in the Ambedkar movement.[47] Early writings of Dalit women in the periodical *Janata* also provide insights into the issues and practices of the Ambedkarite women's publics. Anjanabai Deshbhratar, narrating her experiences of the Nagpur Conference of the AIWC, in 1938, comments that the Savarna sister's behavior towards their untouchable sisters was distant, cold, mean and of lowly attitude. During the lunch hour, the untouchable women delegates, Jaibai and others had been asked to sit aside and had felt humiliated. The Conference of Ambedkarite women at Nagpur had condemned this act of the AIWC through a resolution and announced the formation of a separate Srimati Ramabai Ambedkar Sangh. The third All India Untouchable Women's Conference in 1945 critiqued the agenda of the AIWC as being hollow and underscored the need for separate organisation of untouchable women.

In the late 1930s, Mahila Parishads became a regular feature of the conferences of the Independent Labour Party and passed resolutions to reserve one out of three seats for women in the Provincial Legal Councils for Dalit women and to appoint Dalit women as honorary magistrates. There were other important

47. By far the best documentation of women's participation in the Ambedkar movement is to be found in Pawar and Moon (1989; 2000).

resolutions against the cuts in wages of women textile workers, for promotion of compulsory education for Dalit girls through freeships, appointment of Dalit teachers and ban on marriage of girls until the completion of education.

The modern feminists had relegated caste to the 'social', addressed untouchability as 'retrograde tradition' and 'a disgrace to Hindu community'. In opposing the Communal Award of separate electorates for 'common good' and 'unity' they had, naturalised the claim of upper caste women to represent the modern Indian woman. The Ambedkarite women's publics articulated caste not just as retrograde tradition but as a form of inequality reproduced in modern institutions like state bodies and women's organisations. Sisterhood across castes was not a given but achievable through a programme of a direct onslaught on *brahmanism*. The conflicting relationship between women of different castes and the possibilities of collaboration evident in Dr Ambedkar's thought appear in women's oral compositions about Dr Ambedkar's second marriage to Savita Kabir, a *brahman* woman. Printed critical works of memory have sometimes recorded these verses composed by women in the Ambedkar movement and which became a part of popular memory. In one such composition, the Dalit women imagine the sisterhood made possible by Bhima:

> Ramabai and Savitabai—though both of different castes,
> Eat in the same plate—it's for the sake of their Bhima

In another composition, a Dalit woman advises the *brahman* girl to learn the ways of the Dalit community:

> O girl-from brahman family, drape your sari well to cover yourself.
>
> Baba is busy with his work—sitting on the chair,
>
> He's not looking at you.

Such a prioritisation of the community over conjugality is a repeated theme in women's compositions and stands out distinctly from the middle class discourse of the 'educated companionate' conjugality that alienated women from the community without granting autonomy. The Ambedkarite women's publics in contesting the dominant opposition between political claims of 'untouchables' and the rights of women, thus held a promise of a more emancipatory modernity.

We see that until the first decade of the 20th century, *brahman* men largely dominated the Marathi public sphere through which the women's question came to be debated. The kind of fractured modernity, fashioned by bringing together Mill and Manu helped men to create new forms of control but also created spaces for middle class, upper caste women to contest male domination and pursue their interests. If the end of the 19th century is marked by the nationalists relegating the women's question to the private, the period also saw intensified activity in the form of caste conferences among the non-*brahman* castes like the *marathas*, *mali*, *bhandari*, *ramoshi* and *dhangars*. It may be argued that the relegation of women's question to the private had been contested and the women's question continued to dominate debates in the journalistic literature of women and the 'lower and middle caste' associations of the early 20th century. In the caste journals, a growing concern with the status of the caste came to be linked to the status of the women of that particular caste. *Bahujan* women in their editorials, writings and speeches underlined the relative lack of education of their menfolk as compared to *brahman* men and linked progress of the caste community to the education of women. The women of the *bahujan* castes wrote claiming their *jnanti* (caste) and gender identities; and in doing so, caste was often privileged over the nation.

The closing decades of the 19th and the early decades of the 20th century saw several educated middle class women contesting through journalistic writings, the relegation of the woman's question to the private. Women wrote on the question of enforced widowhood, dowry, the importance of education, age at marriage, physical exercise, health and sexuality. There seem to have been some debate among the upper caste *shenvi* and *prabhu* women on whether the narration of their experiences would create a negative image of their caste. Women write as if on behalf of *stree samaj*, *stree varg* or *stree jaat* (community, class, caste of women) while in practice suggesting differential education and occupations for women of different strata. Writing in 1890s, they explain how labouring in the mills or vegetable vending was not suited for women of higher castes and that tailoring was the best source of livelihood. In the post-war period as women of these classes began to enter the sphere of paid service, several writings began to outline arenas like primary education, post and telegraph offices, medicine and nursing as appropriate areas for women. They argued that women competing with men in these arenas was in the interest of the nation; however, women competing with men in the mills was dangerous. Small workspaces, long hours of work, illiteracy and 'low caste' were seen as causes of immorality in such workplaces. The politics of these early feminists which consolidated the notions of stree *samaj/varg/jati* was not autonomous of the fractured modernity of their class and therefore articulated both a critique of and complicity with *brahmanical* caste and gender codes. They articulated *navmatavaad* (modernity) as a practice, which did not hinder old ideas while developing new viewpoints among the new generation. They only reminded them of some existing theoretical perspectives.

A review of the extraordinary number of autobiographies written and published in Marathi by women since the early 20th century further suggests the ways in which elite women exercised the power to name and represent the modern. More than half of the 35 autobiographies representing Marathi middle class life of the late 19th and early 20th centuries are narratives of companionate marriages or life sketches of a famous husband. The post first world war period is marked by autobiography of the middle class upper caste women making spaces in the public arenas of education, music, cinema and dance. An extraordinary number of autobiographies in the period 1976-2000 are narratives of women artists and wives of famous men. The earlier stress on perfect companionship is replaced with a predominance of expressions of marital discord. Caste rarely appears in the autobiography of the Marathi middle class women, it always belongs to someone else especially to the 'lower caste' women in the mills or vegetable vendors or to a by gone past. In the taken-for-granted categorisation of autobiographies practised in Marathi literature departments too, caste belongs only to Dalit women. If we reflect on this categorisation and pose a reversal—why is the autobiography of companionate marriage, marital discords or making spaces in public sphere not referred to as the modern *brahman* women's autobiography? It is because much of the autobiography of the modern Marathi woman has been the narrative of the upper caste woman, her struggle with tradition and desire to be modern. It is this self that claims to be universal, modern, unmarked by caste through its journeys of companionate marriage, modern institutions and marital discord. Caste as the 'other' of the modern as if belongs only to the Dalit women. The common sense of the women's movement and rehearsed frames of feminist analysis too render Dalit women's narratives of struggle as not feminist enough because of what is perceived as a prioritisation of community over 'own issues'. This claim of the upper caste women's autobiography to represent modern Marathi/Indian woman serves on the one hand to render invisible their complicity in privileges of *brahmanical* patriarchy; on the other hand, it classifies the narratives of women whose self-definition is located explicitly in caste as a relational identity as if the 'other' of the modern and feminist.

The collection of translated, historically and relationally located *testimonios* put together as learning-teaching materials though not exhaustive brings together writings that reinscribe histories spanning a period from 1920 to the present. Six of the writers inscribe memories of different phases of the transition from Mahar to a neo-Buddhist community. Two *testimonios* inscribe into the histories of Dalit feminism, voices of the *gopal* and *gondhali* castes, which are marked in Maharashtra as nomadic communities. While all writers belong to the larger universe of Dalit movement, their politics differs by region, community and their ideological position. Babytai Kamble and Shantabai Kamble (both located in Western Maharashtra) foreground the life of the Mahar community in the pre-Ambedkar era highlighting thereby the transformation that came with the emergence of Ambedkarite counterpublics. Muktabai Sarvagod outlines the tensions between Gandhian and Ambedkarite politics, while Shantabai Dani's *testimonio* maps the gender ideology of the Ambedkarite movement. Kumudtai Pawde reflects on life in the Varhad region characterised by the early entry of Mahars into textile labour, a legacy of self-reform and strong base of Ambedkarite movement. She writes on practices of *brahmanical* patriarchy, intercaste marriages, and 'sisterhood' in the movement, the question of class among Dalit women among other issues. Urmila Pawar's *testimonio* brings details of Dalit life in the Konkan region while also charting a Dalit feminist map of the relationships between the different and new social movements in Maharashtra. *Testimonios* of women of the nomadic communities, Janabai Girhe and Vimaltai More centre on life in the temporary settlements and the resistance to the patriarchal practices of the caste *panchayat*. Together, the accounts map the agitation of Dalit women into the spheres of Ambedkarite politics, school education, the literary and academic. Too much has been presumed about the 'silent years of Dalit feminism', without really interrogating the cursory search for Dalit feminist voices in spaces and times predefined by upper caste feminisms. The *testimonios* provide an opportunity to map spaces of Dalit feminist activism in the Republican Party, Buddhist Mahila Mandal movement, school education and literary movement and invite an engagement with histories of anti-caste feminisms in general and Phule-Ambedkarite feminisms in particular.

The *testimonios* seek an engagement with the category of Dalit women not as an automatically unitary group or as defined by 'same problems' but as emerging in a context of struggles and viable oppostional alliance. An engagement with 'translations' of eight Dalit women's *testimonios* invites participants to interrogate received theoretical frameworks that negate the agency of Dalit women in their misrecognition of Dalit feminism as 'new practice' emerging solely out of the practices of exclusion of women's movement and Dalit movements. Following Nora, I conclude that in the current conjuncture, the passage of these *testimonios* from acts of memory to history is happening in a moment of redefining of Dalit feminism through a revitalisation of history.[48]

I shall move on now, to the second project, which seeks to build empirically researched histories from below of the institutions and practices of the Ambedkarite counterpublics.

48. See Nora (1989).

Introducing Ambedkarite Music and Print Cultures in the Curricula: Countering Erasure of Dalit Intellection

As discussed earlier, the debate on Dalit modernity has been significant for opening up the experience of the Indian-modern for interrogation. It has challenged the too–neat–a dichotomy between western modernity and alternate Indian modernity. This suggests the need to explore, recover, and contest sites on which caste was publicly stated on 'its own terms' and the power of the elite to represent and name modernity. Interpretative engagements with the public practices of caste struggles that surround us have only rarely received sociological attention.

A usual middle class 'commonsensical' reading of the annual Ambedkarite gatherings, like the one at Chaitya Bhoomi in Mumbai on 6 December is one that declares these events as irrational/emotional and even as causing civic problems related to traffic and hygiene. Comments by social scientists on these annual gatherings suggest more continuity than differences with the commonsensical. This expression of caste identity in modern public spaces is read as reiteration of the 'tradition bound' character of the lower castes. A focus on the leaders' discourse in the academic engagement with Dalit movements has meant that the public cultural practices have been relatively ignored. There is very little in the way of sociological documentation of these gatherings as the interactive work among individuals, groups and parts of the Dalit movement. Social scientists, with notable exceptions, have continued to explain these 'publics' through a thesis of either 'deification of Ambedkar' or 'manipulation of the masses by the leadership'. Some of them contrast the rationality of Dr Ambedkar's thought and practice with the 'irrationality' of these annual gatherings; the 'public' is then seen as 'undeserving' to claim the legacy of Dr Ambedkar. The need to empirically document the publics that constitute and are constituted by the Ambedkarite calendar propelled this work into action. 'Listening' to the 'public' guided us to trace the legacy of these publics to the *Satyashodhak* counter publics of the late 19th century.

The institutions and practices that combine the 'print' and 'popular music' modes of publicity have been the distinctive character of Satyashodhak and non-*brahman* counterpublics of the late 19th and early 20th centuries. Scholarly efforts of *Dalitbahujan* individuals and organisations[49] that recovered the writings of the *Satyashodhak* and non-*brahman* movement have noted the loss of large number of pamphlets, of the tremendous efforts that were needed to trace booklets, even those written by prominent leaders. The long-term aim of this project is also to archive the Ambedkarite modes of publicity, both booklets and music and routes of their circulation.

The Ambedkarite calendar[50] refers to the calendars published yearly by several Dalit groups or publishing houses. These calendars are distinct with the presence of blue colour and the cover pages in different styles establishing the historical lineage from Buddha, Phule, Shahu Maharaj to Dr Ambedkar. The advertisements (mostly middle-level entrepreneurial efforts from the community) occupy a very small space at the bottom of the page. Each of these calendars is a documentation of history in that while marking the days, each day is represented as a day in the history of Dalit doing. The calendars (the largest sale is generally on 6 December) have become a mode in which critical memory and history of the Dalit counterpublics is reiterated, reinterpreted and reindexed.

The project has sought to document over five years the annual gatherings on Chaitya Bhoomi in Mumbai (6 December), Diksha Bhoomi in Nagpur (14 October), Kranti Stambh in Bhima Koregaon (1 January) and in Mahad (12 March and 25 December). While it is apparent that each of these places has a special value in their being connected to Dr Ambedkar, the question that we explored was how do these places continue to be culturally and politically meaningful year after year. Why

49. The writings and compositions of the *Satyashodhak* and non-*brahman* movement had been rendered invisible until their recovery by untiring scholarly efforts of Baba Adhav, Y.D. Phadke, Gail Omvedt, Hari Narke, S.G. Mali, and Shriram Gundekar among others. More recently, Nutan Malvi has been recovering the voices of *Satyashodhak* women in particular. Institutions like the Samta Pratishthan, Pune, the Shahu Centre, Kolhapur and more local libraries like those at Kakadwadi have helped preserve and circulate these texts.

50. There are also calendars published by the Buddhist society of India, which are not included in this inquiry. Our collection includes special calendars published in Nagpur on centenary celebrations of the Reservation Policy of Shahu Maharaj, published by the Samata Sainik Dal and the Dr Babasaheb Ambedkar Urban Co-operative Bank.

do thousands of people come year after year? We asked people to tell us about themselves and why they visit these places, the costs of the visits, the way it is organised and their experiences of travelling without tickets that often place the groups in direct confrontation with the state authorities. We also documented the trade in these gatherings—the activities at the different stalls exploring questions of: Who puts up these stalls? What do they sell? What sells? the problems in acquiring the stalls, and so on. The stalls sell a wide range of items varying across brass vessels from Muradabad, Jai Bhim caps, statues, posters, calendars, prints of Dr Ambedkar, statues of Buddha, lockets, watches, pens, key chains, ribbons and night lamps with images of Dr Ambedkar. There are other stalls that sell household items, toys, cosmetics and food and tea stalls. In the last decade, stalls offering free medical services, stalls put up by various banks, those giving career advice and matrimonial data have been on the rise. The stalls offering free food have been on the increase and this has been controversial. Some groups argue that 'acceptance of free food' goes against the Ambedkarite culture of self-respect and that this free food could be a strategy of co-option by Hindutva forces. Two kinds of stalls, which were documented in detail, the book stalls and stalls of *gayan parties* (singing troupes) with their audio cassettes sideline others by their very number and the crowds that they draw.

On this occasion, there is a lot of unease expressed about buying and selling of good by Dalits, which is most often expressed as "these events have gotten commercialized". Typically buying by Subaltern groups has been explained either through the alienation or resistance thesis. We realised that there is yet very little information about commerce and co-operative building efforts among Dalit communities. What we are proposing to explore is not really a neat hypothesis that equates consumption of commodities that iconise Dr Ambedkar to a form of cultural politics. Nevertheless, in order to explore the processes of circulation, the flow of the vendors to these sites, the design of the particular iconic products, and the distinctly marked aesthetic and the informal economies built around them, this mapping has suggestions for the interconnections between expressive and symbolic issues and the practical.

The mass gatherings of Ambedkarites at Nagpur and Mumbai are viewed by the 'unmarked' publics as days of 'traffic nuisance', 'packed trains' and days on which the Shivaji Park grounds in Mumbai get littered with food packets and other things.[51] These are reactions to 'unmarked public spaces' being occupied (physically) on certain days in a 'marked manner'. Space and spatial strategies of appropriation, deployment and control have been of crucial significance in maintaining hierarchical relations of caste. The Ambedkarite counterpublics had contested this through claiming the right to public water resources, temple, educational centres, by dropping negative rights to spaces such as the *Watan*[52] and denouncing the 'space' within Hinduism. At the level of ideology, the spatial strategies can be seen as articulating the physical—material and mental—imaginative aspects of social space. The Ambedkarite utopia (a community based on the call to Educate, Organise and Agitate) represents a search for society in a perfected form but like all utopias, it does not have a fixed address or determinate physical space. It may be argued that the Ambedkarite calendar events link the utopia to real places thereby constructing Dalit 'heterotopias,'[53] real places that exist on a map, and which can be visited. They mediate in a mirror-like fashion between utopias and ideological subjects and link people with a possible political moral identity that they could assume.

The printed booklet and music have been historically the two most distinctive features of the Dalit counterpublics. In contemporary time too, these modes perform considerable ideological labour in sustaining the heterotopias. The Dalit Panthers had commented on the Marathi mainstream publishing order arguing that the two major publishing houses of Maharashtra have been the major obstructions in the way of any experimentation in Marathi literature. The ideological impact of the Panthers and later the 'Namantaar' movement initiated processes that

51. From collection of interviews conducted with 'unmarked public' at Dadar and other parts of Mumbai on 6 December 2001.

52. *Watan* refers to the lands that the Mahars received in return for the discharge of caste-based village duties. The *Watan* was not fixed on individuals but on the entire community. Dr Ambedkar introduced a Bill for Abolition of Mahar *Watan* in the Bombay Legislative Council in 1927.

53. The term heterotopia is a medical term, introduced in the social sciences by Michel Foucault in Foucault (1986).

culminated in the emergence of several small publishers dedicated to producing literature for Dalit readership. By interviewing at length the publishers, bookstall keepers and the buyers, we attempted to document the circulation of booklets (who writes, on what themes, who publishes, sells and reads).

The booklets play a distinct role in organising the counterpublics as the Dalit counterpublic emerges as a distinctive social space through the reflexive circulation of these booklets. Most of these booklets not only assert their own position, but also characterise its relation to all other positions—in the imagined horizons of circulation. Circulation is neither indefinite nor continuous—there are rhythms and distinct moments. Every year 14 October to 14 April is marked as the 'season'; 14 October and 6 December being underlined as distinct moments of circulation. How do we understand these booklets as constituting a 'counter' public—is it their claims to the oppositional that constitute the counter? Alternatively, is it the host of the alternate publishing and circulating institutional practices and sites that make them 'counter'? To some extent, it is both. But more importantly, it is also in the awareness of the subordinate status and of the conflict of ideas, modes of address, speech genre that it marks itself off from the dominant public.

While the booklets lend largely to the rational-critical dimension of the Dalit public sphere, a dimension of social imagination and promise is lent by the *gayan parties*, which constitute the second largest number of stalls at these gatherings. In the pre-Ambedkar era, since the Mahar community had been traditionally associated with singing, there had been several *bhajan mandalis* who used the *ektara* and sang compositions in the Varkari tradition. With the expanding reach of Dr Ambedkar's message, there was a dramatic change in these *bhajan mandalis.* Old forms of publicity like the community *bhajan* were thematically reformulated[54] while private forms of expression, like women's compositions of the *ovi* (songs of the grinding stone), *palana* (songs of the cradle), adopted overtly political themes of a caste society. A new mode of publicity, the Ambedkari Jalsa, emerged in

54. See Guru (1997).

which the comedian of the Jalsa (a man dressed as a woman) would seek to convey the message of Dr Ambedkar through comical dialogues often using parody. The Jalsas would be performed after the meetings and conferences and the translations of the themes—from the public speech to the verse were swift. Jalsas, like the famous one entitled "Dialogue between a Congress Devotee and an Untouchable" would, after public speeches, present a critique of the term *Harijan*.[55]

The first generation of Ambedkari Shahirs (1920-1956)[56] who composed these Jalsas while seeking to spread the message of Dr Ambedkar used the idioms that contested the dominant ones of the day. For instance, V.D. Savarkar's composition *Tumhi Amhi Bandhu Bandhu* ("You and Us—We are all Brothers") is contested by Shahir Patitpavandas:

> You are human beings, we too are human beings,
>
> We are Hindus, you too are Hindus,
>
> Yet when it comes to temples,
>
> Its always—you above and we in our place.

Shahir Keruji Ghegde contested the claims of the political parties of the period in his composition "The Market of Indian Politics". He imagines the marketplace of Indian politics:

> To the marketplace of Indian politics, goes the old Congress woman,
>
> She is really obstinate, she is possessed by non-violence,
>
> Has lost her principles—lost her path, How can she get Swarajya?
>
> To the marketplace of Indian politics, goes a Hindu Mahasabha woman,
>
> She is obstinate, she is possessed by Hindutva,
>
> Has lost her principles—lost her path, How can she get Swarajya?[57]

55. Kardak (1978).

56. The first generation of Ambedkari Shahirs include Patitpavandas, Bhimrao Kardak, Keriji Ghegde, Arjun Hari Bhalerao, Keruba Gaikwad, Keshav Sukha Aher, Ramchandra Sonavane and Amrutbhuwa Bavaskar.

57. See Kirawale (1992).

The second generation of Ambedkari Shahirs[58] composing after 1950s, while carrying on the earlier genres created a new genre of *Bhimgeet* and *Buddhagee* which underlined the strong linkages between Dr Ambedkar and the Dalit masses. The *palana* (songs of the cradle) of Phule, Dr Ambedkar, Shahu became a popular genre with women. The primary theme in the compositions is the message of modernity; to provide a quality of life for Dalits as also to legitimise Buddhist ways as modernist expressions. This counter-public of jalsas and their audiences was in dialogue and contestation with other strands of politics most evidently the communist jalsas and the *kalapathaks* (cultural troupes) of the socialists that mobilised modernity in a language of universal freedom.[59] The *kalapathaks* and jalsas became central to the Buddhist conversion movement as well as the land grab movement led by Dadsaheb Gaikwad in 1959 and 1964. The decline of the jalsa in the late 1960s has been explained by scholars in terms of the political sub-ordination of Dalit politics to the Congress. The neglect of the tradition by Dalit political leaders, the rise of electronic media and young Dalit musical parties are also seen as contributing to this decline.[60] While the impact of these forces cannot be denied, it may be argued that the issues of tension between preservation and expansion of cultural forms cannot be settled at once and need further probing. We therefore documented in detail the cassette culture of the *gayan* parties.

As the jalsa troupes began to close in the post-Ambedkarite period a new generation of composers emerged. These came to be referred to as *gayan* parties or *quawal* parties. In keeping with changing times, they reshaped the folk form thereby creating a new genre of the Ambedkari *quawalis*.[61] These *gayan* parties travel throughout the year most extensively from 14 April (Ambedkar Jayanti) to the end of May (Buddha Poornima) performing public programmes centring

58. The second generation includes Wamandada Kardak, Sridhar Ohol, Rajanand Gadpayle, Deenbhandu Shegaonkar, Annabhau Sathe, Dalitanand and Vithal Umap.

59. For a more detailed reading and collection of communist Jalsas, particularly the work of Annabhau Sathe, see Sathe (1998).

60. See Guru (1997).

61. Londhe (2001).

around *Geet Bhimayan*, a kind of dramatised and lyrical performance of the life history of Dr Ambedkar. Buddha *geets* (songs) and Ambedkar *geets* form the other popular aspects of the programme. The compositions move across regions and generations so that often (unless mentioned in the composition or obvious by individualised style) the original composition is difficult to trace. The rich genres of Ambedkarite music cannot be reduced to 'organising tool for politics' or something all too 'readily appropriated by market forces'. In 1990s, the possibilities opened by locally produced inexpensive cassettes have meant a revolution in quantity and variety of music and it has sometimes revitalised the *gayan parties*. It has brought more women singers and parties into prominence. This has so far not eroded the base of the live performances. At Chaitya Bhoomi and Diksha Bhoomi the audio cassette stalls are the most colourful with posters announcing new cassettes with live performances of artistes at regular intervals. A preliminary documentation of cassettes sold at Diksha Bhoomi and Chaitya Bhoomi suggest that recurring themes include a rereading of events in modern Indian history as also a mapping of the struggles both in everyday life of Dr Ambedkar and the sociopolitical domain.

The Pune Pact (1932) is the theme that appears repeatedly in the cassettes. The conflict between the two great men, Gandhi and Ambedkar is imagined to be an 'intellectual *akhada* (wrestling ground)' in which Ambedkar is imagined as revealing the true face of the 'loin cloth clad ascetic'. The focus is on 'unethical and morally incorrect' behaviour of Gandhi in withdrawing from a signed agreement. The repeated chorus underlines the defeat of Gandhi (Gandhi *Harla*) and his betrayal of the ex-communicated communities. The interesting and repeated imaginary in the compositions on the Pune Pact is the request made by Kasturba Gandhi to Ambedkar to grant *jeevandan* (boon of life) to Gandhi.[62] The songs in the genre of Bauddha *mahila geet* (songs of/for Buddhist Women) include those that convince women to give up rituals and temples by outlining Dr Ambedkar's

62. Listen to, for instance, the song *Vachava Gandhi* (Save Gandhi) in the popular cassette "I Love You Ambedkar" (Mumbai: Wings, 2000).

advice to Ramabai who wanted to visit the temple of Vithoba at Pandharpur.

No Rama-No Rama

Say no to Pandhari.

What kind of Srihari is he,

who hates some human beings.

Yet another *mahila geet* imagines the true celebrations of Jayanti as constituted by a bullock cart full of women; breaking new paths, taking revolutionary steps constituting a true Bhimwadi (a politically vibrant Ambedkarite settlement). The compositions in the much circulated popular cassette, "I love you Ambedkar" outlines the contours of conjugal relations in the new Ambedkarite community. The four compositions on Side A present an interesting mix—the first one "Lucy I love you Ambedkar Mhanali" (Lucy said, "I love you Ambedkar") narrates the story of a British woman Lucy who expresses her love for Ambedkar. Her lack of control over her feelings, her plans to seduce Babasaheb are underlined:

She drops her books and then says sorry sorry.

All these efforts of Lucy are seen as lost on Ambedkar who tells her that she was like a sister to him, for fidelity and commitment were to him most important.

The second composition *Baba Mhanio Samaj Mala—Lagna Konashi Karu* (The community calls me 'Father'—who can I marry) imagines doctors as advising Babasaheb to marry a second time, after the death of his first wife Ramabai. Babasaheb replies that the entire community called him 'father' and that the welfare of his nine crores of Dalit children was his real aspiration and work. The whole composition as if places on record why Dr Ambedkar might have married Savitabai, a *brahman* doctor as also the secondary importance of conjugality as compared to the community.

The third composition outlines a young Dalit boy's precondition for marriage. He agrees to marry if the women can find him a bride like Ramai (Dr Ambedkar's first wife) whose contribution to Babasaheb's work is then underlined. While the fourth composition—

Tumcha Kahi Nahi Mala Akaycha (I will listen to nothing you say) is the voice of woman's determination to attend the Jayanti celebrations at her paternal village where the celebrations are more grand than her conjugal home. She warns her husband that her mind has been made up and that she will hear nothing that stops her from going. The four songs together weave patterns that contest upper caste bourgeois ideals of conjugality. The musical meanings of ideals of faithfulness and loyalty of the man, priority of community over conjugality, supporting and giving wife—who can challenge the husband if he stands in the way of her commitment to the Ambedkarite ideology are grounded socially and in Dalit historical struggles. The musical meanings, it is apparent, are grounded socially and historically in struggles and operate on an ideological field of conflicting interests, institutions and memories.

This documentation of the calendar events is a beginning and has several limitations especially the weakness of a survey-based method. Nevertheless, when introduced in the classroom, to an extent it serves to contest the 'deification' and 'manipulation of masses' theses practiced by dominant frameworks in the social sciences. It seeks to recover Dalit intellection erased by Marxist, liberal and subaltern frameworks in the study of collective action. Furthermore, most social science curricula discuss caste within the troublesome conceptual division of state and society, thereby limiting the discussion to reservation policy on one hand and rites and rituals on the other. This project seeks to foreground the notion of public sphere as it impels explorations into the received demarcations of public and private. Furthermore, in the debate on the public sphere in colonial India, the concern with 'authenticity' and 'real Indian public', has so far overshadowed engagement with deep segmentations of the public sphere in colonial India. Dalit citizenship therefore has come to be viewed as passive, morally inferior that which is incapable of thinking in general terms and engaging only with everyday mundane problems. Our pedagogical project seeks to problematise these issues and to raise questions historically and empirically about the ways in which *Dalitbahujan* participation changes the nature and quality of the public sphere.

Coda

In putting together learning and teaching materials from Dalit collective action for interpretative and political engagement with caste, I am making a case for Dalit studies as Phule's *Tritya Ratna* (third eye)—a medium for interrogating misrecognition of the social world perpetuated by the dominant. The practices of such a Dalit studies must move within and across disciplines, back and forth between assumptions of theory, institutional spaces in the academy and democratic struggles outside it. On this matter, there are several notes to be shared with feminist comrades in the academy for both Dalit and feminist studies have emerged through an interrogation of the canonical opposition between 'scholarship' and 'commitment'. However, like all inheritances, much about this inherited relationship has come to be assumed and discussions on the matter are but few. We need more of loud thinking and sharing on the relationship between researchers and social movements and intellectuals and the academy. How may intellectuals in their pedagogical practices reinvent their relation to the Dalit movement in ways that move beyond relations of instrumentality or fusion? How may scholars guard against a scholastic bias but also a bias of 'campus radicalism' that confuses the things of logic for the logic of things? Dalit studies as pedagogical practice has to encounter these questions in producing instruments both for defence against the symbolic domination of the academy as also for a merciless critique of its concepts, metaphors and modes of reasoning. For at stake, is no longer just a space in the *brahman galli*, or an 'expert view' in the neo-liberal corridors of power but claims to 'universalising the conditions of access to the universal'.[63]

63. This phrase and several ideas in developing the conclusion are influenced by Bourdieu (2003).

References

Aloysius, G. (2005). "Inscribing Dalit Concerns within the Curricula of Higher Education: Some Comments", in Arun Kumar and Sanjay Kumar (eds.), *Dalit Studies in Higher Education*. Deshkal Publication. pp.12-17.

Anand, S. (2003). *Untouchable Tales: Publishing and Reading Dalit Literature.* Chennai: Navayana.

Bhagwat, Vidyut (1988). "Shree, Shreepad Mahadave Mate", in Sumant Yeshwant and Dattaray Punde (eds.), *Maharashtratil Jatisansthavishayak Vichar.* Pune: Pratima Prakashan. pp.196-206.

Bhagwat, Vidyut and Pratima Pardeshi (eds.) (1998). *Abrahmani Streevaadi Itihasalekhanachya Dishene.* Pune: Women's Studies Centre, University of Pune and Krantisinha Nana Patil Academy

Bourdieu, Pierre (1990). *In Other Words: Essays Towards a Reflexive Sociology*. Cambridge: Polity Press.

———. (2003). *Firing Back: Against the Tyranny of the Market.* The New Press.

Chakravarti, Uma (1993). "Conceptualising Brahmanical Patriarchy in Early India: Gender, Caste, Class and State", *Economic and Political Weekly:* 579–85, April 3.

———. (2003). *Gendering Caste: Through a Feminist Lens.* Calcutta: Stree.

Chatterjee, Partha (1997). *Our Modernity*. Rotterdam/Dakar: SEPHIS and CODESRIA.

Cohn, Bernard S. (1987). "African Models and Indian Histories", in Bernanrd S. Cohn, *An Anthropologist Among Historians and Other Essays.* New Delhi, Oxford University Press. pp.224-54.

Dahiwale, S.M. (ed.) (2005). *Understanding Indian Society: The Non-Brahmanic Perspective.* Jaipur: Rawat Publications.

Dangle, Arjun (ed.) (1992). *Poisoned Bread: Translation from Modern Marathi Dalit Literature.* Hyderabad: Orient Longman Limited.

Delanty, Gerard (2005). "The Sociology of the University and Higher Education: The Consequences of Globalisation", in Craig Calhoun, Chris Rojek and Bryan Turner (eds.), *The Sage Handbook of Sociology.* London: Sage. pp.530-46.

Deshpande, Satish (2003). *Contemporary India: A Sociological View.* New Delhi: Viking.

Dhareshwar, Vivek (1993). "Caste and Secular Self", in *Journal of Arts and Ideas* 25(26): 115-25.

Foucault, Michel (1986). "Of Other Spaces"', in *Diacritics* 16 (1): 22-27.

Geetha, V. (2001). *Gender*. Kolkatta: Stree.

Guru, Gopal (1997) *Dalit Cultural Movement and Dialectics of Dalit Politics in Maharashtra.* Vikas Adhyayan Kendra.

———. (2000). "Dalits in Pursuit of Modernity", in Romila Thapar (ed.), *India : Another Millenium*. New Delhi: Viking. pp.123-37.

———. (2001). "The Language of Dalit-Bahujan Political Discourse", in Ghanshyam Shah (ed.), *Dalit Identity and Politics*. New Delhi: Sage. pp.97-108.

———. (2002). "How Egalitarian are the Social Sciences in India?", *Economic and Political Weekly:* 5003–10, December 14–20.

———. (2003). "Review of Joothan: A Dalit's Life by Om Prakash Valmiki" (Translated into English by Arun Prabha Mukherjee), in *Seminar* 530: 70-71, October.

Ilaiah, Kancha (2001). "Dalitism vs Brahmanism: The Epistemological Conflict in History", in Ghanshyam Shah (ed.), *Dalit Identity and Politics*. New Delhi: Sage. pp. 108-29.

———. (1998). "Towards the Dalitisation of the Nation", in Partha Chatterjee (ed.), *Wages of Freedom: Fifty Years of Indian Nation-state.* New Delhi"Oxford University Press. pp.267-92.

Joshi, Sanjay (2002). *Fractured Modernity: Making of a Middle Class in Colonial North India.* New Delhi: Oxford University Press.

Kardak, Bhimrao (1978). *Ambedkari Jalse: Swarup va Karya.* Bombay: Abhinav Prakashan.

Kirawale, Krishna (1992). *Ambedkari Shahiri: Ek Shodh.* Pune: Kalpana Kirawale.

Kothari, Rajni (1994). "Rise of Dalits and the Renewed Debate on Caste", *Economic and Political Weekly*: 1589-94, June 25.

Kumar, Arun (2005). "Introduction", in Arun Kumar and Sanjay Kumar (eds.), *Dalit Studies in Higher Education*. Deshkal Publication. pp.1-12.

Kumar, Arun and Sanjay Kumar (eds.) (2005). *Dalit Studies in Higher Education*. Deshkal Publication.

Kumar, Vivek (2005). "Situating Dalits in Indian Sociology", *Sociological Bulletin* 54(3): 514-32.

Londhe, Baban (2001). *Anibedkari Lokgeete.* Mumbai: Akshar Prakashan.

Mani, Braj Ranjan (2005). "Core Characteristics of Literature for Dalit Studies", in Arun Kumar and Sanjay Kumar (eds.), *Dalit Studies in Higher Education*. Deshkal Publication. pp.33-45.

Menon, Dilip M. (2006). "Introduction: Thinking Caste in Modem India", in *The Blindness of Insight: Essays on Caste in Modern India.* Chennai: Navayana Publications. pp. i-xx.

Nanda, Meera (2001). "Hitching Dalit Modernity to Anti-Modernist Wagon", *Economic and Political Weekly:* 1480-83, April 28.

———. (2002). *Breaking the Spell ofDharma and Other Essays.* New Delhi: Three Essays.

Nigam, Aditya (2000). "Secularism, Modernity, Nation: Epistemology of the Dalit Critique", *Economic and Political Weekly:* 4256-68, November 25.

Nora, Pierre (1989). "Between History and Memory: Les Lieux de Memoire", *Representations* 26: 15, Spring.

Omvedt, Gail (1994). *Dalit and the Democratic Revolution: Dr. Ambedkar and the Dalit Movement in Colonial India*. New Delhi: Sage.

———. (1995). *Dalit Visions: The Anti-Caste Movement and the Construction of an Indian Identity*. Hyderabad: Orient Longman.

Oomen, T.K (2001). "Understanding Indian Society: The Relevance of the Perspective From Below", *Occasional Paper Series* 4. Pune: Department of Sociology, University of Pune.

Palshikar, Suhas (1998). "Shree Govind Mahadev Joshi", in Sumant Yeshwant and Dattaray Punde (eds.), *Maharashtratil Jatisansthavishayak Vichar.* Pune: Pratima Prakashan. pp. 239-63.

Pandian, M.S.S (2002). "One Step Outside Modernity: Caste, Identity, Politics and Public Sphere", *Economic and Political Weekly:* 3763-74, September 9.

Pandit, Nalini (1979). "Caste and Class in Maharashtra", *Economic and Political Weekly* (Annual Number): 425-37, February.

Partha Chatterjee (ed.), *Wages of Freedom: Fifty Years of Indian Nation-State.* New Delhi: OUP. pp.267-92.

Patel, Sujata (2006). "Beyond Binaries: A Case for Self Reflexive Sociologies", in *Current Sociology* 54(3): 381-95, May. London, Thousand Oakks, C.A. and New Delhi: SAGE.

Patil, Sharad(1994). *Marxvaad-Phule-Ambedkarvad.* Pune: Sugava.Prasad, Chandra Bhan (2006). *Dalit Phobia: Why Do They Hate Us?* New Delhi: Vitasta.

Pawar, Urmila and Meenakshi Moon (1989; 2000). *Aamhihi Itihas Ghadawla: Ambedkari Chalvalit Streeyancha Sahabhag.* Pune: Sugava Prakashan.

Prasad, Chandra Bhan (2006). ***Dalit Phobia: Why do they Hate us?*** New Delhi: Vitasta.

Rege, Sharmila (2006). *Writing Caste/Writing Gender: Narrating Dalit Women's Testimonios.* New Delhi: Zubaan.

———. (forthcoming). *Caste, Identity and Public Sphere: Documenting Ambedkarite Counterpublics.* Kolkatta: Samya Publications.

Rodrigues, Edward (2003). "Dalit Struggle for Recognition within Indian Sociology", in Maitrayee Chaudhari (ed.), *The Practice of Sociology.* Hyderabad: Orient Longman. pp.221-58.

Sathe, Annabhau (1998). *Lokshahir Annabhau Sathe: Nivdak Vagmay.* Bombay: Maharashtra State Sahitya aani Sanskriti Mandal.

Satyanarayana, K. (2005). "Dalit Studies as a New Perspective in the Indian Academia", in Arun Kumar and Sanjay Kumar (eds.), *Dalit Studies in Higher Education: Vision and Challenges.* Delhi: Deshkal. pp.81-95.

Smith, Dorothy (1974). "Theorising as Ideology", in R. Turner (ed), *Ethnomethodology.*London: Penguin. pp.39-54.

Stanley, Liz (2000). "For Sociology, Gouldner's and Ours", in John Eldridge, John Masinnes, Sue Scott *et al.* (eds.), *For Sociology: Legacies and Prospects.* Durham: Sociology Press. pp.56-83.

Talpade, Chandra Mohanty (2003). "Under Western Eyes' Revisited: Feminist Solidarity through Anticapitalist Struggles", in Chandra Mohanty Talpade (ed.), *Feminism without Borders: Decolonizing Theory, Practicing Solidarity.* Durham and London: Duke University Press. pp.221-51.

Thorat, Sukhdeo and Uma Kant (eds.) (2003). *Caste, Race and Discrimination: Discourses in International Context.* Jaipur: Rawat and IIDS.

6

RAMACHANDRA GUHA

The Challenge of Contemporary History

A Paradox and a Puzzle

History is demarcated from its sister disciplines principally by its method of gathering information. According to custom and convention, historians work in the archives, sociologists do field research, political scientists conduct surveys. In the Indian academy, however, the demarcations are also marked by a single moment in time. Thus when the clock struck midnight on 14th/15th August 1947, India was freed (and also divided), history ended, and political science and sociology began.[1]

This division made sense in the first years of Independence. The British Raj had definitively ended; it could therefore be treated as 'history'. The new nation was being made; its making (and unmaking) could be fruitfully studied through the participatory methods of the ethnographer and the political scientist. But as the 1950s gave way to the 1960s and the 1970s, the division made less sense. Yet it has persisted. Even now, 60 years after Independence, 15 August 1947 remains a *lakshman rekha* observed faithfully on either side of the divide. Historians of India do not transgress beyond that date. Sociologists and political scientists do not look back before that date.[2]

The overwhelming importance in the academy of that single date has led to a paradox—namely, that while India is the most interesting country in the world, we know very little about its modern history. And what we do know about independent India is chiefly the work

1. In this essay, I use 'sociology' to mean 'sociology and social anthropology'.
2. This *lakshman rekha* is also carefully observed by foreign scholars of India; the historians dealing with colonialism and before, the political scientists and sociologists with independence and after.

of sociologists, economists, political scientists, and journalists—not historians. In fact, the works of history, properly so called, on any aspect of India since 1947 are so few that they can be counted on the fingers of one hand or, at most, two.

The paradox is also a puzzle. For it is not as if history as an academic discipline is underdeveloped in India. To the contrary, there is a large and visible community of historians of India, so large and so visible that they are, in fact, the envy of their colleagues in sociology and political science. These historians are British and American and French and Japanese as well as Indian. Some are Marxist, others post-Marxist or subalternist, still others professing to be non-ideological, faithful only to the canons of empirical research. Arguing vigorously among themselves, these historians constitute an incredibly productive community of scholars, who have influenced intellectual debates well outside the borders of the Indian Union.

Perhaps even more than Indian economists, Indian historians have left their mark on global scholarship. Their special field of interest has been colonialism, or stated more precisely, the encounter between colonialism and nationalism. In contrast to the handful of works on independent India, there are perhaps several thousand books and articles on the history of British India. Among the areas most intensively mined are the high politics of Viceroys and English-speaking nationalists; the subaltern politics of peasants and workers; environmental histories of water, forest and wildlife; the economic histories of agrarian and industrial structure; feminist histories of women in the household and in the factory; and cultural histories of art, architecture, and literature.

The historiography of India is a very rich and very well-tilled field. It is also a very narrow one. For it has focused closely—some would say obsessively—on the period "from Plassey to Partition" (to invoke the title of a recent survey of the field).[3] The narrowness of the time frame has come at a cost—in fact, a double cost. In recent years, historians have begun to challenge this obsession with colonialism

3. Bandopadhyay, 2004. Bandopadhyay's book has an excellent bibliography, listing the important books and articles on different aspects of the history of colonial India.

from one, that is to say the prior, side of the divide—with regard to the period of Indian history before 1757.[4] It is past time that the obsession is challenged from the other, that is to say the latter, side of the divide—with regard to the period of Indian history after 1947.

Some Things We Do Not Know About the History of Independent India

I have referred to independent India as the most interesting country in the world. This is the impartial judgement of a historian, not the partisan claim of a citizen. For India may also be the most exasperating and the most hierarchical and the most degrading country in the world. But whatever qualifier or adjective one uses or prefers, it remains the most interesting country, too. This 'interestingness' lies in the facts that it is very large and populous, containing one-sixth of humankind; that this territory is astonishingly diverse, its people differentiated by religion and language and caste and ethnicity, as well as by ecology and technology and dress and cuisine; and that this massive and very diverse population is simultaneously undergoing four fundamental transformations. The Indian economy was once very largely based on agriculture; now, it increasingly depends upon industry and services. An overwhelming majority of Indians once lived in the villages; now, more and more Indians are making their homes in cities and towns. India was once a territory colonised by and ruled over by Europeans; now, it is an independent and sovereign country. The political culture of India was once feudal and deferential; now, it is combative and participatory.

There were, and are, four revolutions occurring simultaneously in India: the urban revolution, the industrial revolution, the national

4. For too long precolonial history was identified largely with the history of the Mughal Empire, and with a Marxist interpretation of that Empire. Since the Mughals, at their zenith, controlled at most 40 per cent of what is now India, and since Marxism is but one historical approach among many, this dominant paradigm was doubly limited. A new generation of scholars are now focusing on southern, eastern and western India (all areas scarcely touched by the Mughals), and writing sensitively about social, cultural, ecological and aesthetic matters that the economic determinism of orthodox Marxism was unable to adequately take account of. Among the pioneers of this new precolonial history are Muzaffar Alam, Richard Eaton, Sumit Guha, Sheldon Pollock, David Shulman, Sanjay Subrahmanyam, Cynthia Talbot, and Philip Wagoner.

revolution, and the democratic revolution. The key word here is 'simultaneously'. In Europe and the United States (US), for example, these revolutions were staggered. The US became a nation (or least proclaimed its national independence) in the 18th century; urbanised and industrialised in the 19th century; and became democratic only in the 20th century, after first women and then people of colour were granted the vote. In Europe, a continent broken up into many different nationalities, the pace of these different revolutions varied greatly across and within countries. Crucially, in every country the national revolution preceded the democratic one by several decades or more; that is, the residents of a geographically defined and circumscribed territory came together under a single flag and currency well before they were all allowed to vote to choose a single set of rulers.

India has three times as many people as the US; as many major languages as Europe; and far greater religious diversity than either the US or Europe. Besides, it became a democracy at the same time as it became a nation (in striking contrast to its great Asian neighbour, China). In any event, the urban and industrial revolutions would have produced major conflicts and upheavals (as they have elsewhere in the world); but only in India have these conflicts and upheavals been articulated through the processes of political mobilisation and rhetorical expression that a democracy permits and even encourages. The size of its territory plus the diversity of its people plus the simultaneity of these four great social revolutions—this is what makes India the most interesting country in the world.

However, in focusing on the period of the Raj, the substantial and very sophisticated community of Indian historians has very largely ignored these multiple churnings. Take for instance those two words, and categories, and processes, which are of central importance to the history of modern India: 'caste' and 'elections'. Sociologists and anthropologists have done numerous field studies of caste in every decade since Independence. They have worked on single-caste villages, on multi-caste villages, on marginal castes like fisherfolk and pastoralists. They have investigated the relationship between the caste system and the agrarian economy, and between caste and politics. Likewise, political scientists have undertaken surveys and opinion polls at the time of every election since Independence. Their studies have sometimes focused on a single constituency; at other times on the dynamics of party competition in an entire state. Scholars have investigated voter behaviour, styles of campaigning, means of finance, and much else.

There must be, by now, hundreds of books on caste in independent India, as well as many hundreds of articles on elections. Yet we do not have a single work by a historian that analyses or interprets the evolution of the caste system since Independence. Nor do we have a historical study that can illuminate our understanding of how elections and electioneering have changed over these 60 years.

The sociologist John Goldthorpe (1991) has argued that one advantage his discipline possesses is that it can generate its own evidence through fieldwork, interviews and surveys. The historian, he believes, is limited by his reliance on the world of the dead, that is, on what Goldthorpe calls "relics". But he omits to mention the other side of the coin—namely, that sociologists and political scientists, precisely because they deal with the world of the living, are seduced into predictions about the future which often, or perhaps even usually, turn out to be off the mark. The graveyard of the social sciences is littered with the corpses of failed forecasts, predictions by sociologists about the retreat of religion from public life, for example, or predictions by political scientists about the coming extinction of particular political parties or political institutions.

On the other hand, because they deal with the past, and hence with a completed social process, historians are in a position to pass reasonably considered judgements on a particular society in a particular slice of time—on what happened there, how it happened, and on its larger significance. For the historian, the incomplete or fragmentary nature of evidence is compensated for by the completeness of the narrative. Seen from the perspectives of the disciplines, the orientations of the historian are different from that of the sociologist and the political scientist; seen from the perspective of human knowledge as a whole, they are also complementary.

The studies by sociologists and political scientists of caste and/or elections were all conducted synchronically, that is, at a single point of time. A historical approach would differ in being diachronic, or across time. It would differ also in the kinds and varieties of sources used. Thus, for example, a historian writing a social history of elections would make use of the studies by political scientists, and supplement them with unpublished correspondence (whether personal or official), periodical literature (in English and other languages), posters and pamphlets, and oral histories. Writing several years or decades after the event, the historian has the distance and detachment denied the participant observer. He[5] has the ability to take a retrospective and panoramic view, using these varied sources to track changes in patterns of party funding, or forms of propaganda and rhetoric, or the mobilisation of voters, or the incidence of electoral violence and crime. In the same manner, a scholar writing a history of caste since Independence would, to the published accounts of sociologists, juxtapose evidence from newspapers and journals, court records (civil and criminal), and parliamentary and legislative proceedings to interpret the changing role and significance of this very influential social institution.

There is not a single book on the social history of caste in independent India; not a single book either on the social history of Indian elections. But the neglect runs far deeper than that. Last year, 2006, saw the 50th anniverary of the reorganisation of Indian states. Normally, anniversaries are a spur to the publication of historical works—remember how many books were published in 1997 to commemorate or deplore the Partition of India?[6] And yet, the 50th

5. My use of the conventional 'he' to denote 'he or she' should not be taken as a manifestation of male bias. It is just that I find the alternatives—'s/he' or 'he or she'—clumsy and cumbersome.

6. There is a veritable 'Partition Industry' in India, comparable to the 'Holocaust Industry' in Israel. The 60th anniversary of Partition prompted a fresh slew of books on the subject. As with the Holocaust, historians and writers have focused so closely—one dare not again say 'obsessively'—on the catastrophic event that they have tended to ignore or underplay its impact on later generations and decades. The residues of Partition, its impacts on the economic and social history of independent India, have only recently, and very belatedly, begun to receive scholarly attention. See, for instance, Tan and Kudesia, 2000; Kudaisya, 1995; Chatterji, 2001; Kaur, 2007; and, perhaps above all, Chakravarti, 1999). (The original, Bengali, edition of Chakravarti's book came out several years before its English translation.) The imbalance is palpable. There are hundreds of books and articles on Partition itself, but only a handful on its equally interesting (and important) aftermath.

anniversary of the formation of most Indian states was met with a resounding silence. No historian, living in any of the 28 states of India, thought it worth his while to write a social, or political, or cultural—or 'total'—history of the state he was working in.

Some of the states of India are larger than a large European country. Their history has been as colourful and tumultuous as the modern histories of, say, France or Germany. But whereas there might be a 50 or a 100 worthwhile histories of postwar France, there is not a single history of West Bengal since its formation in 1947. I mention this particular Indian state because it has a very active community of historians. These historians have restricted themselves almost wholly to the colonial period. There are hundreds of books and PhD theses on the agrarian structure of British Bengal, but not—so far as I know—a single historical study of Bengal agriculture since 1947. In this respect, at least, what Bengal thinks today the rest of India thinks today as well. Go to a bookshop in Thiruvananthapuram, and find there histories of colonial Malabar and the Maharaja's Travancore, old district gazetteers and manuals, but not a single history of modern Kerala. When the advanced intellectual cultures of India have been so remiss, how can we expect there to be decent histories of Gujarat or Karnataka?

Move now from history to biography. There do exist some fine lives of our pre-eminent 'national' leaders, such as Jawaharlal Nehru, Vallabhbhai Patel, and C. Rajagopalachari (Rajaji), written by accomplished historians and biographers. Since their subjects all died after 1947, these biographies do also illuminate the history and politics of independent India.[7] The second generation of national leaders, for example, Indira Gandhi and Jayaprakash Narayan, have also had serviceable lives written about them, albeit by journalists rather than historians.[8]

Although these major national leaders have been written about, for a deeper historical understanding they need to be written about much more, and from many different angles. We need not

7. See Gopal, 1975-1984; Gandhi, 1991; 1995. Cf also Gopal, 1989.

8. Frank, 2001; Malhotra, 2006; Bhattacharjea, 2004.

one biography of Patel (which is all we have at the moment) but at least half-a-dozen. Moreover, we need to juxtapose these leaders to one another, to illuminate the rivalries and controversies that they initiated or responded to. For instance, a student of colonial India knows a great deal about how Jinnah and Nehru differed with regard to the Hindu-Muslim question, or about how Gandhi and Ambedkar disagreed about the past and future of the caste system. What, however, of the debates in independent India between Nehru and Rajaji on economic policy, or between Indira Gandhi and Jayaprakash Narayan on the proper role of the state? Should we not know about these, too? Till the 1970s at least, politics in India had a strong moral and ideological core—it had not become, as it is now, wholly cynical and instrumental. The policy and political debates of the 1950s and 1960s are interesting in themselves: more importantly, they had a defining impact on the career of the nation.

The major 'national' leaders have not been wholly ignored by historians and biographers. However, if one moves a level below the 'nation', one draws a complete blank. If one excepts, as one must, hagiographies and party pamphlets, then there are no lives of such remarkable and historically significant figures as E.M.S. Namboodiripad, C.N. Annadurai, Sheikh Abdullah, A.Z. Phizo or Master Tara Singh.

From the perspective of India as a whole, the likes of E.M.S. and Anna might be considered 'provincial' politicians. But their province is the size of a large European country. These leaders shaped, for good and for ill, the lives of 40 or 50 million people. Their policies profoundly altered the economic, social, and cultural histories of the states they lived in and led. At every major turning point in the history of Jammu and Kashmir, which also means the history of India and of Pakistan, one finds the hand of Sheikh Abdullah or of the party (and political dynasty) he founded. Likewise with Namboodiripad and the history of Kerala, or of Indian communism.

That we have no lives of such Indians is a commentary only on the impoverishment of our historical imagination. Not having a life of E.M.S. of Kerala, or of the Sheikh of Kashmir, is like being French and not being able to read a single life of Charles de Gaulle. Like de

Gaulle, these individuals are significant enough, from a historical point of view, to merit not one biography but several.

The individuals mentioned in the preceding paragraphs were all oppositional figures, who set themselves against the Central Government and, in some cases, against the Union of India. But there are no biographies either of other influential politicians who did not 'challenge' the system, but worked within to reshape and rework it. I have in mind here such Indians as K. Kamaraj, Chaudhury Charan Singh, Devaraj Urs and Karpoori Thakur, whose life and work likewise impacted many million people.

But it is not just lives of politicians that historians need to research and write about. Often, the history of a society can be illuminated by taking, as one's entry point, a middle-ranking figure, whose life and work touched both the top and the bottom, the decision-making élite as well as the humble farmer and labourer. Three such people in the history of independent India are the campaigning journalist and film-maker P.K. Atre, the novelist and activist Mahasweta Devi, and the novelist, journalist, film-maker and activist Kota Shivarama Karanth. One could write a wonderful social history of modern Maharashtra through Atre, or of modern Bengal through Mahasweta, or of modern Karnataka through Karanth. These names are thrown up for illustrative purposes only. Surely, in a country so large and so interesting, one could think of 30 or more Indian writers and thinkers, all of whom would, in a more sensitive and responsible intellectual climate, have already found their biographers.[9]

Move now from biography to policy. It is now the conventional wisdom that the autarkic model of economic development adopted in the 1950s, where the state occupied the 'commanding heights', was a consequence of the preferences and prejudices of our first Prime Minister, Jawaharlal Nehru. In fact, the claim that Nehru

9. Nor should one restrict oneself to politicians and writers. The poverty of the Indian biographical tradition could equally be illustrated by the fact that there are no biographies of a musician of truly global reach, such as Ravi Shankar, or of an entrepreneur who, for better or for worse, radically reshaped our political econony, namely, Dhirubhai Ambani. While a life of Ambani is awaited, we do have a valuable study of the most politically astute businessman of the previous generation, namely, G. D. Birla. See Kudaisya, 2003.

imposed a state-controlled economy on an unwilling nation is a claim made solely on the basis of the prejudices and preferences of the industralists of today. The industrialists of Nehru's day were by no means laissez-faire. In their Bombay Plan, they themselves asked for a strong and interventionist state. They even went so far as to quote the Cambridge economist A.C. Pigou to the effect that socialism and capitalism had to find a common meeting ground. And both Nehru and the Bombay capitalists were merely reflecting the spirit of the age. Across the board, among politicians, businessmen, scientists and economists, there was an overwhelming consensus in favour of a self-reliant, state-directed, 'mixed economy' model for India's development. This consensus is richly reflected in the private correspondence, official memoranda, scholarly literature, and newspaper commentary of the 1950s.[10]

If the conventional wisdom with regard to the evolution of India's economic policy is all too different from the historical truth, then there is no one to blame but the historians. Or, more specifically, the economic historians. These have scrupulously stayed on the far side of the *lakshman rekha,* writing many books and articles about the economic policies of the colonial state, while restraining themselves from examining, in an equally rigorous fashion, the economic policies of the successive governments of independent India.

The failure of the historian has led to gross misperceptions in the popular imagination, as in the myth of 'Nehru the economic czar'. More seriously, it has led to colleagues in kindred disciplines making elementary errors for which, again, it is not them but the historian who is to blame. For instance, in a newspaper article published in March 2005, a political scientist at Delhi University claimed that the "Hindu code bills, passed in 1955 and 1956, did not reform Hindu personal laws, they merely codified them, that is, brought them into conformity with what was assumed to be the 'Indian' norm—north Indian, upper-caste practices."[11] Three months later, writing in another newspaper, another political scientist from the same

10. See Guha, 2007.

11. Menon, 2005.

university claimed that the Rashtriya Swayamsewak Sangh (RSS) "had not opposed any legal or social reforms of Hindu society. It had proactively supported such efforts. The support to the introduction of the Hindu Code Bill can be cited as just one example."[12]

Both these claims were false. The modernisation of Hindu personal laws was orchestrated by B.R. Ambedkar, who was admittedly male, but not north Indian, and certainly not upper caste. The reforms marked a substantial departure from (and improvement on) tradition and orthodoxy, allowing Hindu women, for the first time, to choose their marriage partners, to marry outside their caste, and to divorce (the reforms also substantially enhanced a woman's right to her husband's or father's property). And far from supporting these reforms, the RSS and kindred organisations in fact bitterly opposed them. Jana Sangh and Hindu Mahasabha members sought to stall the new laws in Parliament. The RSS organised hundreds of demonstrations calling on Nehru and Ambedkar to leave their posts for daring to tamper with Hindu tradition.[13]

That, in everyday discourse, the common folk display a comprehensive ignorance of the history of the 1950s is bad enough; but that this ignorance is manifested also by trained academics writing in newspapers is simply shocking. The fault lies with the historians. By turning their backs on the formative decades of Indian independence, when the economic, foreign and social policies of the Republic were shaped, they have allowed the events and happenings of those decades to be distorted and misrepresented according to the whims and fancies of the individual (or scholar) concerned.

Given the richness and diversity of the historical literature on modern India, the fact that so little of it deals with the period after 1947 is a paradox, a puzzle, and a pity. Other nations and intellectual cultures have been more fortunate. There is no reliable study of the formation of economic policy in independent India, but there are many excellent books on the formation of the Welfare State in

12. Sinha, 2005.

13. See Guha, 2007: Chapter 11, for a flavour of these debates as they occurred at the time. For a more comprehensive and authoritative account, see Chitra Sinha's forthcoming book, *Hindu Code Bill and the Shaping of Modern India*.

postwar Britain. Historians have not written with depth or insight about the (often very fertile) debates among writers and social scientists in independent India. Yet there are many outstanding studies of intellectual life in postwar France. No Indian historian has written a proper historical study of our wars with Pakistan. In contrast, studies by American historians of their postwar adventures in the Middle East and Asia are so numerous that they could stock a decent-sized library.

The history of independent India is mostly unwritten. Even so, one knows that it will be more diverse and more exciting than the postwar histories of France and the United Kingdom and the US. This is because, as a culture, a society, and a nation, India is altogether more diverse and exciting than France or England or America—or any of the other 100 odd members of the United Nations.

Hurdles and Impediments

The historian who writes about the recent past faces difficulties very different from (and sometimes unknown to) the historian who writes about the more distant past. One problem is the availability of sources. Government archives and private papers generally become open only after 30 or more years. Relevant secondary sources may also not be abundant, since memoirs and biographies of key historical actors tend to be written or published some years or decades after the events which they helped shape or determine.

A second challenge faced by the contemporary historian is that his audience often has strong notions about the topics he is writing about. A historian of the Vijayanagara Empire or a biographer of Krishnadevaraya expects that his readers will know little about the subject. His own scholarly expertise, and the depth and originality of his research, carry great authority and value. In such cases, the historian speaks or writes, and the reader listens or reads, and learns. But a historian of modern Kerala or the biographer of E.M.S. Namboodiripad cannot count on such willing passivity. For his readers already have decided opinions about the subject. Facts or interpretations that tend to confirm these opinions will be endorsed; those that tend to dispute them will be dismissed.

The reader of contemporary history, unlike the reader of medieval or early modern history, is not willing to take the historian on trust. He comes to the text with his own, and often long-held, political and ideological preferences. The reader, in other words, knows the 'truth' even before the historian offers it to him. The reader's truth is usually based on hearsay and prejudice rather than evidence or research; for these very reasons, it is clung on to fiercely, even though the alternate, historian's, truth, may be based on solid research and scholarship.

The farther back one goes in time, the more comfortable the historian is, the more in command of his material, the more secure of his terrain. No reader would challenge the historian of the Mughal Empire in the same, direct, combative way as he might challenge the historian of the 1950s. The biographer of Akbar, or even Aurangzeb, will not face the same searching, skeptical audience as will the biographer of Nehru or Indira Gandhi. The reader's confidence in his own opinions decreases in proportion to the distance in time. The reader knows that there are some things recent rulers or politicians, say Nehru or Namboodiripad, should have done differently. But when it comes to individuals or institutions of a 100 or 200 years ago, the reader is more hesitant—he may wish that things had turned out other than they had, but he is not so certain that they could have.

The reader of contemporary history is a critical reader—an active participant in the historical dialogue. But it is not only the reader who brings his prejudices to bear on the facts of history. The historian might sometimes do so, too. This, then, is the third challenge of contemporary history, namely, that the historian of the recent past can himself have strong, and preconceived, opinions about his subject matter. Before he enters the archives, he may already know what kind of conclusion he is looking for. Evidence that fits his line of thinking will be eagerly seized upon; evidence that confutes it disregarded. It is not easy for a historian of modern Kerala to stand completely apart from the Communist-Congress polemics of the present day. On the other hand, the historian of the Vijayanagara Empire is less likely to bring his political preferences to bear on his scholarly research.

Both the writing and reception of contemporary history are suffused with passion and prejudice. For the world that the historian and his reader live in, and share, has been profoundly shaped by the personalities and policies of the recent past. The imprint of E.M.S. Namboodiripad and his party hangs heavy on modern Kerala, just as the imprint of Jawaharlal Nehru and his party hangs heavy on modern India. Every Malayali has an opinion about E.M.S. and Communism, every Indian an opinion about Nehru and the Congress. On the other hand, the imprint of rulers and political regimes of ages more distant is less easy to recognise. Thus for both the reader and the historian, the farther back in time one goes, the more easy it is to stand apart from the din and clamour of political controversy and debate. The farther back one goes, the more willing is the reader to respect and seek to learn from the historian. The farther back one goes, the less likely is the historian to let his personal or ideological agenda have a bearing on his scholarship.[14]

These three challenges—namely, that the sources can run thinly on the ground, that the reader is a critical reader of the text, and that the historian can himself be strongly prone to bias and prejudice—are common to contemporary historians everywhere. But they operate with especial force in India. Here, the sources are even more scarce than they are in some other countries. For instance, very few of the records of the Government of India for 1947 and later have been transferred to the National Archives. The official papers of India's first Prime Minister, Jawaharlal Nehru, remain in the control of his descendants; only two foreign scholars and two Indians have been allowed to consult them. The official correspondence as Prime Minister of Indira Gandhi has not been shown to anyone outside the family. That these official papers are not available to scholars is possibly illegal. That they remain closed is certainly an impediment to the deeper understanding of the policies of the Government of India between 1947 and 1964, between 1966 and 1977, and between 1980 and 1984.

---

14. There are, of course, exceptions to this rule, as in the Ayodhya controversy, where a political and religious controversy of the 1980s influenced how Indians understood—or misunderstood—events that took place—or did not take place—in the 1520s.

Outside of the Nehru-Gandhi family, too, the private or official papers of influential individuals are also not nearly as abundant or accessible as one might wish them to be. For Indians in general are indifferent to records and artefacts; thus when a distinguished Indian passes away, his records are often burnt or disposed off as *raddi*. Alternately, they may be guarded with an almost paranoid vigilance, secreted and kept away from scholars. (The former is the case usually with writers or social workers; the latter is the case usually with politicians or demagogues.)

The compulsions and pressures of academic fashion also act as a deterrent to contemporary history. For some time now, the agenda for Indian history-writing has been principally set by the currents of post-modernism and post-structuralism. These tendencies tend to under privilege archival research; they have little time for political history; and they are actively hostile to biography. Finally, these fashions and trends are obsessed with the impact of European colonialism.

Those in thrall to academic fashion may not be so easily persuaded to fill the gaps in our historical understanding identified in this essay. To write about Bengal of the 1920s is to connect oneself to grand and ostensibly universal themes such as 'colonialism' and 'modernity'; to write about West Bengal in the 1950s, when the whites had all departed and the truncated province was merely part of the Republic of India, is to run the risk of appearing, at least among your peers, 'provincial'. This may be one reason why the historiography is so disproportionately biased towards the first half of the 20th century, why, for every historical article or book written about Bengal in the 1950s there are perhaps 500 written about Bengal in the 1920s.

And How to Overcome Them

The preceding section underlined some of the hurdles placed in front of the historian of contemporary India. This concluding section is an exhortation to my colleagues to disregard or overcome them.

To begin with, the sources for contemporary history are perhaps more abundant than many Indian historians allow. True, the National Archives in New Delhi, and the India Office collections of the British

Library in London are filled mostly with records of the colonial period. But the Nehru Memorial Museum and Library (NMML) in New Delhi has painstakingly built up a magnificent collection of private and institutional papers. A handbook issued by the Nehru Library in 2003 lists as many as 681 separate collections. These include the papers of major political parties, as well of influential and important writers, scientists, civil servants, diplomats, and above all, of politicians from all sides of the ideological spectrum.[15] Some state archives have also collected the papers of Indians who lived and worked after Independence.

From these collections one can, if one chooses, reconstruct many aspects of the political and institutional history of independent India. In that endeavour, the historian can also draw upon the fabulous riches of India's periodical press. The Nehru Library itself has a very rich collection on microfilm of daily newspapers in English, Tamil, Hindi, Bengali, and other languages; as well as runs of important weeklies. Newspaper and journal offices elsewhere in the country also maintain their own files. Vigorous and independent, documenting and reflecting the social and political currents of the day, the Indian press is a wonderful resource for historians, if somewhat under-utilised by them.[16]

A third source that can be used is, of course, oral history. Here the contemporary historian has a decided advantage over his more backward-looking colleagues. The biographer of the 19th century Bengali reformer Raja Rammohun Roy can only know of his subject at third or fourth hand. But the biographer of the 20th century Bengali politician Dr B.C. Roy can actually meet, in the flesh, many individuals who knew his subject, sometimes intimately. The same is true for social history: for instance, there are many people around who participated in the all-India railwaymen's strike of 1974, whereas the rebels of the Santhal *hool* of 1855 have all been dead a century and more. It would be unwise for a historian to rely wholly on oral

15. *NMML Manuscripts: An Introduction*. New Delhi: Nehru Memorial Museum and Library, 2003.

16. Two works of contemporary history that have made skilful use of press reports are Gupta, 1966 and Chakravarti, 1999.

testimonies; however, when used judiciously, along with and as a complement to contemporary documents—whether private letters or notings or newspaper reports—they can be of much value in reconstucting the somewhat recent past.

Contrary to what is sometimes supposed (or claimed), the sources for writing contemporary history in India do exist. The research into these sources will be laborious; the writing up of the material, perhaps harder still. For the historian of the recent past has to work his way around the prejudices of the present. We know that Indian history is a most contentious terrain. The battles over our nationalist heritage are very bitter indeed. There are those who see Gandhi and the Congress as the real deliverers of India's freedom: others who would accord the accolade to Savarkar and Hindutva; still others to Bhagat Singh and revolutionary socialism; yet others to Subhas Chandra Bose and the Indian National Army.

The historian of Indian nationalism has to negotiate a perilous path between these competing interpretations and claims. Who is to say that the task of the historian of independent India will be any easier? If anything, it will be more difficult still. The passions generated by Jawaharlal Nehru are even more heated than those generated by Mahatma Gandhi. Dispassionate analyses of the period of Indian history since 1947 are even more likely to be silenced or intimidated by sectarian identities based on caste and religion.

There is the worry that anything a historian will say or write about the recent past will be 'politicised'; but the historian cannot escape his obligations, his academic duty, his professional calling, for that reason alone. However, to write contemporary history in a coherent, plausible, independent way, the historian must approach his sources with a completely open mind. He cannot completely abandon his own beliefs and prejudices; but he can at least try to hold them in abeyance.

How best can the historian face up to the challenge of contemporaneity? How best can he rise above the arguments and animosities of the present day, to which he, as much as his reader, is also prey? Two maxims might be useful here. The first is from F.W. Maitland: "What is now in the past was once in the future."

The second is from George Orwell: "The writer must not be a loyal member of a political party." Maitland's maxim warns us against using the privilege of hindsight. Orwell's warns us against imposing the political preferences of today on our renditions of the past.

My own view is that the historian needs a generation's distance to write dispassionately and seriously about the past. In the 1960s, the 1950s could not be treated as 'history'; but in the first decade of the 21st century it certainly can. After 25 or 30 years have passed, one can view events and processes away from the partisan passions they gave rise to at the time. The happenings of this and the previous decade are the stuff of currrent affairs; the historian has no business passing judgement on them. For example, one does not yet know whether economic liberalisation will decisively end the endemic poverty of the people of South Asia. One does not know either whether the Hindutva wave has peaked, and will pass.

On the other hand, the period of independent India upto and including the Emergency can be viewed through a properly historical lens. Living through the 1970s, it was hard not to take sides in the rivalry between Indira Gandhi and Jayaprakash Narayan, to see one (either one) as a protector or liberator, and the other as a destroyer. Now, so many decades later, with so many new sources available, and with the distance that comes with time, one does not have to take sides any more in that once intense rivalry (the fact that the rivals are both dead also helps). One might even see those fierce competitors as being, in the long run, collaborators—in the undermining of constitutional democracy from above and from below.

My own hope is that the study of the first decades of independent India will become, for historians old and young, Indian and foreign, the real growth area of the future. The India of the 1950s, the 1960s, the 1970s—this was an extraordinary country living through extraordinarily interesting times. It was an unnatural nation; and an even more unlikely democracy. Never before had a society so large and so diverse sought to make itself into a single territorial unit; never before had a population so overwhelmingly poor and illiterate based its political system on universal adult franchise.

As a political experiment, the Republic of India has no parallel or precedent. But there was, as I have noted, a social and economic churning too. A society based on deference was learning to live with the language of rights; an economy based on the land was diversifying into other forms of productive activity. In the different states of the Union, and in the different regions and districts within them, these transformations were manifesting themselves in different ways. The variations in language, social structure, and ecology made for different local and regional histories, all articulated within a wider history of India as a whole. These histories were sometimes marked by contention and conflict; at other times, by consensus and collaboration. The claims and desires of various social groups were expressed directly by themselves, and indirectly through the representations of artists, writers, musicians, and film-makers.

The year 1947 marked a watershed in Indian history; as, long before that, did the year 1757. For the colonial impact on the subcontinent was wide-ranging as well as long-lasting. The British brought with them new technologies of production and communication; new forms of political authority; new ideas on society and culture; and, of course, a new language to expresses these in. The different parts of the sub-continent did not experience British rule in the same uniform pattern. The interventions of the rulers varied widely; one land system was imposed on eastern India, for example, but a very different one in the South. The indigenous response varied, too; some groups in some periods met the new institutions with resigned acceptance; others with militant opposition; yet others with a critical engagement. The languages of resistance and incorporation varied from province to province and often within a province as well.

When India became independent, a long, deep look back at the period of British rule seemed a necessary task for the historian. For the economy, society, polity, and ecology of the Indian sub-continent was shaken up by colonialism; and shaken up in a hundred different ways. One can understand why the colonial encounter, in all its variations and manifestations, became the 'boom' area of historical research. One can appreciate and admire the very many excellent books and essays that came out of this preoccupation. One must still insist that the historian's obsession with colonialism has gone on far too long.

This insistence stems from the understanding that the changes unleashed by that momentous year, 1947, have been at least as far-reaching as those set in motion by the outcome of the Battle of Plassey. But they have been much less written about. Take, again for illustrative purposes only, the social history of West Bengal in the decades after the British had departed. The 1950s saw the massive influx of refugees from the east, which transformed the demography and social life of the premier city, Calcutta. The 1960s witnessed scarcity, food riots, and the rise of the Naxalite movement. The 1970s began with bloody battles between two kinds of Communists, continued with the Emergency, and ended with the unseating of the Congress from political power (for the first time since Independence). The 1980s saw the CPM consolidate its hold over the countryside through agrarian reform and political decentralisation. The 1990s began a partial reversal of the anti-urban bias of the Bengal Communist; the present decade has seen the reversal continue further, with unexpected effects (as in the bitter battles about land acquisition).

These are the bare, skeletal facts, as put down by someone who does not read Bengali and does not know Bengal particularly well. But once—or if—the trained historian puts flesh and blood on them, who is to say that the history of postcolonial Bengal will turn out to be any less interesting than the history of colonial Bengal? On the political and economic fronts, it appears to have been scarcely less tumultuous. And we haven't even mentioned the cultural side yet. For the West Bengal of these years also showcased the films of Satyajit Ray and Ritwik Ghatak, the plays of Utpal Dutt, the stories of Sunil Gangopadhyay and Subhas Mukhopadhyay, and the poetry of Sudhin Dutta.

I am confident, too, that the postcolonial histories of other parts of India, when written, will be as absorbing. The state I live in, Karnataka, has certainly enjoyed its own roller-coaster ride. Here, the first decade of freedom was dominated by the Samyukta Karnataka movement, by the struggle to create a single political unit within which all Kannada speakers could dwell. The second decade was dominated by a tussle for political dominance between the Vokkaligas of the southern parts of the state and the Lingayats of the north. The third decade saw these two major castes being temporarily sidelined by an alliance of backwards and Muslims. The fourth decade witnessed (as in Bengal and elsewhere) the end of the Congress hegemony, and a fascinating but ultimately failed experiment with *panchayati raj*. The fifth decade saw impressive strides by the software industry, a movement of agrarian capital into manufacturing and real estate, and a rise in Hindu-Muslim violence. The sixth decade was marked by the emergence of Bangalore as a favoured destination for foreign investment, and by unprecedented levels of political corruption.

Taking the period as a whole, the political and economic transformations were profound, and their cultural expressions varied and effervescent. For the history of modern Karnataka has also featured, among other things, the stories of U.R. Anantha Murty and Devanoor Mahadeva; the plays of Girish Karnad, Chandrasekhar Kambar, and K.V. Subanna; the films of Rajkumar and of Girish Kaseravalli; and the poetry of Kuvempu and Adiga.

Academic fashion calls the scholar to focus on the period of British rule. Political partisanship calls him to pass quick and motivated verdicts on the history of the recent past. But these calls are not compulsions. They can be resisted, and they must. As an ordinary citizen, one might certainly be more content in Sweden or England; but, as a historian, where else would one want to live in and work on than contemporary India? There are so many archives to dig into it, so many narratives to construct and share. To turn one's back on these stories is to live in the most interesting country in the world, and yet to abuse that privilege.[17]

17. I remember an interview with Vikram Seth that I once watched on television. Seth had just published a new novel, which had a musical theme. The interviewer commented on the striking coincidence that two writers of Indian origin—Salman Rushdie being the other one—had published, in the same year, novels inspired by music. Seth saw it somewhat differently. If two Norwegian writers were to simultaneously publish books on the pencil, he said, now that would be a surprise. But music was a large and capacious, almost universal, subject; so, too, was India. Why should the fact of two Indian writers publishing books on music be seen as a coincidence?

Whether one is a political historian, a social historian, a feminist historian, an environmental historian; whether one is an urban historian, an agrarian historian, a film historian, a literary historian—in sum, whatever branch or style of history one owes an allegiance to, there are diminishing returns from working on the colonial period. The history of independent India after 1947, and of its states and regions, is easily as interesting as the history of British India, and of its provinces and Presidencies, before 1947. And it is so much less studied. Why write the four hundredth book on some aspect of the social history of colonial Bengal, when you can write the first book on all (or at least most) aspects of the social history of Bengal after Independence? Why write the twentieth or thirtieth book on Bankim Chandra Chatterjee, when you can write the first life of Mahasweta Devi?

References

Bandopadhyay, Sekhar (2004). *From Plassey to Partition*. Hyderabad: Orient Longman.

Bhattacharjea, Ajit (2004). *Unfinished Revolution: A Political Biography of Jayaprakash Narayan*. Delhi: Rupa and Co.

Chakravarti, Prafulla (1999). *The Marginal Men: The Refugees and the Left Political Syndrome in West Bengal*. Calcutta: Naya Udyog.

Chatterji, Joya (2001). "Right or Charity? The Debate over Relief and Rehabilitation in West Bengal, 1947-50", in Suvir Kaul (ed.), *The Partitions of Memory: The Afterlife of the Division of India*. Delhi: Permanent Black.

Frank, Katherine (2001). *Indira: The Life of Indira Nehru Gandhi*. London: Harper Collins.

Gandhi, Rajmohan (1991). *Patel: A Life*. Ahmedabad: Navjivan Press.

———. (1995). *The Rajaji Story*. New Delhi: Penguin India.

Goldthorpe, John (1991). "The Uses of History in Sociology", *British Journal of Sociology* 42(2).

Gopal, Sarvepalli (1975-1984). *Jawaharlal Nehru: A Biography*. Three volumes. London: Jonathan Cape.

———. (1989). *Radhakrishnan: A Biography*. New Delhi: Oxford University Press.

Guha, Ramachandra (2007). *India after Gandhi: The History of the World's Largest Democracy*. London: Macmillan. Chapter 10.

Gupta, Sisir Kumar (1966). *Kashmir: A Study in India-Pakistan Relations*. Bombay: Asia Publishing House.

Kaur, Ravinder (2007). *Since 1947: Partition Narratives among Punjabi Migrants in Delhi*. New Delhi: Oxford University Press.

Kudaisya, Gyanesh (1995). "The Deomgraphic Upheaval of Partition: Refugees and Agricultural Resettlement in India, 1947-67", *South Asia* 18(1).

Kudaisya, Medha M. (2003). *The Life and Times of G. D. Birla*. New Delhi: Oxford University Press.

Malhotra, Inder (2006). *Indira Gandhi*. New Delhi: National Book Trust.

Menon, Nivedita (2005). "A Debate among Men', *The Telegraph*, March 23.

Sinha, Rakesh (2005). "Nasty, Brutish and Shorts", *The Hindustan Times*, July 23.

Tan, Tai Yong and Gyanesh Kudesia (2000). *The Aftermath of Partition in South Asia*. London: Routledge.

7

YOGENDRA YADAV

Whither Survey Research?

Reflections on the State of Survey Research on Politics in Most of the World

Survey Research Then and Now

When I was a student, doing Masters in Political Science, the worst thing you could say about any political scientist was that he or she "did survey research". The label 'survey research' stood for what was considered to be most inappropriate in the third world imitations of the American science of politics: it was methodologically naive, politically conservative and culturally inauthentic. Perhaps my academic socialisation bore a strong impress of the institution where I studied then: the Jawaharlal Nehru University (JNU) in general and the School of Social Sciences in particular, was strongly left-wing in its orientation. In those days, a radical orientation in political science was associated with taste for certain kind of subjects (revolutions rather than constitutions, land reform rather than affirmative action, protest movements rather than voting behaviour), preference for some approaches (political economy over analysis of political institutions, history of ideas over conceptual analysis) and strong methodological partisanship (theoretical and not empirical, diachronic and not synchronic, qualitative and not quantitative). In retrospect it is less obvious why these preferences were associated with radicalism. But it should not be hard to see why survey research did not then fit into what a young political scientist wanted to do then.

Some of it may have been specific to the JNU or to political science in India. But it may not be unfair to say that milder or stronger versions of this orientation towards survey research characterised the cutting edge of third world political science such as it was. Survey research was not merely a technique of data gathering, as keeping beard was not merely hair-style. It was a cultural package with a political orientation. It meant focusing on mainstream politics of parties, elections and voting. It went with liberal political orientation; to be 'liberal' was as conservative as one could get in a self-consciously left-wing discipline. It also meant relying on sample surveys of political opinion and behaviour and drawing simple-minded, often harmless if inane, conclusions from the quantitative data thus gathered.

I must confess that I shared with my contemporaries much of this disdain for survey research.[1] After completing my Masters, I took to political theory and did research on the history of the idea of socialism in modern India. It was not surprising therefore that my professional friends and well-wishers were quite puzzled and upset when I started doing survey research, and that too on voting behaviour. Many of them tried to dissuade me from this strange move of 'giving up' on political theory and 'taking to' something as crass as survey research. Some of them have never understood why I did so; some have never forgiven me for doing so.

As I received the news of my selection for the Malcolm Adiseshiah Award, my thought went back to that initial response of my professional colleagues. Not because this honour vindicates my choice; as would be clear from what I say, I continue to harbour deep unease with the practice of what is often called survey research. In any case I have never managed to gather enough energy to participate in methodological crusades in social sciences and could not care less if one or the other carried the day. The reason I turned to my initial encounter was that my initial reaction and that of my professional colleagues was very typical of those times. This award recognises some of my work and much of the work done by other colleagues in the Lokniti network, for which I get underserved credit—in gathering and analysing empirical data on Indian politics. It occurred to me that perhaps this recognition marks a silent shift

1. I think I was only reflecting this commonsense in one of the first essays that I published on a critique of positivist ambition of creating a science of politics. See Yadav, 1986.

in the discipline from largely derivative 'theoretical' debates to addressing our own agenda with the help of systematic gathering and sifting of information, maybe with some of our own conceptual tools. In that sense my work happens to be a part of a much larger body of work as much a product of the work by political theorists as of empirical studies on Indian politics that has ushered the discipline of political science in India into its own. I take this award not so much as recognition of work already done but as an encouragement to work in this direction so as to earn this honour and as a signal about the direction in which the study of politics in our country should proceed.

From what I said about my disposition towards survey research in my student days, you might expect my lecture to be a story of conversion, a story of how I discovered the virtues of survey research and found that the charges against it were unfounded or irrelevant. I'm afraid I am not going to do that. It is true that a closer encounter with the practice of survey research has made me appreciate some of its subtle aspect more than I did initially. I do believe that some of the criticism against survey research reflected (and continues to do so to this date) the fear and the prejudices we all have against things we know little about. Ignorance about the basics of survey research is not confined to public and media; I have found that my fellow political scientists are no less innocent and often give in to the temptation of making a virtue of it. But that is not the burden of my argument here. As I said earlier, fighting disciplinary crusades on behalf of survey research cult doesn't engage me.

Looking back at it a quarter of a century after I first encountered survey research and as someone who has come to be seen as a practitioner of survey research, I am not sure if the charges against survey research were mistaken. Nor can I say with any confidence that these charges do not apply to the practice of survey research today, including to some of my own work. I would suggest instead that the encounter between the package of cognitive practices that we call survey research and the socio-political reality of what used to be called the third world continues to be a very difficult encounter, full of pitfalls and possibilities. I would therefore seek your indulgence to use this opportunity to think aloud about the dangers and the promise of this epistemic encounter.

A quick word of clarification about what I mean by survey research here. I do not use the word in its generic sense[2] that covers census as well as sample survey. I use it in the sense in which it is used commonly by political scientists, as a technique of data gathering in which a sample of respondents is asked questions about their political preferences and beliefs to draw conclusions about political opinions, attitudes and behaviour of a wider population of citizens. In this sense, survey research is associated with but not limited to election studies and research on voting behaviour on the one hand and public opinion research on the other. It includes academic as well as commercial use of this data gathering technique.

In my paper, I draw upon two contexts that I am somewhat familiar with. The first, the more obvious and familiar context is that of political science in India. In sharp contrast to many other social sciences, the discipline of political science in India has had a fraught relationship with things empirical.[3] The unease originated in conditions that are not difficult to understand with hindsight. Empirically oriented study of politics came to our country as a part of the package of American Science of Politics which was, understandably viewed with deep suspicion by the students of politics in our country. This suspicion initially released creative energies that involved philosophical and political interrogation of the new fangled science of politics.[4]

2. A recent textbook defines survey in this generic sense as follows: "A 'survey' is a systematic method for gathering information from (a sample of) entities for the purposes of constructing quantitative descriptors of the attributes of the larger population of which the entities are members." See Groves *et al.* (2004).

3. The contrast is, for example, with the discipline of history in India that has been robustly empirical without giving up on theoretical ambitions. Irrespective of their ideological hues, Indian historians are very attentive to their 'sources' in sharp contrast to the attitude of most political scientists to the nature of 'evidence'. Marxist economists in India have never shunned quantitative information, unlike their counterparts who study politics. The most influential tradition of social anthropology has also been deeply empirical in nature, with 'field work' being seen as a rite of passage. The discipline of political science did not develop any such protocol of external reference to archive, ethnographic field-work or surveys.

4. For two examples of this initial energy see Kaviraj (1978) and Singh (1967).

As a first reaction, this was understandable. Arguably this response saved the discipline of political science in our country from becoming an intellectual colony of American Political Science. But protests have a tendency to degenerate into rituals and serve as shields for vested interests. This I think is what happened to the early critique of positivist political science in India. Since this critique was not backed by a vigorous and creative search for alternative modes of thinking about politics, the discipline of political science soon degenerated into a loose if fashionable way of talking about politics, poorly grounded in theory and devoid of anchors in reality.[5] As radical posturing replaced serious thinking, every empirical enquiry was dubbed empiricist, anything to do with numbers was shunned.[6] In this intellectual climate there was simply no space for developing skills for data analysis, though the universities continued with the ritual of teaching some abstract statistics as a part of the Research Methodology courses. As political scientists in India try to come to terms with survey data, they face a larger question that has relevance beyond the disciplinary context: Must the late comers to survey research confine their intellectual ambitions to 'catching up' with the advanced survey research tradition and data analysis techniques offered by the dominant discipline of political science? Or can they use the latecomers' advantage to reflect on the state of the discipline and chart out a course of their own?

This question acquires a wider significance if we turn to the other context that I draw upon for my reflections here. This is the context

5. These remarks are aimed at the mainstream of the discipline of political science. Needless to say, there were some exceptions and creative interventions from within the Marxist and the non-Marxist camp that defied the limitations of the mainstream.

6. Ironically, one of the biggest casualties of this radical orientation in the discipline has been a systematic study of class in Indian politics. While Marxist economists and political practitioners spent a good deal of their intellectual labour in going over empirical data, including a lot of survey data, on land relations to understand the structure of class in agrarian economy of India, Marxist political scientists have never cared to sift through the existing evidence on how class operates in the domain of politics. If anything the irony has deepened in the last decade or so: as evidence of operation of class as a variable in electoral politics begins to mount in these years, political analysis of radical persuasion has moved further away from any attention to this kind of evidence. It is not surprising that one of the few attempts at using empirical information for the study of class character of Indian politics came from an economist. See Pranab Bardhan, ...

of expansion of survey research on politics outside the academia and beyond the boundaries of India. One of the by-products of the global march of democracy in our times is the expansion of public opinion research all over the globe. Much of this research takes place outside the academia and is driven by the institutional imperatives of the opinion polling industry in close collaboration with the mass media. Often the focus of this industry is very narrow. In India, survey research on politics has become synonymous with 'exit poll' that has come to be the generic name for all the pre and post election polls that aim at predicting electoral outcomes.[7] This is occasionally supplemented by analysis of electoral outcomes and by opinion polls that are not election related.[8] In most of the newly democratising countries, a similar pattern is being replicated, except that there is even less academic input into opinion polling than in our country. Opinion polling organisations, often the local branches of global corporate companies, are rapidly spreading in all these countries, introducing polling into the newly developing democratic culture. This has had its academic counterpart: some countries with social science capacities have evolved public opinion research. But much of serious public opinion research in these countries has been carried out by cross-country, international surveys by academics in the global North with local collaborators. A little later I will say something about the nature and effect of this type of expansion of survey based public opinion research. But at this stage, let me just use this to pose a question: what happens when survey research is taken to 'most of

7. I have had the misfortune of commenting repeatedly on this art of the so-called 'psephology' in our country without much success. See Yadav (1991). For a more technical analysis of election forecasting models, see Karandikar *et al.* (2002).

8. Although the number of such polls is now huge, there is little academic reflection on the findings of these polls or on their methodology; there is not even a simple compilation of the reports of such surveys. India Today's 'Mood of the Nation Poll' done in association with ORG-MARG is one of the most reputed and long-standing series of public opinion polls in the country. In recent years, the CNN-IBN and the CSDS have come together to institute a six monthly 'State of the Nation Survey' that combines the functions of political barometer and general purpose public opinion research.

the world?'[9] Must the growing research on public opinion in most parts of the world replicate the dilemmas and infirmities of the art in the older democracies? Worse, must the practice of polling citizens opinions, attitudes and behaviour in the global South follow the intellectual and political agenda set in the global North?

To anticipate, I shall argue that public opinion research can take one of the two paths as it expands beyond the global north to most of the world. The first—the more likely and decidedly less promising—path is that public opinion research in the rest of the world will replicate a discipline that is yet to come to terms with its foundational assumptions. This expansion might expose and accentuate the inherited flaws of survey research, especially its Euro-centricism and political conservatism. Instead of serving democracy, public opinion research can become a tool of the powerful local and global interests. I do not however think that this is the only path possible. The encounter between the inherited toolkit and the new political reality opens a second path as well. This would involve not just reflecting on how the techniques should be 'applied' to a new setting but to rethink and reshape the methodological self-image of public opinion research. This encounter offers an opportunity to rescue survey research from its unreconstructed positivist self-image and to learn from the 'linguistic turn' of the social sciences. It invites us to consciously bracket many of the western assumptions and meanings that have crept into the standard toolkit of public opinion research. This encounter also provides us with a powerful tool to restore the 'public' that is increasingly elusive in the 'public opinion' manufactured by the mass media.

A Case Against Survey Research

Let me go back to the three charges that I mentioned right at the beginning and try to review where we stand on each of these today. I would not even attempt to offer an overview of the vast literature that exists on debates and controversies concerning

9. I borrow this phrase from Partha Chatterjee who uses it to draw our attention to the fact that what used to be described as the 'Third World' or the global South is not just a small appendage; this comprises most of the world. See Chatterjee (2004).

survey research on political opinions, attitudes and behaviour.[10] I am interested here in summarising the basic questions and the answers that these elicited or failed to elicit. Just to remind you, the three charges leveled against survey research in its early days were that it was methodologically naïve, politically conservative and culturally inauthentic or neo-colonial.[11]

Right from the beginning, survey research was imagined within the four walls of the larger project of developing a 'positive' science of society on the lines of the natural sciences. That its findings could be presented in terms of hard numbers and therefore lent itself to a lot of precision and sophistication that comes with quantification tended to confirm this self-image of survey researcher as a scientist in the mould of a natural scientist. Ironically, largely unknown to the practitioners of survey research in political science, this grand project was interrogated and its methodological foundations rendered suspect just when survey research was beginning to take off. This is not the place to offer a bird's-eye view of the positivist debate in the philosophy of social sciences; the debate is very well recounted in more than one place.[12] Suffice to say here that the critique of the positivist claim came not only from the intellectual traditions like hermeneutics and phenomenology that have offered strong reasons why social phenomenon could not be treated like natural objects. Some of the most powerful critique came from historians of natural sciences and philosophers of language who questioned the impression that the kind of science that the students of society sought to imitate

10. For a quick overview see Splichal (1999). For a summary of theoretically informed critique of survey research on public opinion, see Beniger (1992). For a political critique of the polling industry, see Miller (1995).

11. The literature on philosophy of social sciences and method in political science, which the current section draws upon, is so vast that I have avoided making specific references. Some of the classical critiques aimed generally at the follies of the new empirical science of politics were Taylor (1967); MacIntyre (1973). For extracts from the larger philosophical debate in the philosophy of social sciences, see Delanty and Strydom (2003).

12. Giddens (1977); Bernstien (1983). For extracts from the larger philosophical debate, see Delanty and Strydom (2003).

was ever practices in natural sciences or could in principle be achieved in any branch of knowledge.[13]

Survey researchers in general and survey researchers in the discipline of political science in particular offered very little by way of response to this critique. The critique and the 'linguistic turn' in social science did dent the prestige of survey research and served to subordinate these within the American academia to the theoretical enterprise within which surveys could measure whatever they sought to measure, but it is not clear if this critique changed in any way the practice of survey research on political opinions, attitudes and behaviour. The study of political opinion, attitudes and behaviour was split between two groups that co-existed in a relationship of back-to-back neighbourliness. Most of the radical students of politics went in for ethnographic case studies, completely disregarding whatever information was gathered by survey researchers. For survey researchers it was business as usual, as if the Emperor Science still had his clothes on. There was no doubt about the methodological sophistication, but it was largely confined to data analysis. Search for grand theory of value shift in contemporary world did bring some conceptual sophistication as well; but this was confined to Anglo-Saxon political culture. Arguably the currency of large-N studies and search for cross-national data actually led to a decline in the quality of survey data in post-colonial countries. Survey instruments conceptualised and designed in North America and Europe were lifted and hastily transferred to other parts of the world, generating many a dubious insights. Be as it may, the fact is that survey researchers and those who shunned surveys have largely been two different sub-disciplines, almost two different sects, that hardly spoke to one another. One could say that the methodological dispute regarding a science of society has left political science on the whole a wiser and a more modest if fractious discipline, but it would be difficult to make a similar case about the sub-discipline of survey research. It may be

13. The critique surfaced with Thomas Kuhn's (1962) classic *The Structure of Scientific Revolution*. An examination of the implication of the debate following Kuhn's work, see Fuller (1993).

unkind but not very unfair to say that we stand on this question exactly where we did 25 years ago.

The second charge of political conservatism may not stick as easily today as does the first one. But that is not necessarily a function of learning or improvement in survey research practices. One could argue that this critique was always somewhat misplaced. It was a critique of the political conclusions of the scholars who happened to do survey research; the method itself was free of political bias. It is true that in the heat of the methodological debate it was argued that the method itself was tied to status quo, but it is hard to see the merit in that reasoning today. Survey research on political opinions and attitudes is bound to be a surface investigation, but it is not clear why a conversation in a survey setting is more likely to be status quoits than textual interpretation or ethnographic description. All one can say is that (like in all other branches of knowledge) established routines of knowledge tends to favour the existing configuration of power and that one needs to be very creative to be able to break this.

There is another, weaker, version of this charge that deserves a closer scrutiny. It could be argued that the association of survey research with status quoits politics may not be a necessary function of its method, yet this association is not just a coincidence. It reflects a theoretical inadequacy or laziness that has always characterised survey research. The community of survey researchers has not been vigilant about interrogating the values implicit in its measures. The absence of caution has led to a wholesale and unconscious importing of unexamined political values that reflect the dominant values of the society that exports survey research. This is what accounts for the evident political conservatism of much of survey research on politics. The question we need to answer is whether the practice of survey research has improved in this respect in the last quarter of a century. I am not very sure of my judgement on this score, for such a judgement presupposes a familiarity with substantive conclusions of survey research based studies of politics in different parts of the world that I do not possess. I look forward to corrections and refutations of my reading. But on balance it seems to me that the verdict cannot be very positive on this score as well. Survey research continues to be imprisoned within the frame of liberal democracy that may not appear conservative in Europe and North America, but that has a built-in drag in the context of the post-colonial societies. I think it is possible to counter this drag while using the survey method, but I am not sure the community of survey researchers has done very much about it. From a largely passive application of 'modernisation' and 'development', we have moved to equally uncritical application of 'democracy' and 'civil society'. A check list model of democracy dominates the discourse on democracy; survey research applies it to different parts of the world to measure how they measure up to it. Cross-sectional surveys use more or less the same framework as was used by elite measures like Freedom House index; Washington consensus on democracy dominates both of these. I see very little attempt to use survey research to expand the meaning of democracy. Let me reiterate that I do not see this as the limitation inherent in survey research but as a weakness of the way it has been practiced.

Let me now turn to the third charge, that of cultural inauthenticity. To be sure, this is not how the charge was originally framed, and this is not how many critics of survey research will like to articulate it: the charge presupposes a notion of authenticity that is not shared by all. Some critics might wish to call it the neo-colonial nature of the survey research enterprise; others might point to the intellectual heteronomy in the practice of survey research. Whatever the label, the substance of the criticism is not very different: survey research is accused of mindless imitation of ideas and concepts of one society in a different and inappropriate context. This criticism in similar to the previous one in that it is political in its substance, but it is different from calling it politically conservative. The charge of political conservatism could apply in any context, but that of cultural inauthenticity is specific to the practice of survey research in post-colonial setting. It involves three related arguments: that survey research has external origins, that its currency draws its strength not from its intrinsic intellectual charm but from the field of power and that its application creates an incongruence or a mismatch between the method applied and the reality that it seeks to capture. Please note that the criticism about cultural inauthenticity is not confined to a simple-minded complain about its external origins alone; at the heart of this charge is an intellectual criticism. I am not sure if survey researchers have responded to this criticism seriously. It might be useful to contrast the response of survey researchers with the response of anthropologists to the charge of being instruments of colonial knowledge;[14] survey research on political opinions has never undergone that kind of self-criticism and transformation.

This is not just an academic point. The link between survey research and colonial power is not just a matter of archeology of knowledge as it were. It is a contemporary and pressing political concern. It is not a coincidence that there has been a proliferation of comparative survey research precisely at a point when the world is more unipolar than was the case before and when the USA is on a mission to export liberty and democracy by using, shall we say, rather unconventional means. In a world where knowledge is power, the sudden proliferation of US sponsored research on mass political opinions cannot be an unmixed blessing. At least the students of politics cannot pretend that this is a pure diffusion of scientific knowledge. Not to put too fine a point on it, I fear that survey research on political opinions and attitudes can serve as instrument, more effective and therefore more dangerous, of neo-colonial surveillance of global population. In this respect, I'm afraid we do not stand where we stood a quarter of a century ago; we may be in a much more precarious position today. That much of survey research in global South is done now by 'local' researchers, does not take away from what I am saying. We know that colonial power (or for that matter white racist regime) was defended by largely 'native' army.

Transfer as Transplantation

The extension of democracy to most parts of the world following the third wave of democratisation was also accompanied by the expansion of polling and other forms of survey research. This globalisation of survey research took many forms, but in each case it

14. See, for example the powerful critique of Western descriptions of the non-West in anthropology in Clifford and Marcus (1986). Edward Said's classic *Orientalism* had already had this influence on humanities in general and literary criticism in particular.

meant a transfer of the established survey practices from the global North to the rest of the world. This may be described as 'transfer as transplantation'. Expansion of survey research has meant an extension of field sites but it has not been matched by corresponding expansion of theoretical and methodological imagination. Before turning to the deficiencies of this mode of transfer as transplantation, let us first understand the dynamics of globalisation of survey research.[15]

The demand for more and better survey research outside the global North has been fuelled by a shift in the agenda of media, academia and global financial institutions. The fall of Berlin wall was accompanied by opening up of a new world that was both accessible and newsy. Similarly the story of rise and fall of democracies in other parts of the world also served to shift the media attention in the global North to politics in most parts of the world. This was particularly so for the 'emerging economies' that now held the key to economic transformations all over the world. All this meant greater media attention to political developments in democracies outside North America and Western Europe. This was accompanied by a shift from area study to comparative design in the academic research on politics, especially within the discipline of political science in the USA. This has meant greater comparative attention to democracies outside the USA. The methodological premium on putting theoretical models to empirical test fuelled the need for greater data from these parts of the world. Partly as a result of these two, there occurred a shift in the thinking of the global lenders and donors. They discovered that politics mattered, perhaps in fundamental ways, to economic and human development. It began with the World Bank's emphasis on what it called 'governance'. But the agenda, and the number of institutions that subscribed to it, expanded rapidly. An intellectual desire to understand quality of governance soon gave to a quest to index and rank countries by their quality of governance. Thus came together curiosity, intellectual tools and the funds to support public

15. This section draws upon the limited literature on globalisation of survey research on politics. See Smith and Jibum (2007); International Organization for Standardization/Technical Committee 225 (2005); Harkness (1999); Heath *et al.* (2005).

opinion research in most parts of the world. While the initiative may have come from within in some cases as in India that can boast of a large economy, mature media and social science academia, for most countries the push came from outside.

The supply side of globalisation of survey research took three forms. First, there was a rise of cross-national surveys in a comparative design. Some of these surveys were one-off cross-national comparisons of political behaviour, attitudes and opinions. But this gave rise to some very large and regular cross- national surveys that have increased their scope. The trend began with the World Values Survey (WVS) in 1981.[16] By the time the WVS carried out its fourth wave in 2004, it covered as many as 80 countries. Over the years it has also tried to shed its dependence on North American concerns and vocabulary, though it continues to retain a large residue of that. One could add the Pew Global Survey and the Transparency International survey to this list.

The second source of cross-national survey data is the rise of regional barometers all over the world that offer at regular intervals a reading of political opinions, attitudes and values of cross-section of citizens in several countries. Taking its inspiration from the Eurobarometer that began in 1960 and that covers countries of the European Union, a series of regional barometers started in the 1990s. Beginning with 1991, the New Europe Barometer has come to cover 16 post-communist countries. The Latinobarometer has run continuously since 1995 and covers 17 countries of Latin America.[17] Afrobarometer began in 1999 and covers 19 democracies in Africa.[18] Finally, the East Asian Barometer began in 12 countires of East and South-East Asia in 2001[19] and has joined hands with the State of Democracy in South Asia study that covered 5 countries of

16. For introduction to the World Values Survey and access to its data and findings see *http://www.worldvaluessurvey.org*

17. *http://www.latinobarometro.org/*. Latinobarometer also serves as the headquarter for a coalition of all these regional barometers called the Global Barometer Surveys, see *http://www.globalbarometer.net/*

18. *http://www.afrobarometer.org/*

19. *http://www.asianbarometer.org/*

South Asia in 2005.[20] The regional barometers of the global South, beginning with Latinobarometer have tried to foreground different concerns and are sensitive to the vocabulary of politics in each region. Although the regional barometers began independent of one another, they have come to ask a core set of comparable questions on political participation, institutional trust, support for democracy and its alternatives, sources of political information.[21]

The third source has been the rise of commercial opinion polling in most of the new democracies. While some of these countries witnessed local companies take initiative in this regard, the general trend has been the entry of some big global corporations like the Gallup, MORI and A C Neilsen in most of these countries. Commercial opinion polling works closely with market research and draws some support from local media.

There is no doubt that the globalisation of survey research has widened the base for generalisations about public opinion on some key issues of our time. We have comparable data from more countries than ever before on what the citizens think about, say, democracy. We have data on many new issues of global concern, such as global warming, corruption and terrorism. At the same time, it is only fair to say that the expansion of survey research has as yet not brought corresponding theoretical divident to social sciences. Much of the quest in cross-national research is about confirmation of the existing wisdom drawn from a small part of the globe. There is some attempt at statistical sophistication in analysing data from different countries, but it is hard to avoid the conclusion that much of this sophistication is at the expense of contextual understanding of each of these countries. Anchored in 'democratisation' paradigm, much like the modernisation paradigm that characterised the first wave of studies of 'developing societies', the new wave of survey research shares the same naïve teleological approach that expected the rest of the world to traverse the golden path taken by Europe and America. In sum,

20. *http://www.democracy-asia.org/* for introduction to the survey and to the *State of Democracy in South Asia* study.

21. For some of the findings from the barometers on support for democracy, see articles in the symposium on Democracy Barometers, *Journal of Democracy*, January 2008

more than presenting us with an opportunity, the globalisation of survey research brings us face-to-face with a real danger of a new 'parochial universalism'.

Transfer as Transformation

By now some of you must be wondering where this onslaught on survey research is headed and whether it does not cut the branch on which I am perched. If survey research faces such fundamental questions and if these are only deepened as a result of the recent globalisation, isn't it time to give up on it? If the advanced and well-funded academia in the first world could not respond to these questions, how would the practitioners of survey research in the global South cope up with the challenge?

But as many of you can guess, I do not share this line of reasoning. Let me say with all the emphasis at my command that doing survey research on political opinions, attitudes and behaviour of the citizen is not an optional activity in modern democracies. If we are at all serious about the democratic project, we cannot but record and register public opinion. And if we are even marginally aware of the contemporary setting when exposure to mass media and homogenising political practices shape rapid shifts in mass political opinions, we cannot but need an instrument like survey research that can sketch the broad contours of changing public opinion. Those of us who have chosen to or are condemned to live under conditions of modernity that are usually not of our making have simply no choice except to use modern cognitive tools that enable us to make sense of the world that we inhabit. In that sense, modern social science and survey research on public opinion is essential for those who wish to make sense of modern politics, democratic or otherwise.

There is a stronger, democratic argument for taking survey research seriously. We face a paradox in the global discourse on democracy: while democracy is expanding all over the world, our notion of what it means to be democratic is shrinking. A one-dimensional, check list model of democracy seems to dominate our imagination today along with institutional quick-fixes about how to build democracy. Survey research can play a very significant role here by recovering and foregrounding 'public opinion' in an age where democracy is all about institutional forms and correct rituals. As a tool for recovery, reconstruction and amplification of subaltern/ marginal voices, survey research can become an ally of the project of radical democracy. This is not to say that every form of survey research is an ally of radical democracy. Such an enterprise would require considerable change in the dominant mode of comparative survey research. Surveys will have to be not just carried out but also imagined in different parts of the globe. Designing surveys specific to the political culture, might mean giving up on some universal questions and checking some of our global theoretical ambitions. Above all, it would mean focusing surveys to excavate the 'social imaginary'[22] that envelops democratic practice in different parts of the world and gives a different character to this word in different political settings. By pluralising the concept of democracy to reflect the diversity of opinions across the globe, we might forge one of the strongest counter to neo-colonial domination of the world.

In the post-industrial societies of the global North, public opinion polling as an institution may have become a way of shutting out the critical voices by drowning them into the mainstream voice of the majority. But in the global South, the real challenge is to establish that the opinion of the public and the voice of the majority heard. In this context, a simple-minded aversion to 'positivist' social science and complete abandoning of empirical enquiry into political behaviour, attitudes and opinion has done a lot of harm to the understanding of politics in many countries of the global South. I know I am making a fairly strong and largely unsubstantiated case here, but I hope that by now I would not be accused of being partisan to survey research.

I do not believe that survey research in the global South is condemned to producing a poor copy of the comparative survey research practiced in the global North and thus reproducing its fundamental flaws in its worst form. I think what appears to be a grave problem, of carrying the tools of survey research to a radically

22. This concept is drawn from Taylor (2004).

different situation, is in many ways a big opportunity of tackling afresh some of the foundational questions that have always dodged survey research on public opinion. This would require us to diverge from the prescription of a pure methodologist in the global North: giving up omnibus surveys, better sampling, living up to standards set by 'proper' surveys and greater emphasis on sophisticated data analysis. Instead the approach we need to pursue may be described as 'transfer as transformation'. This involves innovation in a different direction so as to explore the distinct character of public opinion research in the South. This calls for nothing short of rethinking the method, substance and protocols of survey research in a radically different setting and reflecting on the political practice embedded in survey research. In what follows, I offer a synoptic overview of this approach. I do so in the hope that these remarks will generate a debate that can lead to a more careful consideration and reflection on the future direction of survey research.

First of all, truth claims of survey research could do with some clarity and modesty. If the current state of philosophy of social science dictates a mood of methodological modesty, survey research too needs to partake of this modesty. While methodological debates have shaken the foundations of survey research, it has questioned other hallowed ground as well. Philosophy is seen as no more than a form of writing.[23] If hermeneutic engagement with texts or ethnographic involvement with the subjects was not assured of recovery of meaning, survey research had all the less reasons to pretend to do so. It is time we saw and presented survey research as a craft, as an art form, rather than get entangled with claims of scientificity. This can help survey research get rid of a lot of excess baggage that the previous generation of survey researchers carried on their shoulders. In particular, this would free survey research from carrying the burden of the positivist project of a science of society. This would also alert the researchers to the profoundly political nature of survey research on politics. Survey research on political opinion, attitudes and behaviour is no different from any other form

23. Rorty (1979).

of inquiry on this subject in that it is inextricably enmeshed with concepts that are 'essentially contested'. Embedding such concepts in a questionnaire and presenting the evidence in statistical tables does not absolve the researcher from the responsibility of demonstrating that the concepts are appropriate to what they seek to measure. This would necessitate establishing a conversation between survey-based inquiries with political theory.

This reorientation would affect the design of surveys as well as the analysis of survey findings. Survey research in most parts of the world need not adopt the latest, the most fancy state-of-the-art techniques; 'appropriate technology' is a good slogan in this context. In the last few years, the routine and flat-footed understanding of causality deployed by mainstream researchers has attracted serious criticism within the American Political Science.[24] This awareness of the complex nature of causality is vital for the study of most parts of the world. Since the formal models of politics are usually distilled from the historical experience of European and North American societies, they can be specially debilitating in the study of other societies. There is a need therefore to build in an understanding of the context of different countries, especially in cross-national surveys. In this effort, some of the state-of-the-art techniques can be quite useful. I have in mind the use of vignettes as a way to control for the variations in base-line expectations in different societies and the use of field experiments.[25] But we need to resist the have-data-will-regress mood of the discipline and the fad for the latest techniques of data analysis. No matter how sophisticated the technique of data analysis, it offers no more than an interpretative suggestion that needs to be fitted with other links in the logical chain to arrive at a causal inference. Regression by itself is not causal determination, though carefully testing of models with sophisticated techniques is a necessary tool for arriving at any serious conclusion about mass political behaviour. The outcome may be even weaker in the case of

24. Cameroon and Morton (2002). For a critique of mechanistic models of explanation that dominate statistical analysis of survey data in political science see, Achen (2005).

25. For suggesting use of vignettes within surveys, see King *et al.* (2003). For field experiments, see Green and Gerber (2003).

survey data on opinions and attitudes, for what one can conclude from such an inquiry is severely constrained by the conceptual design and interpretative frame.

The second change would have to do with how survey research relates to other forms of inquiry. Once we give up the monopolistic claims of survey as a method to understand the structure of mass beliefs, survey research can serve as a reality check for much of social science research on democracy and democratisation. It can do so by sketching the big if rough picture of the changes in mass political behaviour or mass opinions and attitudes. Even if survey based investigation does not offer a satisfactory explanation of the phenomenon, it can set the agenda for what needs to be explained. Nature and pattern of political participation in contemporary India provides an apt illustration. Earlier both popular and academic commentaries had assumed that India had followed the global pattern of growing disinterest and apathy among the citizens, especially in the lower orders. It took survey based investigation to show that this was simply not true: levels of political participation in India were good by global standards, did not experience a secular decline and that citizens from the lower order of society actually participated as well if not more than the upper castes and classes.[26] This finding does not by itself explain this outlier, but it does specify what needs to be explained. It now opens itself to ethnographic enquiries of what goes into political participation,[27] comparative investigations of the patterns and theoretical disputes about meaning and significance of political participation. Similarly for a country like India where we have some credible survey based data for several points in its post-colonial history,[28] there needs to be a better conversation between political historians and survey researchers. The need for dialogue is more pronounced if we take the instrument of survey research to newer democracies in most parts of

26. Yadav (2000), for subsequent modification see Palshikar and Kumar (2004).

27. Banerjee (2007).

28. Much of this data is available at the CSDS Data Unit, perhaps the richest data archive on politics anywhere in the global South. See, *www.lokniti.org*. For an introduction to its flagship survey series, see Lokniti Team (2004).

the world. Research designed on formal models of politics is unlikely to be of much help here, simply because these models have not been distilled from the political realities of these societies. If one has to pose meaningful and researchable questions in the survey, one has to draw from anthropology, political history and in some cases post-colonial studies. The less insular survey research on politics becomes, the more its dialogue with other related disciplines, the higher we can expect its yield in terms of a better understanding of politics.[29]

The third domain of 'transformation' is really about restoration of a fundamental tenet of survey research, namely its privileging of probabilistic sampling. Random sampling is usually seen and discussed in technical terms, as the ideal method for selecting a sample that mirrors the attributes of the larger universe. It is time we viewed this technical practice with a political lens. In the new democracies of the global South, random sampling is a radical device to ensure that the subaltern and suppressed opinions are made public. This is a way to find out if a collusion between the political elite and the opinion makers may have kept the public opinion out of public policy. The introduction of policy package of 'liberalisation' in many countries including our own is a case in point. In most of these cases, these new policies have been pushed with the help of a political consensus. In our own country the New Economic Policy was a political surprise, was a matter of political contention but has over the years come to be seen as a subject of political consensus for all parties that govern at the centre or at the state level. However a series of studies of public opinion on this question has demonstrated that the public does not share this political consensus, that the public opinion is still for state intervention in the economy, for public sector as a provider of basic services and uneasy with though not hostile to globalisation.[30] Afrobarometer found a similar dissonance between public policy of Structural Adjustment Programmes and public opinion in many countries of Africa. I am not here to make a case for

29. For a plea for such a dialogue between ethnographic and survey research on elections, see Yadav (2007).

30. Suri (2004).

or against neo-liberal economic policies. My only point here is about ensuring that public opinion really reflects the opinion of the public.

In this context sticking to random sampling acquires a new salience. If the opinion polling in India is any indication, the expansion of polling in most parts of the world has meant a step back in methodological terms. Crude quota samples, where even the quota does not represent the population profile, are the norm. Much worse are urban or metro polls that do not even try to cover the national population that they seek to represent. Even academic surveys do not use the principle of randomness; purposive sampling is the norm as and when the researchers use survey methods to study public opinion.[31] Well-regarded global surveys accept utterly unrepresentative samples when it comes to countries outside the global North. Insisting on random sampling in this condition would require some innovations. We need to work on sampling techniques in conditions where background information is very low and the listing of the population is not always available. Another area of attention will be devising protocol of reporting the sample profile that takes into account the various dimensions of exclusion and marginalisation. In India, for instance, it should be mandatory for every poll to make public its sample profile in terms of urban-rural divide, gender and major caste-community groups.

The fourth transformation is about ensuring that survey research is imagined and conceptualised in the language of the subjects whose opinions it seeks to capture. It is ironic that nearly two decades after the 'linguistic turn'[32] in social sciences was recognised, survey research is yet to take that linguistic turn. Surveys on political opinion, attitudes and behaviour are still imagined and conceptualised in the languages of the global North. Concepts distilled from the political

31. The CSDS surveys have been an exception in this regard. Ever since the 1960s when the survey tradition started there, the CSDS teams have followed multi-stage random sampling procedures and have used the official electoral rolls to draw the sample. For discussion of the evolution of sampling practices, see Lokniti Team (2004).

32. The expression is used wisely to refer to the move in social and human sciences away from objectivist orientation to one that takes language and subjectivities more seriously. Rorty (1992). There is very little reflection on the question of language in survey research. For a few examples of some technical work see, Behling and Law (2000); Harkness *et al.* (2004).

practice of Europe and North American democracies are often applied all over the world without serious debate on the appropriateness or otherwise to most parts of the world.[33] And this applies not just to cross-country surveys. The entry of global firms in the polling industry all over the world has meant a mechanical replication of survey items designed in the older democracies to all other countries. In this respect as well, the expansion of survey research has meant methodological regress: some of the elementary rules of survey research are given a go by when exporting it to most parts of the world. Methodological discussions on cross-national surveys rarely mention language as a key issue. In a multi-linguistic context like ours, the challenge is multifold: the survey instrument needs to be developed in several languages and dialects.[34]

The challenge is not merely that of accuracy of translation that can be checked by back-translation: the real challenge is of conceptual translation and the appropriateness of the concept itself. I would like to reiterate emphatically that we are not discussing nuts and bolt issues here: if the enterprise of survey research derives some of its relevance from the project of pluralising the idea of democracy, then recovering the 'social imaginary' embedded in political practices is one of its key tasks, one that it cannot even begin to take up unless the surveys are imagined and designed in languages of the subjects. Survey research must recognise language of political practice as a conceptual resource.

The fifth and related domain is that of survey fieldwork protocols. Here is another area where survey research tradition has experienced a decline in the recent times. Since face-to-face interviewing has

33. The wide currency of concepts like social capital and civil society and the battery of questions on trust and membership of organisations in most global surveys appear to me to be an example of this trend. The application of the concept of 'self-expression values' drawn from post-industrial societies is another instance of lack of fit between the concept and the world that it seeks to capture. For the latter see Inglehart and Welzel (2005).

34. The question of 'dialects' or languages without a script or state recognition is a vital question waiting to be attended to in our context. The National Election Study, with its research instrument in 18 languages, has attempted to address this question with the help of transliteration in the case of Kok-Borok, a language spoken by the *Adivasis* of Tripura. The real challenge is to attend to more than a dozen 'dialects' of Hindi that can be mutually incomprehensible.

become prohibitively expensive in North America and Western Europe, the focus of methodological sophistication has shifted to telephonic and now internet-based interviews. As a result very little attention is now paid to refining the original and the best practice of face-to-face interview, which is still possible in most parts of the world. Anthropology has produced a good deal of reflection on how should an 'outsider' gain entry into a new culture, but there is no equivalent reflection in survey research on how to establish a rapport with a respondent who is from a very different class, caste-community or gender and speaks a different register of the same language, as is often the case while doing surveys in India. There is a real need to develop fieldwork manuals and training modules to attend to these questions.

Let me pick up two questions for special attention here. Survey researchers often approach respondents who are either not literate or are not exposed to media and draw a blank when they ask them questions about controversies of national politics or questions involving remote institutions. The standard protocol requires them to put these responses under a dustbin category of "Can't say/ Don't know". This category actually masks three different kinds of responses: when the respondent is unable to comprehend the question, when the respond understands the question but has no clear opinion about it and when the respond has an opinion but does not wish to disclose it. Since the proportion of those who fall in this category can be anything from a quarter to half of the respondents for some of the complex questions, we need much more reflection on fieldwork protocols for identification of these different responses. A related issue is that of survey research in conflict zones. The current protocols of fieldwork are about the ordinary or normal situation that simply does not occur very often in our setting. Think for example of survey researchers in the Maoist controlled areas in Nepal before the restoration of democracy, or for that matter in Salwa Judum affected areas of Chhattisgarh today.[35]

35. For some reflections on survey at the height of Maoist insurgency in Nepal, see SDSA Team (2008). The CSDS teams have carried out surveys in the Kashmir valley, Manipur and Nagaland in the recent years but the lessons remain to be written about.

Finally let me turn to the externalities of survey research: Who carries out surveys? At whose behest? To what end? These questions are more pertinent to survey research than any other form of social science inequiry, for survey research is a resource-intensive team game. More than any other kind of research, surveys require institutional support. The history of evolution of surveys in the older democracies has meant a close collaboration of public opinion research with private interests. Opinion polling is done by private companies and is dictated by their bottom line. Mass media and political parties are the biggest funders of public opinion. A good deal of public opinion research never makes it to the public domain, for it is for-clients-eye-only. No wonder, the agenda of 'public opinion' is dictated by organised private interests. The situation gets even more complicated when we look at public opinion research in the global South. The agenda is not just dictated by private interests, but by those situated outside the country. Very often the nationally owned media simply cannot afford to sponsor or does not see value-for-money in such surveys. The surveys are supported by media outside the country, global corporate houses, instruments of global finance or multilateral donor agencies. While the investigators are local, the intellectual leadership and the toolkit comes from outside. No wonder, survey research of this kind is viewed within these countries with deep suspicion if not active hostility.

It is time therefore that we start thinking of the questions of funding and the institutional setting of survey research as political questions that require policy responses. First of all, it would require infusing some public funds into the collection of public opinion on some key questions on a regular basis. Our country has a rich tradition of data collection on economy and demography, thanks to institutions like the Census of India and the National Sample Survey Organisation (NSSO). I am not suggesting that a governmental agency should be set up to investigate public opinion on politically sensitive questions. We are fortunate to have autonomous agencies like the Indian Council of Social Science Research that can be used to funnel public funds into regular monitoring of public opinion. Other countries that do not have a similar set up will have to think of different mechanisms. Nor am I arguing for banning private or foreign funding: such bans are either superfluous or counter-productive. What we need is greater public spirited philanthropy and at any rate more transparency in reporting of funding sources for every kind of survey. Besides funding we also need to think of other resources like institutional space, intellectual capacity and skills. Very often a rapid expansion of polling in the absence of trained personnel leads to a decline in quality of survey research. I believe that this is what has happened in our country in the last decade or so. Pioneers of academic survey research and commercial opinion polling in our country had achieved for their time fairly high international standards of quality of research. The expansion of commercial opinion polling in the last decade has led to a visible decline in the quality of research, accuracy of findings and the extent of transparency. There is clearly a need to invest more into the R&D of survey research and into training of the personnel. Improving the standards of survey research would also require learning across national boundaries. In this respect, the survey researchers in the global South can learn quite a lot from one another.

Conclusion

I began by talking about the days when I was a student. It may be appropriate therefore to conclude by reflecting on what it could mean to be a student of politics today and what role, if any, could survey research play in that. We live in different times today and the world of political science in our country has, at least partly, moved with the times. There is a grudging acknowledgment that the students of political science should study politics, and not just socio-economic structures. There is a desire to understand popular opinions and attitudes, and not merely as false consciousness. There is also a willingness to entertain a suspicion that understanding India may require modification in some of the received categories and theories of social science. All this has happened at a time when Indian politics has witnessed a democratic upsurge, new social groups are making claims to political power and new social alliances and political coalitions are being forged. These are exciting times to be a student of politics in India.

This is not my case that survey research has to be at the fulcrum of the engagement for a student of politics in India today. As would be clear by now, I would consider it nothing short of an intellectual catastrophe, were the entire discipline of political science to swing now to survey research of the kind that we have received. My plea, rather, is that theoretically oriented yet empirically grounded engagement with politics should be at the fulcrum of the future of the discipline of political science in India. This engagement can and should take multiple forms: conceptual analysis, intellectual history, political history, comparative analysis, ethnography and survey research, among others. I do believe that survey research of the kind suggested above would constitute one necessary ingredient of the toolkit for a student of politics in India. I do hope at least some of those who are students of politics today would make it their business to not just transfer but transform the tradition of survey research and make it relevant for most parts of the world.

Acknowledgment: Delivered as the Malcolm Adiseshiah Memorial Lecture on 21 November 2008 at Chennai. Some of the ideas here were presented as a plenary speech at the session "Probing Public Opinion,Interpretations, Deliberatios" of 38th World Congress of the Internatinational Institute of Sociology at Central European University, Budapest, 27 June 2008. An earlier version was presented as a talk "Setting standards for international survey research" at Afrobarometer Round 3, Planning Workshop, Accra, 7-11 February 2005 and as valedictory address to the Summer School in Research Methodology in Political Science organised by India Institute of Advanced Studies, Shimla with Lokniti, Centre for the Study of Developing Societies, Delhi at IIAS, Shimla, 2-14 July 2007. Comments and feedback from participants at Budapest, Accra and Shimla are gratefully acknowledged.

References

Achen, Christopher H. (2005). "Let's Put Garbage-Can Regressions and Garbage-Can Probits Where They Belong", *Conflict Management and Peace Science* 22(4), January.

Banerjee, Mukulika (2007). "Sacred Elections", *Economic and Political Weekly* 42(17).

Beniger, James R. (1992). "The Impact of Polling on Pubic Opinion: Reconciling Foucault, Habermas and Bourdeieu", *International Journal of Public Opinion Research* 4(3).

Behling, O. and K.S. Law (2000). *Translating Questionnaires and Other Research Instruments: Problems and Solutions*. Sage.

Bernstien, Richard (1983). *Beyond Objectivism and Relativism: Science, Hermeneutics, and Praxis*. University of Pennsylvania Press.

Cameroon, Charles M. and Rebecca Morton (2002). "Formal Theory Meets Data", in Ira Katznelson and Helen V. Milner (eds.), *Political Science: State of the Discipline*. Washington: APSA.

Chatterjee, Partha (2004).*The Politics of the Governed: Reflections on Popular Politics in Most of the World*. Delhi: Permanent Black.

Clifford, James and George E. Marcus (1986). *Writing Culture: The Poetics and Politics of Ethnography*. School of American Research. Santa Fe: University of California Press.

Delanty, Gerard and Piet Strydom (eds.) (2003). *Philosophies of Social Science: The Classic and Contemporary Readings*. Maidenhead: Open University Press.

Fuller, S. (1993). *The Philosophy of Science and its Discontents*. 2nd edition. New York: Guilford.

Giddens, Anthony (1977). "Positivism and its Critics", in *Studies in Social and Political Theory*. London: Hutchinson.

Green, Donald P. and Alan S. Gerber (2003). "Reclaiming the Experimental Tradition in Political Science" in Ira Katznelson and Helen V. Milner (eds.), *Political Science: The State of the Discipline*. W.W. Norton & Company.

Groves, Robert M., Floyd J. Fowler, Jr., Mick P. Couper, James M. Lepkowski, Eleanor Singer and Roger Tourangeau (2004). *Survey Methodology*. New Jersey: John Wiley. p.2.

Heath, Anthony, Stephen Fisher and Shawna Smith (2005). "The Globalization of Public Opinion Research", *Annual Review of Political Science* 7.

Harkness, J. (1999). "In Pursuit of Quality: Issues for Cross-national Survey Research", in *International Journal of Social Research Methodology* 2.

Harkness, J., B-E. Pennell and A. Schoua-Glusberg (2004). "Survey Questionnaire Translation and Assessment", in S. Presser *et al.* (eds.), *Questionnaire Development Evaluation and Testing Methods*. Wiley Series in Survey Methodology. New Jersey: John Wiley and Sons Inc.

Inglehart, Ronal and Christian Welzel (2005). *Modernization, Cultural Change and Democracy: The Humna Development Sequence*. New York: Cambridge University Press.

International Organization for Standardization/Technical Committee 225 (2005). *Market, Opinion and Social Research Draft International Standard*. Madrid: AENOR.

Karandikar, Rajeeva L. Yogendra Yadav and Clive Payne (2002). "Predicting the 1998 Indian Parliamentary Elections", *Electoral Studies* 21: 69-89.

Kaviraj, Sudipta (1978). *State of Political Theory: Some Marxist Essays*. Calcutta: Research India Publications.

King, Gary,Christopher J.L. Murray, Joshua A. Salomon and Ajay Tandon (2003). "Enhancing the Validity and Cross-Cultural Comparability of Measurement in Survey Research", in *American Political Science Review* 97.

Kuhn, Thomas (1962). *The Structure of Scientific Revolution.* University of Chicago Press.

Lokniti Team (2004). "National Election Study 2004: An Introduction", *Economic and Political Weekly* 39(51), December, 18.

MacIntyre, Alisdair (1973). "Is a Science of Comparative Politics Possible? ", in Alan Ryan (ed.), *The Philosophy of Social Explanation.* Oxford: Oxford University Press.

Miller, Peter V. (1995). "The Industry of Public Opinion", in T.L Glauser and C.T. Salmon (eds.), *Pubic Opinion and the Communication of Consent.* New York: Guilford.

Palshikar, Suhas and Sanjay Kumar (2004). "Participatory Norm: How Broad-based is it?", *Economic and Political Weekly* 39(51) December 18.

Rorty, Richard (1979). *Philosophy and the Mirror of Nature.* New Jersey: Princeton University Press.

———. (1992). *The Linguistic Turn: Essays in Philosophical Method.* University of Chicago Press.

SDSA Team (2008). *State of Democracy in South Asia.* Delhi: Oxford University Press.

Singh, Randhir (1967). *Reason, Revolution and Political Theory: Notes on Michael Oakeshott.* New Delhi: PPH.

Smith, Tom and Kim, Jibum (2007). "The Globalization of Survey Research", Paper presented at the *Annual Meeting of the American Sociological Association.* TBA. New York. August 10. Online <PDF> *http://www.allacademic.com/meta/p175569_index.html.*

Splichal, Slavko (1999). *Public Opinion: Developments and Controversies in the Twentieth Century.* Lanham: Rowman & Littlefield.

Suri, K.C. (2004). "Democracy, Economic Reforms and Election Results in India", *Economic and Political Weekly* 39(51), December, 18.

Taylor, Charles (1967). "Neutrality in Political Science", in Peter Laslett and W.G. Runciman (eds.), *Philosophy, Politics and Society.* Oxford: Blackwell.

———. (2004). *Modern Social Imaginaries.* Durham: Duke University Press.

Yadav, Yogendra (1980). "Political Science: Positivist Method and Philosophic Critiques", *Indian Journal of Political Science*: 502-17, October-December.

———. (1991). "The Problem and Polls, Predictions, Psephology", *Seminar* 385 [Beyond the Vote: A Symposium on 1991 Election and After], September.

———. (2000). "Understanding the Second Democratic Upsurge: Trends of Bahujan Participation in Electoral Politics in the 1990s", in Francine R. Frankel, Zoya Hasan, Rajeeva Bhargava and Balveer Arora (eds.), *Transforming India: Social and Political Dynamics of Democracy.* Delhi: Oxford University Press.

———. (2007). "Epilogue: What Does Fieldwork Do in the Field of Elections?", in A.M. Shah, *The Grassroots of Democracy: Field Studies of Indian Elections.* Delhi: Permanent Black.

8

C.P. CHANDRASEKHAR[1]

Global Imbalances and the Dollar's Future

In the tradition of the early nation builders, Dr Adiseshiah combined a deep commitment to development in newly independent countries with a belief in the role of ideas and institutions in that process. I don't need to elaborate on Dr Adiseshiah's role in promoting ideas, innovations and institutions. The strand in his thinking which I want to pursue was his concern for not just national but global problems and his conviction that researching the real world and defining the area of control that we have open to us is the only basis for assessing what can and cannot be done to address pressing economic and social problems. It is in that spirit that I seek to examine an issue that is of global concern: the future of the world's reserve currency, the dollar.

Talk of the dollar's demise as the world's principal reserve currency does appear grossly exaggerated (Fisk, 2009). That prediction has been periodically heard at least since the early 1970s when the United States (US) brought the Bretton Woods arrangement to an end by breaking the link between dollar and gold. As is obvious, whatever else may be said of the role of the US in the world system, this expectation of the dollar's displacement as the currency that is as good as gold has not materialised. However, with the strength of the US economy once again in question, the dollar has begun to slide. Between the low of 1.2932 to the dollar it touched on 21 April 2009 and its value at the end of September 2009, the euro had appreciated by 13 per cent *vis-á-vis* the dollar.[2] This (and other similar tendencies)

---

1. I am grateful to Jayati Ghosh and Prabhat Patnaik for detailed comments on an earlier draft of this paper.

2. Figures from the European Central Bank available at *http://www.ecb.int/for transactionsstats/exchange/eurofxref/html/eurofxre f-graph-usd.en.html*. Accessed October 12, 2009.

has triggered predictions of the demise of the dollar as lead currency. Should and will a new currency replace the dollar as the paper that is treated as good as gold?

There is a noteworthy feature of the debate sparked by the revival of interest in the question of the dollar's worthiness as a reserve currency. Most participants in the debate who argue that it is time for the dollar to go, are not basing their argument on the greater strength of an alternative currency (like the euro, the yen or the Chinese RMB) which should take the dollar's place. Rather, the most popular alternative is the IMF's Special Drawing Right (SDR) which is more a unit of account than a currency and whose value is itself linked to that of a weighted basket of four major currencies. There are three implications here. First, even when the weakness of the US and the dollar is accepted, the case is not that the dollar should be completely displaced, since even in the basket that constitutes the SDR the dollar commands an influential role. Second, there is no other country or currency that is at present seen as being capable of taking the place of the US and its dollar, at least in the near future. And third, the search is not for a currency that can be used with confidence as a medium for international exchange, but for a derivative asset that investors can hold without fear of a substantial fall in its value when exchange rates fluctuate, because its value is defined in terms of and is stable relative to a basket of currencies.

The need for a reserve currency in an economically integrated world is well known, but the issue bears considering once again. Put simply, the international transactions undertaken by agents of different kinds in every country in any time period are not fully balanced in the sense that the expenditures of residents undertaken abroad are equal to that which foreigners undertake within the country concerned. Unlike in the case of domestic transactions, the difference in deficit countries cannot be settled by the legal tender of the country concerned (unless, of course, it happens to be the reserve currency). In the days of the metallic standard, when the value of a currency was determined by the value of the metal that constituted it, the difference could be financed through the flow of precious metals across borders, assuming agreement on the international price of the metal concerned. But even in times when countries operated with metallic currencies, rarely was the deemed value of coinage equal to the value of the metal that constituted it, which too in any case was variable. Acceptance of the value of coinage was predicated therefore on the belief, grounded on the backing provided by the state, that holding a certain value of coinage ensures command of an equivalent value of goods or resources.

The acceptance of deemed value grounded on backing by the state essentially meant that when it came to international transactions the global community was unwilling to accept the currency of just any country as legal tender, being unsure whether the value it claimed to represent in global transactions would actually materialise into an equivalent command over goods and resources. A combination of the competitive strength of the economy in which the currency originates, confidence in the strength of the state to ensure that the value of the currency it backs would be stable relative to goods and resources in general, and (as a consequence) the willingness of others to accept that currency in payment is what is required to ensure that a particular currency is acceptable as a reserve currency. However history suggests that in practice, it is confidence in the state rather than the competitive strength of the economy it governs that is crucial for generalised acceptance of a currency as reserve.

It must be noted that even when the world moved to an environment where the reserve currency was one which was in the nature of fiat money, such as the pound sterling or the dollar, the global strength of the currency derived also from the fact that it was representative money, in the sense that there was a sovereign promise that the currency concerned would on demand be exchanged for gold by the state of the country from which the currency originated. Not surprisingly, despite the economic strength and political and military supremacy of the US at the end of the Second World War, the dollar's role as the undisputed reserve currency of the world was backed with the solemn promise that the US government would on demand convert dollars to gold at the rate of $35 for an ounce.

The Pound Sterling and the Dollar as Reserve

But there are two, among other, differences between the dollar and the pound sterling as reserve currencies that need to be noted. First, during the period when Britain rose to be the leading imperialist power in the world and the pound sterling emerged as the world's reserve currency, not only was England (the first site of the industrial revolution) a dominant economic power and a nation that ruled the seas because of its maritime and military prowess, but it was also a colonial power. Being a colonial power it had access to unrequited flows of surpluses from and the benefits of enforced and unequal bilateral trade with its colonies, allowing it not only to balance its trade through multilateral arrangements, but also find the surpluses to finance its investments overseas, especially in the regions of recent settlement. The strength of the sterling rested on Britain's political subordination of much of the world. In fact, starting from around the 1870s, Britain had begun to lose its international economic competitiveness and recording trade deficits, though for some time, the current account remained in surplus because of profit and interest inflows resulting from past capital exports. But having risen to dominance based on colonial possessions and having retained many of those possessions and won new spheres of influence, Britain and the pound sterling continued to dominate the world economy till the First World War and were not displaced fully even during the inter-War years.

As compared with this, during the inter-War years when the US was rising to dominance but was not unchallenged, especially by France and Germany, it had no colonies to speak of. Subsequently, the process of decolonisation proceeded apace, and the US could not politically subordinate much of the globe. Domination had to occur within a framework of independent nation states, though the substance of such independence varied considerably across countries. This deprived the US of one of the forces that anchored the role of the sterling as the reserve currency. In fact, the dollar's supremacy was only established with the Second World War, when it derived the benefits from the War while Europe was left devastated by it.

A second major difference between the pound sterling and the dollar as reserve currencies was the fact that after 1971, the value of the US dollar was not stable and linked to gold, but was delinked from gold and unstable. Yet, much of world trade continued to be denominated in dollars and much of the world's wealth holders and most governments chose to hold their surpluses and reserves in dollar-denominated assets.

The Economic Decline of the US

This persistence of faith in a currency not founded on the economic strength that came from colonial possessions nor backed by the confidence that the government of the country in which it originated would redeem it for gold at a stable value was in itself remarkable. But, what was even more noteworthy is that it occurred in a period when the US was losing its economic competitiveness.

Figure 8.1

US Balance on Goods and Services

(US $ billion)

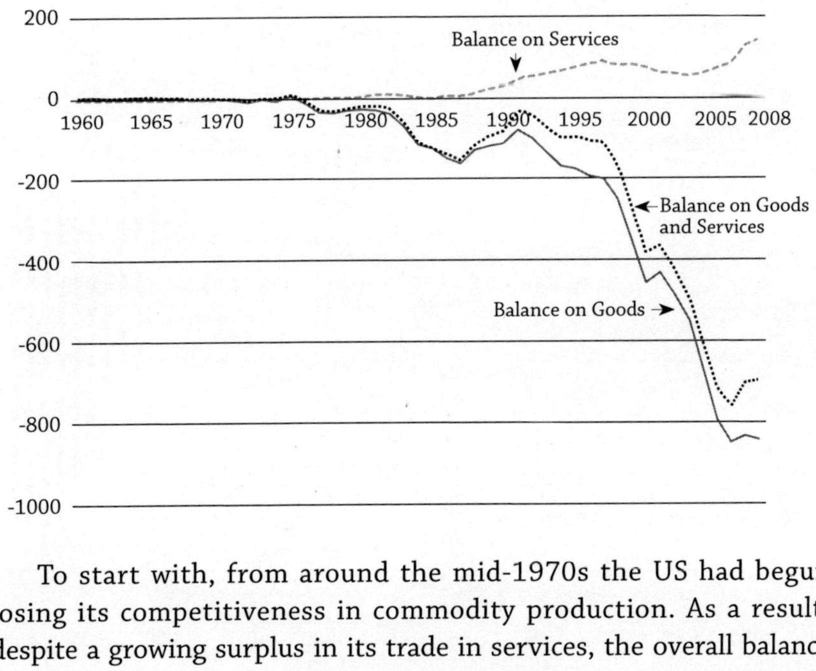

To start with, from around the mid-1970s the US had begun losing its competitiveness in commodity production. As a result, despite a growing surplus in its trade in services, the overall balance of trade in goods and services has been substantially negative during the last two decades (Figure 8.1). That is, the dollar has remained the world's reserve currency not because the US is the world's most competitive economy, but despite the growing loss of its competitiveness.

A concomitant of the loss of competitiveness has been the transformation of the US from being a net exporter to a country that was a net recipient of capital. The current account deficit of the US which had to be financed with capital inflows, was in balance or reflected small surpluses between 1960 and 1982. Subsequently, partly as a result of the second oil shock the deficit widened, only to fall again in the period after 1987 and turn into a surplus in 1991. Since 1991, however, that deficit has continued to widen and touched 6 per cent of GDP in 2006 as compared with 0.17 per cent in 1982. However as a result of the slowdown in growth and the depreciation of the dollar, it stood at a smaller but still large 4.89 per cent of GDP in 2008.

Figure 8.2

Balance on Current Account

(US $ billion)

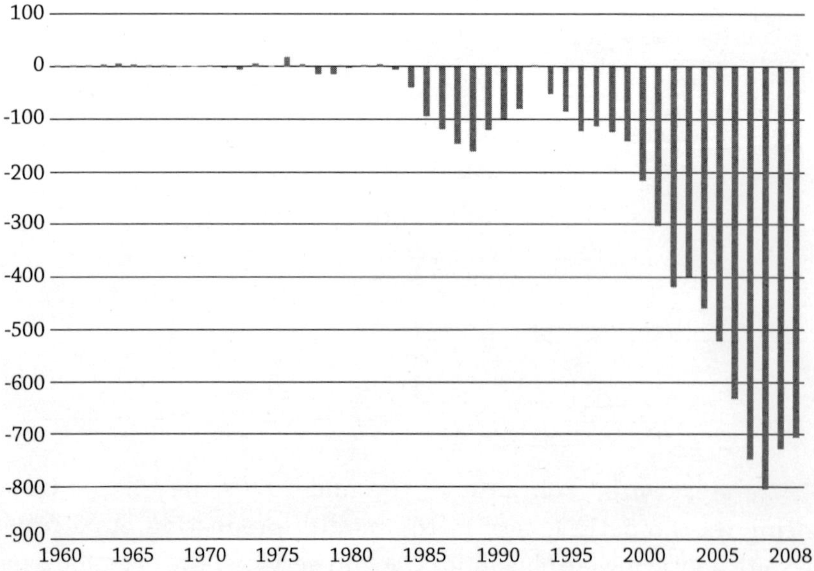

The transition from balance to a large deficit on the US current account has important implications for the state of dollar liquidity in the global economy. Whether the reserve currency is backed by gold or not, there must be enough of it to finance the requirements of countries that need to import more than they earn from exports and there must be ways to reach the surplus dollars to countries that need it. In practice this was not a problem, because the supply of liquidity was more than the offtake by countries which could access that liquidity, which excluded those that were considered too risky by private capital or were not favoured by bilateral and multilateral donors. Netting this out, during the years when the competitive strength of the US ensured that its current account was in balance, global demand for the reserve currency was met because of the expenditures abroad by the US in the form of grants and loans (to developing countries and to Europe under the Marshall Plan), investments by US firms and US military expenditures abroad or expenditures incurred on policing global capitalism. All of these expenditures reflected the costs of building and maintaining the US empire, or as Sweezy and Magdoff (1972) put it, of financing "the United States role as organizer and leader of the imperialist system". However, because of these expenditures, the US delivered on the requirements that Kindleberger (1996) had argued a global leader had to meet: that of discounting in crisis, offering countercyclical financing and providing a market for other countries' exports so that they could meet the commitments associated with the capital inflows they relied on.

The difficulty of course was that even though the US was running a current account that was in balance, the overall balance of payments of the US was continuously in deficit, even when US technological leadership and investments abroad yielded revenues in various forms (dividends, royalties, technical fees, etc.). Needless to say, within the framework of the gold exchange standard, the US could indulge in this luxury only so long as other nations were willing to hold dollars or dollar-denominated securities as reserve assets without wanting to convert them to gold. Normally that willingness would exist so long as the value of the dollar *vis-á-vis* gold was stable and returns on dollar-denominated assets were attractive. This creates the oft-quoted Triffin (1968) dilemma. On the one hand, the US whose national currency is also the globally accepted reserve currency, needs to ensure there is an adequate amount of dollar liquidity to meet the current account transactions and investment demands of the rest of the world. On the other hand, it cannot allow the dollar 'overhang' to reach levels where fearful of a decline in the value of the currency investors and governments chose to trade in dollars for gold. So, if the dollar overhang becomes large, the US would have to either reduce its current account deficit (increase its current account surplus) and/or raise interest rates to attract dollar inflows, both of which could be deflationary for itself and for the rest of the world that relies on its markets.

There is, however, one difficulty in framing the problem in this manner. The excess of dollars in the world system in the run up to the breakdown of the Bretton Woods arrangement in 1971 was not because the US kept its mint active in order to supply adequate amounts of dollars needed to lubricate necessary global economic transactions. Rather, this was the result of the US (government) (mis)using the benefit of being the home of the reserve currency. Facing no immediate national budget constraint, it exploited the 'mint in its backyard' that the dollar standard gave it to finance the costs of empire.

The policing costs incurred by the US during the years of the Cold War benefited not just the US, but also the other developed industrial countries. Having come out successfully from the devastation of the Second World War, these countries had begun accumulating balance of payments surpluses/reserves that were invested in dollar assets. The dilemma relating to the reserve currency applied not so much to the US but to these countries, which benefited economically and strategically from US military and military-related expenditures. If those expenses were to continue, the burden of managing what undoubtedly was and is a world divided in ways that created multiple threats to security was off their shoulders. But if this task was left solely to the US, then while its military supremacy would remain unchallenged and the costs of policing capitalism would be taken care of, the dollar overhang would assume proportions that challenged the relative value of the US dollar defined by its link to gold. This implied, in turn, that the probability of an erosion of the real value of official reserves and private wealth would increase inexorably.

Figure 8.3

Price-Adjusted Major Currencies Dollar Index

This dilemma initially resulted in the fact that inter-imperialist rivalry that could spill over in forms that challenged the dollar's supremacy was subdued. Structurally the system was geared to generate a form of super-imperialism with limited rivalry and substantial collaboration between the imperialist powers, however tenuous that arrangement may be. On the other hand, the subdued nature of imperialist rivalry (combined with US' role as the locomotive for global growth) allowed the US to garner the seignorage benefits associated with the dollar. But with the overseas expansion of the US, especially its engagement in Vietnam, stretching the flexibility that a reserve currency gave the US, the desire on the part of governments and wealth holders to diversify their portfolios and hold, in particular, more gold and less dollars increased. This threatened a run on the US' gold reserves, leading finally to the break in the link between the dollar and gold in August 1971. Once that happened, a shift to a world of floating exchange rates was inevitable, and followed soon thereafter in 1973.

Beyond Bretton Woods

This unleashed the period which is the most paradoxical from the point of view of international monetary affairs. Over three and a half decades since then, the dollar has continued to remain the world's reserve currency. And despite significant fluctuations, it could hardly be said that the dollar was in terminal decline. Periods of a sharp fall in the value of the dollar were followed by remarkable recoveries, keeping the dollar's value around a respectable range *vis-á-vis* the other major currencies (Figure 8.3). This relative strength of the dollar occurred in a period when it was without the benefit of a colonial empire, without a declared even if not actually exercised convertibility to gold, and without the foundation of international competitiveness.

This, however, did not mean that the US gave up its imperial ambitions or its desire to police the world. US direct investments abroad have risen quite significantly since the mid-1980s (Figure 8.4), with US firms increasingly investing in low-cost locations around the world, using them as sourcing hubs for the US market and for markets in the rest of the world. US defence expenditures have also remained high through the 1970s and 1980s, and have shot up in recent years with the country's engagement in Iraq and Afghanistan (Figure 8.5).

Since this occurred at a time when the US current account was in deficit and that deficit was widening sharply over time, the relative stability of the US dollar and its persistence as the reserve currency was a reflection of the willingness and even desire of economic agents outside the US to invest in assets in the US. This has resulted in the peculiar situation where if we examine the net international investment position of the US since the mid-1970s, we find that while it has been characterised by a positive balance on the direct investment account, with that balance rising in recent years, there is a huge and rising net deficit in the portfolio investment account, with foreigners increasing their ownership of financial assets in the US at a much faster rate than the acquisition of assets abroad by US residents and the US government (Figure 8.6). Thus, what we have is a situation where in the period when the dollar was delinked from gold, global investors were not only holding on to the dollars accumulated abroad during the period of the gold exchange standard but acquiring more dollar-denominated financial assets to sustain America's profligate spending abroad, which had now spread from the capital to the current account as well.

Figure 8.4

US Direct Investment Abroad

($ billion)

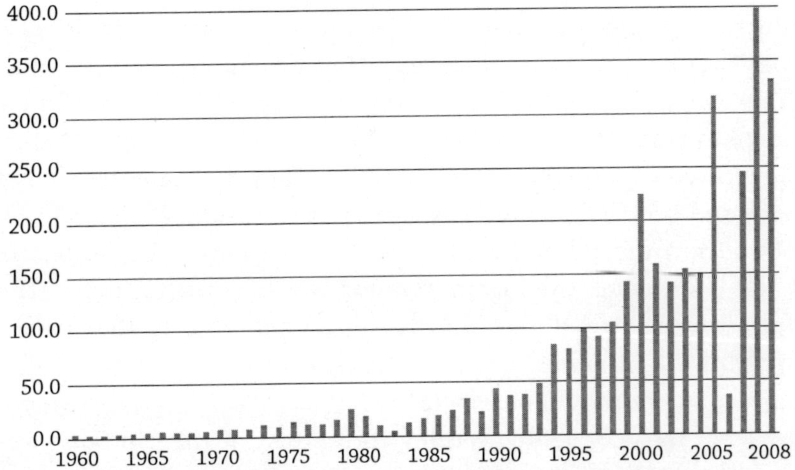

Note: The drop in 2005 reflects actions by US parent firms to reduce the amount of reinvested earnings going to their foreign affiliates for distribution to the US parent firms in order to take advantage of one-time tax provisions in the American Jobs Creation Act of 2004 (P.L. 108-357).

Source: US Department of Commerce, Bureau of Economic Analysis, *http://www.bea.gov/international/xls/table1.xls*

It needs to be noted that not all of this inflow of portfolio investment was on account of the investment of foreign exchange reserves accumulated by central banks. While the increase in foreign official assets in the US did contribute a tidy sum over the last six years, even during that period it was in most years well below a third of the total increase in foreign owned assets (Figure 8.7). This implies that two-thirds of the portfolio investment in the US came from 'non-official' or private sources. Clearly, private wealth holders were also desirous of holding their wealth predominantly in dollar-denominated assets (Ghosh, 2006).

Benefits of Being the Global Policeman

Thus both central banks and private wealth holders were not deterred by the decline of the US as a trading power when it came to choosing the currency of their preferred financial assets. US military and political hegemony rather than economic supremacy seems to have guided their decisions.

US military expenditures do not just sustain the military-industrial complex in the US. They did and continue to allow the other countries to focus their attention on productive investments rather than on 'unproductive' military expenditures, facilitating efforts to restructure production, increase productivity and ensure competitive superiority *vis-á-vis* the US. They generate demands for goods and services provided by countries that compete with the US, both within the US and abroad, and are an important component of the US' role as the locomotive for world growth. Finally, these expenditures ensured that fears of a 'dollar shortage' or an inadequate supply of the reserve currency to sustain the rising volume of global transactions proved to be wrong.

Given these benefits accruing to the rest of the capitalist world from the willingness of the US to bear the costs of managing (however poorly) global capitalism, none of them is willing to challenge US military supremacy and share the burdens of policing capitalism. As Kindleberger (1990) observed:

> As the United States becomes weaker economically and in its resolve to provide the public goods of peace-keeping and economic stability that the world requires, there is no other country in the wings, ambitious to take over the power, prestige and responsibilities of world leadership or hegemony. The dollar survives as a vehicle currency because the authorities of no strong currency are prepared

> to play the role. Japan lends to the United States because it is unwilling to reduce its saving habits, on the one hand, or to lend directly to other debtors, on the other. Germany and Japan have been loyal followers during the period of confident US leadership. Recoiling from the aggressive efforts of the 1930s, they hold back from challenging US proposals. Neither has been ready to take a prominent role in stabilizing political conditions in the Middle East, though both have high stakes in the continued availability of oil from the region. The world seems to be embarking on a transition of power and prestige from the United States to some other country, but it is far from clear which that other country might be.

Finally, it is generally accepted that while a steep decline of the dollar would have adverse consequences for the US, through its impact on interest rates in the US, for example, it would also have deflationary consequences for the rest of the world (Mohi-uddin, 2009).

This had its implication for the attitude of the other developed nations to the value of the dollar. In fact, there have been three occasions in the last three decades when the G7 countries have collaborated with the US to stabilise the dollar. The most important was the Plaza Accord of 1985 when the US managed to persuade the other G7 countries to intervene in currency markets to reverse the appreciation of the dollar *vis-à-vis* the Japanese yen and the Deutsche Mark, so as to strengthen US competitiveness, reduce its current account deficit and help it deal with recessionary conditions. The adverse effect of the resulting appreciation of the yen on Japan's industrial competitiveness paved the way for policies which generated the prolonged crisis of the 1990s in that country.

Then, in 1987, when the depreciation of the dollar was continuing the US got an agreement at Louvre to stall the dollar's depreciation. This was less successful than its predecessor agreement. Finally in 1995, the G7 effort to shore up the dollar led to a sustained rise in the value of that currency.

This ability of the US to work on its partners to achieve compliance with US goals has implications for the degree of confidence in the dollar relative to other currencies. To start with, since there is no single country or adequately unified grouping (which the European Union is not) that is the dominant economic power in the world and there is no challenger to the US as a global military power, military supremacy takes precedence over economic supremacy in determining the global hegemon. Of course, it matters that there was no clear alternative economic leader in the world system. Relocative capital was shifting globally competitive capacities not to other developed countries, but to developing countries or 'emerging market' locations. Capital from all of the developed industrial nations was exploiting this opportunity or being forced to do so. This meant that while industrial leadership was still substantially with the developed countries and some like Germany, for example, were still extremely competitive in certain areas; at the margin export competitiveness was increasingly a developing country characteristic even in manufacturing. This has effectively stalled the emergence of an alternative economic superpower.

Moreover, military supremacy creates the illusion that the hegemon has the ability to keep inflation under control by ensuring adequate supplies of crucial resources at reasonable prices. Besides everything else, inflation in the country which is home to the reserve currency and in whose currency most financial assets are denominated results in the erosion of the real value of financial wealth. Holding down the prices of commodities that can have cascading effects on the price level in that country is therefore necessary in order to sustain confidence in the currency. A typical example here is oil, which is a commodity which still constitutes an important element of costs and consumption in the energy-intensive capitalist economies of today. If inflation is to be avoided it becomes necessary, therefore, that either the price of oil is relatively stable or wage costs are adjusted downwards to neutralise the impact on costs and prices that any sharp increase in oil prices must have. This has led to the important argument (Patnaik, 2008; 2009; Bhattacharya, 2009) that the world is still essentially a commodity money world operating on what is termed an 'oil-dollar standard'.

One way in which wage workers can be forced to bear the burden of an oil price increase to ensure the stability of the dollar is through the adoption of deflationary policies in the developed countries that increase unemployment and adjust downwards relative wage costs. Since this can be politically destabilising and could break the consensus that legitimises capitalism, stable oil prices or at least medium-term expectations of stability in oil prices is crucial to the strength of the reserve currency. As Patnaik (2009) puts it, "The (Oil-Dollar) Standard can survive movements in oil prices provided there are no inflationary expectations with regard to oil prices and provided that jumps in oil prices, if at all they occur, do not lead to significant cost-push inflation."

Such expectations are, in turn, sustained with evidence that the country with the reserve currency (in which oil transactions are also denominated), has the diplomatic and military clout to ensure that oil prices do not remain at high levels even if they rise for a while. The US has made no bones of revealing what its strategy in West Asia is all about, even if that strategy backfired recently in Iraq. What this means is that so long as the price of oil is an important influence on global inflation, the currency of a country seen as capable of keeping oil prices and inflation down has a greater chance of being chosen as the reserve currency. With the task of policing capitalism having been handed over to the US by the rest of the developed capitalist world, they have reduced the likelihood that the world's wealth holders would see the currencies of these nations as being as good as or better than the dollar.

The Importance of Financial Supremacy

Finally there is an element of path dependence that ensures the persistence of the dollar as the reserve currency in a fiat money world. This operates via the role of the country with the reserve currency in the international financial system. Financial investors looking for safe assets that are adequately liquid migrate to financial assets denominated in the reserve currency. This makes financial markets, institutions and instruments located in that country the principal players in the global financial system.

One consequence is that much of the world's surpluses tend to migrate to financial institutions located in the US and a few decision-makers in these institutions would influence the choice of instruments in which those resources are invested. The link between these decision-makers and the US administration is also known to be extremely close, endowing them with even more legitimacy. As this financial system expands, a disproportionate share of the world's financial resources is invested in that market. Small adjustments in interest rates would be adequate to encourage a 'flight to safety' into dollar-denominated assets. And the world's wealth holders are as opposed to any collapse in the value of the dollar as the US government or its citizens may be. This tendency only reinforces the strength of the dollar, making it difficult for any other currency to displace it from its position as the global reserve.

Global Imbalances

The fact that industrial competitiveness was at the margin accumulating with the developing countries while financial activity was concentrating in the developed countries, particularly the US, served the latter well in another sense. An important feature of the global monetary regime of the last three decades is that global imbalances have not undermined the dollar's hegemony. This is reflected in the fact that the US deficit was being substantially financed by developing countries and not largely by the surpluses of other developed countries or the surpluses in the oil exporting countries. Consider 2007, for example. While Japan and Germany are two large surplus earners, the surpluses of these two countries accounted only for 30 per cent of the aggregate surplus of all surplus earners. Even among these two, Germany's surplus of over $263 billion is implicitly being absorbed by deficits in other countries of the Euro area, since the deficit of the Euro area as a whole is estimated at $137.5 billion in 2007.

The corollary is that developing countries and countries in transition have become important sources of surpluses to finance the US deficit. If we take the top ten developing and transition economies in terms of the size of their surpluses, their aggregate surplus accounts for 95 per cent of the US deficit. If we leave out oil exporters and take the top 10 among the remaining developing countries, their surpluses account for 72 per cent of the US deficit. China's surplus alone accounts for 51.1 per cent of the US deficit.

Taking developing countries as a group, we find that the period since the mid-1990s has seen a transformation of their current account deficits into surpluses (Figure 8.6). While this was true initially for a set of countries in Asia, they have since been joined by countries in West Asia, Africa and Latin America, though not Central and Eastern Europe. However, developing and emerging market countries outside Developing Asia have also been recording a surplus as a group, because of the contribution made by oil exporters in the Middle East.

Figure 8.5

Relative Balances on the Current Accounts

($ billion)

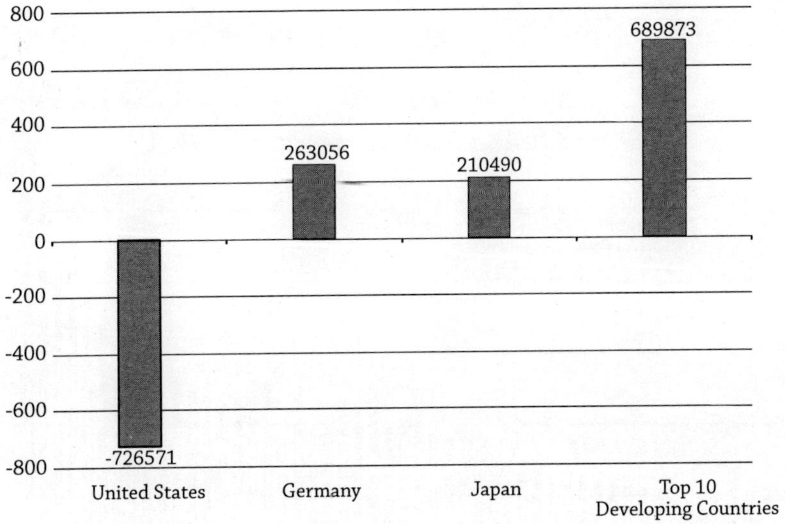

Figure 8.6

Current Account Balances

($ billion)

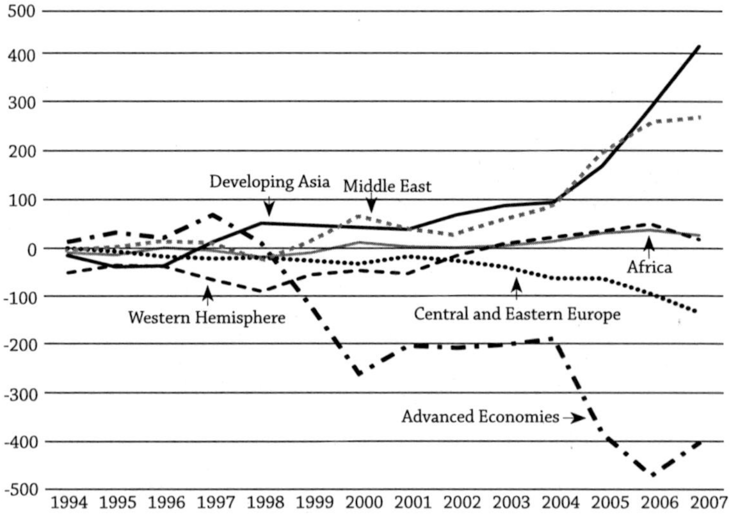

Figure 8.7

Selected Defence Related Expenditures of the US

($ billion)

Note: Figure for 1991 includes a special item titled "Cash contributions received from coalition partners for Persian Gulf operations" that amounted to an inflow for the US of $42.54 billion.

Source: US Department of Commerce, Bureau of Economic Analysis, *http://www.bea.gov/international/xls/table1.xls*

In fact, these developing countries have been even more important from the point of view of financing recent increases in the US deficit. The $602 billion increase in the US current account deficit between 1996 and 2007 was not matched by surpluses in the other industrial countries as a whole, although some individual industrial countries did record increased surpluses. The collective current account of the industrial countries worsened from a surplus of $28 billion in 1996 to a deficit of $366.4 billion in 2008, implying that the increase in the US current account deficit was not offset by surpluses in other industrial countries. The bulk of the increase in the US current account deficit was balanced by changes in the current account positions of developing countries, which moved from a collective deficit of $109 billion to a surplus of $492 billion—a net change of $601 billion—between 1996 and 2007.

There are two sources of accretion of surpluses in the balance of payments of the developing countries, epitomised by China and India. In China's case, these surpluses have been substantially 'earned' in the sense that they reflect its export success and a surplus on the current account of its balance of payments. This has been added to with inflows of foreign direct investment, and more recently foreign portfolio investment. In the case of India on the other hand, its surpluses have been 'borrowed', in the sense that they accrue because small deficits or small surpluses on the current global reserves account of its balance of payments in recent years have been accompanied by huge inflows of capital, especially portfolio capital. If capital inflows are largely borrowed and are of the portfolio kind, the pressure to accumulate reserves is greater, because of the danger that these flows could be reversed, as happened in Southeast Asia in late 1990s.

Figure 8.8

Components of Net International Investment Position of the US

($ billion)

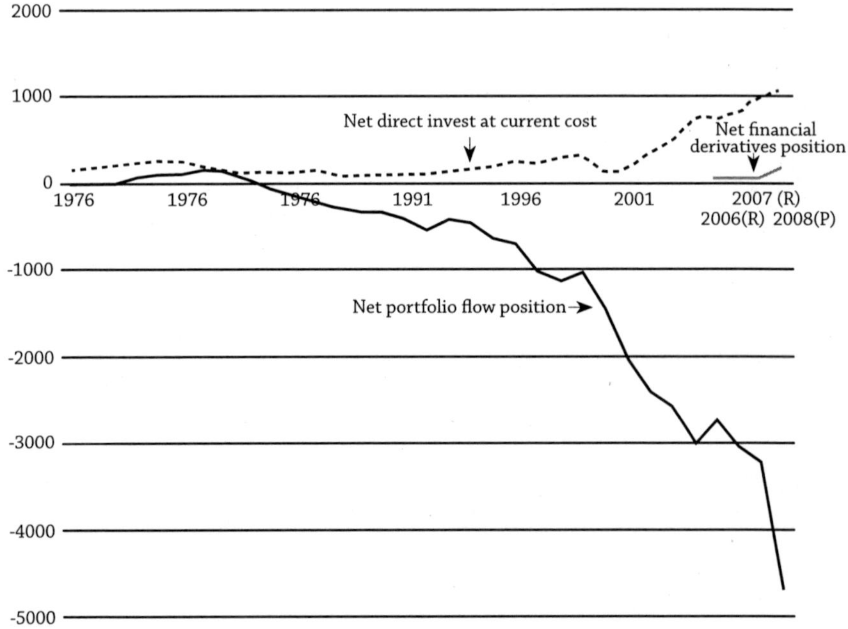

Thus there are two different reasons why developing countries hold reserves. One is because of an accumulation of a 'stock' of dollars in their hands, however temporarily, resulting from movements of financial capital searching for returns. The other is because of a 'flow' of dollars from one country to another to settle the deficit on the current account incurred by former in transactions with the latter. The point to note is that, even in a world where there are no deficits and surpluses, i.e. where the flow argument for holding dollars does not hold, the stock argument still will. This is an argument missed by those who attribute surpluses largely to trade surpluses resulting from 'undervalued' exchange rates.

There is another reason why a significant, even if not dominant part of the recycling of these surpluses to the US occurred through the central banks of these countries. Under liberalised exchange rate regimes, large dollar inflows (whether due to surpluses on the current or capital account) exert an upward pressure on the domestic currency of the countries that receive those foreign exchange inflows, raising the value of the domestic currency against the reserve currency. To prevent such appreciation and shore up the competitiveness of the recipient country's exports, the central bank steps in to stabilise the currency to buy and mop up the excess foreign exchange. This results in the accumulation of large reserves which is then invested in safe and liquid financial assets in the US. Data from the US Federal Reserve relating to US Government agency bonds held by foreign official institutions shows that they increased by $119 billion in 2007, although in the wake of the crisis in 2008 they fell by $31 billion. In the first seven months of 2009, they fell by another $31 billion (*http://www.federalreserve.gov/econresdata/releases/secholdtrans/current.htm*).

Figure 8.9

Foreign-Owned Assets in the US, Total and Official

($ billion)

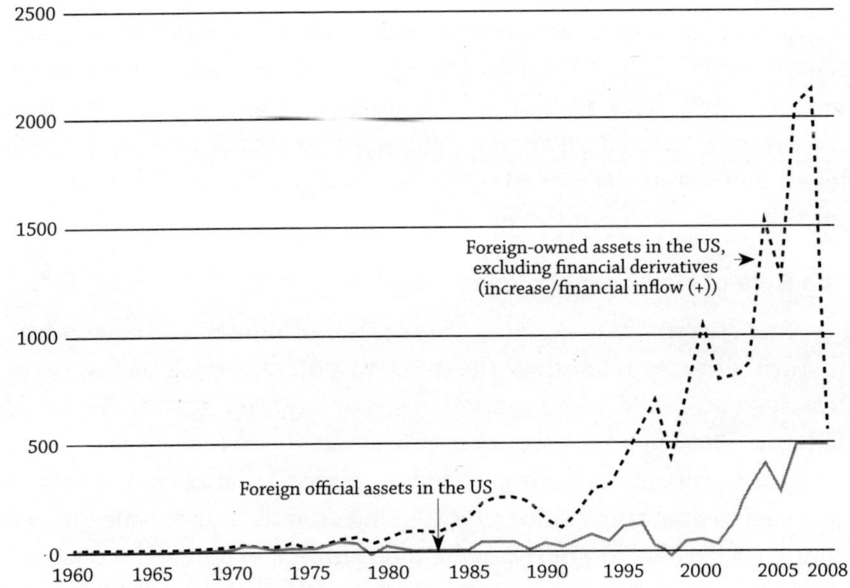

Interestingly, not only was the contribution of non-oil exporting Asian countries significant, it actually continued to be positive even in 2008. Thus Asian holding of US public bonds increased by $131.6 billion in 2007 and $32.4 billion in 2008, while the corresponding figures for China and Hong Kong taken together were $103.7 billion and $40.3 billion. Even in the first 7 months of 2009, total Asian holding of US government bonds remained largely stable, with a small increase of $2.3 billion by Middle Eastern oil exporters and a small decline of $2.5 billion for all other Asian countries.

What is important to note here is that while it is the profligacy of the US that is resulting in the huge deficit on its balance of payments, the deficit country is not the one making the adjustment to correct for global imbalance. This is quite contrary to the experience of developing countries incurring a deficit, who find that they are forced to undertake painful adjustment measures to reduce their own deficit. Instead, in a remarkable reversal, the countries accumulating surpluses, whether earned or borrowed, are the ones making the adjustment. They continue to invest their surpluses in safe and liquid international securities among which US Treasury securities predominate. And that adjustment is not without cost. Large reserves create huge problems for monetary management, and central bank efforts to sterilise foreign exchange reserves to manage money supply have adverse implications for fiscal policy. Moreover, the returns received on reserves invested by central banks are much less than the returns earned by those who bring the foreign exchange into these countries in the first place.

The Role of Neoliberal Policies

This current and evolving international monetary conjuncture is quite directly related to the shift in policy regime in favour of less regulated and more market-friendly regimes across the world (Ghosh, 2006). One consequence of the neoliberal policies associated with that shift is, for example, the increased reliance on exports as opposed to domestic markets for fuelling growth. This has meant that countries that successfully pursue mercantilist, export-led strategies, as China has done, record current account surpluses. This in turn threatens an appreciation of their currencies that could reduce export competitiveness, and encourages them to accumulate foreign exchange reserves to shore up their currencies, necessitating the investment of these surpluses in safe assets. Much of this investment moves to the home of the reserve currency.

Besides, neoliberal fiscal reform imposes fiscal conservatism and deflationary fiscal practices, that have balance of payments effects that imply either a reduction of current account deficits or the emergence or increase of current account surpluses.

Neoliberal policies also contribute to the accumulation of surpluses through the liberalisation of rules governing capital inflows in the form of foreign direct and portfolio investment, besides foreign borrowing. Liberalised foreign direct investment rules help attract relocative foreign capital seeking low cost locations for world-market production, that links direct investment flows with exports, as happened in the past in the second-tier newly industrialising countries in Southeast Asia and more recently in China. Liberalisation of rules relating to foreign portfolio investment and debt flows result in large inflows on the capital account as has happened in India in recent years. In both cases, the effect is to force the central bank to mop up some of the foreign exchange that flows in, so as to prevent the domestic currency from appreciating. Large foreign exchange reserves are a corollary.

Finally, neoliberal policies also involve the liberalisation of rules governing the outflow of capital in the form of investments by residents abroad. The pressure to liberalise these rules is the greater the larger are reserves with the central bank. Once the degree of 'capital account convertibility' is increased, capital tends to flow through private as opposed to official channels from developing countries to the developed in general and the reserve currency country in particular. This contributes to the flow of capital from poor to the rich. It also increases the pressure to accumulate reserves to guard against the reversal of capital flows that could follow any surge in inflows.

These consequences of liberalisation contribute in no small measure to the global imbalance that is otherwise rooted in the uneven development characteristic of capitalism. In sum, today's imbalance is directly linked to the shift to a neoliberal regime. It also strengthens the position of the reserve currency in two ways. First, it creates a constituency of those who are uncomfortable with a depreciation of the dollar, because this would undermine the competitiveness of exporters supplying the US from countries whose currencies are appreciating *vis-á-vis* the dollar, as well as reduce the value of dollar denominated financial assets in which governments and wealth holders from the rest of the world have invested. Second, a depreciating dollar has deflationary consequences in the US in order to reduce the deficit in the US' balance of payments, and this (combined with its continuing domestic recession) reduces its ability to serve as the engine for growth in the rest of the world economy. Thus, the conjuncture created by a combination of uneven development and neoliberalism is partly responsible for the persistence of the dollar as the world's reserve currency.

Put together these features associated with the dollar's position in the current international monetary conjuncture, it becomes clear that in the absence of another country/region and currency that can play a similar role in the world economy, rhetoric alone will not end dollar hegemony. The question, therefore, is whether there is such a currency.

The Fate of the Euro

The first expectations of the displacement of the dollar came with the birth of the euro in 1 January 1999 and the irrevocable fixing of the exchange rates between the then member countries of the European Union (EU). The idea that the euro was an alternative to the dollar came from the evidence that after a brief period of stability and then depreciation of the euro relative to the dollar, from the end of 2000 that currency appreciated from close to $0.8 to the euro to $1.6 to the euro in April 2008. And then, after a further period of depreciation to around $1.25 to the euro in November 2008, the euro has been appreciating once again to reach $1.5 in September 2009.

There are two ways in which to view this relative decline in the dollar's value. The first is to see it as a gradual depreciation of the dollar as part of an effort to correct for the loss of export competitiveness of the US. The second is to see it as a challenge posed to the dollar's supremacy by the new currency.

The supporting evidence to back the second of these propositions is difficult to come by. Consider for example the euro's role in international transactions. By September 2006, 30 per cent of outstanding international securities were denominated in euros as compared with around 20 per cent in 1999. But this was not because of any significant decline of the dollar's role in this area, with its share having fallen from just around one half to 46 per cent. In foreign exchange markets, the euro's share had remained stable at around 20 per cent of all transactions, compared with the dollar's 44 per cent. And, finally, the euro accounted for a stable 25 per cent of the holding of foreign exchange reserves by countries that report the composition of their foreign exchange reserves. All in all, therefore, it appears that the euro has not displaced the dollar as the major reserve currency.

This is not surprising given the fact that the euro is not the currency of a single national political formation with the backing of a single powerful state. Though monetary policy in these countries is harmonised through the European Central Bank, which sets interest rates for all, there is considerable fiscal policy independence (despite the Growth and Stability Pact) of countries characterised by very different levels of development. This does not inspire confidence in the ability of the EU as a formation to be able to influence as desired the value of the euro. And no single state in this formation has the military strength or activism to assert power and stabilise the value of the currency when required.

Put simply, while there are some European nations like Germany that are economically strong, though less so than before unification, if we look at the conditions which helped sustain the dollar's role as the reserve currency, this united formation of still legally independent sovereign states falls short of what seem to be the prerequisites for the euro to displace the dollar as reserve currency.

The Debate over the SDR as Reserve

Besides the euro, the other contender to taking on the role of the world's reserve currency is the SDR (Special Drawing Right) created by the International Monetary Fund (IMF). The debate over the SDR as an alternative currency gathered momentum when in the aftermath of the 2008 global crisis the governor of the People's Bank of China, Zhou Xiaochuan issued a call for replacing the dollar with the SDR as reserve currency. There are, however, many hurdles between this stated desire and the actual transformation of the SDR into the world's reserve.

Created in 1969, the SDR was initially seen as a supplemental reserve which could help meet shortages of the two then prevailing reserve assets: gold and the dollar. The IMF issues credits of SDRs to its member nations, which can be exchanged for freely usable currencies when required. The value of the SDR was initially set to be equivalent to an amount in weight of gold (0.888671 grams) that was then also equivalent to one US dollar. After the collapse of the Bretton Woods system in 1973, however, the value of the SDR was reset relative to a weighted basket of currencies, which today consist of the euro, Japanese yen, pound sterling, and US dollar, and quoted in dollars calculated at the existing exchange rates. The liquidity of the SDR is ensured through voluntary trading arrangements under which members and one prescribed holder have volunteered to buy or sell SDRs within limits. Further, when required the Fund can activate its designation mechanism, under which "members with sufficiently strong external positions are designated by the Fund to buy SDRs with freely usable currencies up to certain amounts from members with weak external positions. This arrangement serves as a backstop to guarantee the liquidity and the reserve asset character of the SDR." So long as a country's holdings of SDRs equal its allocation, they are a costless and barren asset. However, whenever a member's SDR holdings exceed its allocation, it earns interest on the excess. On the other hand, if a country holds fewer SDRs than allocated to it, it pays interest on the shortfall. The SDR interest rate is also based on a weighted average of specified interest rates in the money markets of the SDR basket currencies.

The volume of SDRs available in the system is the result of mutually agreed allocations (determined by the need for supplementary reserves) to members in proportion to their quotas. Till recently, the volume of SDRs available was small. SDRs have been allocated on four occasions. The first, to the tune of SDR 9.3 billion, was undertaken in annual installments during 1970-1972, immediately after the creation of this asset in 1969. The second, for SDR 12.1 billion, occurred during 1979-1981. The third, for an amount of SDR 161.2 billion, was on 28 August 2009. And the fourth for SDR 21.4 billion took place on 9 September 2009. As a result, the total volume of SDRs in circulation has reached SDR 204.1 billion or about $317 billion. It must be noted that these allocations are far short of demands from developing countries both in terms of quantum and distribution across countries. As can be noted, an overwhelming proportion of the allocation has occurred in the aftermath of the 2008 financial crisis.

Does the recent large increase in the amount of SDR's allocated herald its emergence as an alternative to the dollar? There are two roles that the SDR can play, which favour its acceptance as a reserve. First, it can help reduce the exposure of countries to the dollar, the value of which has been declining in recent months because of the huge current account deficit of the US, its legacy of indebtedness and the large volume of dollars it is pumping into the system to finance its post-crisis stimulus package. Second, since its value is determined by a weighted basket of four major currencies, the command over goods and resources that its holder would have would be stable and even advantageous.

There are, however, five immediate and obvious obstacles to the SDR serving as the sole or even principal reserve. First, the $317 billion worth of SDRs currently available are distributed across countries and is a small proportion of the global reserve holdings estimated at $6.7 trillion at the end of 2008 and of the reserve holding of even a single country like China. Since all countries would if possible like to hold a part of their reserves in SDRs, the fraction of this $317 billion that would be available for trade against actual currencies would be small, implying that even with recent increases in allocations the SDR can only be a supplementary reserve. Second, expansion of the volume of SDRs in circulation requires agreement among countries that hold at least 85 per cent of IMF quotas. With the US alone having a 16.77 per cent vote share, as of now it has a veto on any such decision (Table 8.1). Whether it will go along with the decision to deprive it of the benefits of being the home of the reserve currency is unclear. And even if it does, there could be others with a combined vote share of 15 per cent-plus who may not be willing to go along.

Table 8.1

IMF Vote Shares (%)

	Existing	*Proposed*
US	16.77	16.73
Japan	6.02	6.23
Britain	4.86	4.29
France	4.86	4.29
China	3.66	3.81
Russia	2.69	2.39
Belgium	2.09	1.86
India	1.89	2.32
South Korea	1.38	1.36
Brazil	1.38	1.72

Source: IMF

Third, since SDR issues are linked to quotas at the IMF and those quotas do not any more reflect the economic strength of members, the base distribution of SDRs is not in proportion to the distribution of reserve holdings across countries. Reaching SDRs to those who would like to hold them depends on the willingness of others to sell as noted earlier. Fourth, since the value of the SDR is linked to the value of four actual currencies, the reason why a country seeking to diversify its reserve should not hold those four currencies (in proportion to their weights in the SDR's value) rather than the SDR itself is unclear. This would also give countries flexibility in terms of the proportion in which they hold these four currencies (which is an advantage in a world of fluctuating exchange rates, since weights in the SDR are reviewed only with a considerable lag, currently of five years). Finally, as of now SDRs can only be exchanged in transactions between central banks and not in transactions between the government and the private sector and therefore in purely private sector transactions. This depletes its currency-like nature in the real world. It also reduces the likelihood that a significant number of economic transactions would be denominated in SDRs. While this could be corrected (Williamson, 2009), such a correction can throw up a host of additional problems. But this has not prevented suggestions from the likes of John Lipsky, the IMF's First Deputy Managing Director, that the SDR can be used as the foundation to build a new currency that would "be delinked from other currencies and issued by an international organisation with equivalent authority to a central bank in order to become liquid enough to be used as a reserve" (Nicholson, 2009).

The idea of a wholly new currency serving as a unit of account, a medium of exchange and a store of value at the international level does appear a bit far-fetched in a context of nation states with no single global government. The denomination of trade in that currency, the issue of financial assets denominated in that currency, the quantum of such currency issued, and the distribution of that quantum across nations have to be all decided jointly and with consensus. That does appear near impossible in a context of substantial differentials in the level and pace of development across nations. As Kindleberger (1990: 265-66) had commented with regard to the suggestion to substitute the US as world leader with trilateral leadership of the world economy involving, say, the US, Japan and Germany: "Joint ventures in business generally break up sooner or later unless there is a complete takeover, as the interests of the partners almost never converge completely, and any divergence may widen and lead to stalemate." To these basic difficulties associated with treating the SDR as a normal currency must be added the fact that, not being the national currency of any country, the confidence in its ability to serve as a viable reserve currency for the world (even if its value is expected to be stable) cannot be generated by either the economic or the military strength of a state that governs that nation. Put all of these together and while the SDR may be good as a supplementary reserve that aids diversification of the composition of reserves of individual countries, it as yet falls short of the requirements that a true reserve currency must meet. Some form of international currency union or institutionalisation of global economic coordination would be necessary for an independent global currency to serve as reserve. That does appear a distant goal, if achievable at all.

If despite this the SDR is the focus of attention in the search for an alternative to the dollar, that can only be because there is as yet no national currency that can displace the dollar. While the dollar lacks the legitimacy to serve as the world's reserve, it dominates because the time for its substitute is yet to come.

References

Bhattacharya, Jyotirmoy (2009). "Oil Shocks: How Destabilizing are They?", *Social Scientist*, July-August.

D'Arista, Jane (2009). "The Evolving International Monetary System", *Cambridge Journal of Economics* 33: 633-52.

Eichengreen, Barry (2009). "Commercialize the SDR". *http://www.project-syndicate.org/commentary/commercialize-the-sdr*

Fisk, Robert (2009). "The Demise of the Dollar", *The Independent*, October 6.

Ghosh, Jayati (2006). "Making Sense of the World Economy", *Development and Change* 37(6): 1417-23.

Kindleberger, Charles P. (1988). "The Financial Crises of the 1930s and 1980s: Similarities and Differences", *Kyklos* 41(2): 171-86.

———. (1990). *Historical Economics: Art or Science?* Berkeley: University of California Press. Available at *http://ark.cdlib.org/ark:/13030/ft287004zv*. Accessed on 1 October 2009.

———. (1996). *World Economic Primacy: 1500-1990*. New York: Oxford University Press.

Mohi-uddin, Mansoot (2009). "G7 Should Deal with the Dollar", *Financial Times*, London. Septmber 21.

Nicholson, Alexander (2009). "IMF Says New Reserve Currency to Replace Dollar is Possible". June. Available at *http://www.bloomberg.com /appsnews? pid = 20601087 & sid = aUYeJEwZaQrw#*. Accessed on 1 October 2009.

Patnaik, Prabhat (2008). *The Value of Money*. New Delhi: Tulika Books.

———. (2009). "Response to the Discussion on the Value of Money", *Social Scientist*, July-August.

Sweezy, Paul M. and Harry Magdoff (1972). *The Dynamics of US Capitalism: Corporate Structure Inflation Credit Gold and the Dollar*. New York: Monthly Review Press.

Triffin, Robert (1968). *Our International Monetary System: Yesterday Today and Tomorrow*. New York: Random House.

Williamson, John (2009). "Why SDRs could Rival the Dollar", *Policy Brief* Number PB09-20. Washington: Peterson Institute for International Economics. September.

9

PRATAP BHANU MEHTA

The Politics of Social Justice

Dr Malcolm Adeshshiah was an exemplary intellectual in so many ways: a first rate scholar, a superb institution builder, an intellectual with a global reach, but one firmly grounded in the realities of India. His vast erudition was combined with a great social sensitivity. His life-long mission to empower people through education and literacy was just one example of his acute sense of judgment about what is important. I would like to believe that the topic of the paper "The Politics of Social Justice" is one he would have had a great deal of interest in. This paper cannot do justice to the high standards he set, but I hope it will prompt some reflection on a big challenge of our time. India is going through enormous changes. There is, rightly, a great sense of optimism. For the first time in our history real social and economic change seems like a possibility, and the sheer unleashing of aspiration and energy across different sections of Indian society is staggering. But there are some concerns about the form the politics of justice will take, even in this newly buoyant and optimistic era. This is the theme of my paper. The paper is divided into two parts. The first reflects on the limited set of instruments we have that can do full justice to the aspiration of social equality. The second part reflects, somewhat more briefly, on why caste still remains such an entrenched category around which the politics of social justice is constructed, and what the consequences of this entrenchment might mean. The aim of this paper is, to borrow Judith Shklar's phrase, to be more tour of perplexities than a guide for the perplexed.

I

The present challenge of the politics of social justice must be seen against the backdrop of a general, perhaps more global and historical pessimism about the relationship between democracy and equality. Democracies, in principle, derive their legitimacy from a certain form of political radicalism, promising new beginnings, a constantly challenged and renewed social order, and an affirmation of equality. But in practice, democracies have turned out to be remarkably conservative institutions. Perhaps a little historical perspective is in order. In the 18th and 19th centuries, many perceptive observers of 'democracy' saw its conservative potential. Adam Smith had very presciently predicted that a republic, the United States (US), would be the last to abolish slavery, much after many monarchies had done so. Alexis de Tocqueville, the most insightful observer of democracy had commended it in part because democracies make revolutions rare. While democracies relentlessly abolish formal distinctions of social status, they are quite compatible with high levels of economic inequality. Contrary to those who feared democracy, Tocqueville argued that democracies promote stability in property relations. This is so for various reasons. But one reason was quite subtle. In countries where formally inequality has been abolished, and a myth of formal equality becomes part of the self-understanding of a society, it becomes, paradoxically, harder to critique real inequality.

There is a wider debate to be held about why democracies have turned out to be so compatible with high levels of inequality. And this is, in some senses, a truly global debate. In the US, political scientists are puzzled by the fact that the democratic system has allowed inequality to grow immeasurably over the last two decades, with most of the gains of growth going to the top 10 per cent of the population and a decline in real wages for much of the middle class. There are several reasons advanced for this—from the role ideological mystification plays in democratic politics to the susceptibility of democracies to special interests. But in very different contexts, from the debate over democracy in China to the health of democracy in the US, one question is being asked. Is the inability to mitigate inequality a contingent feature of democracy? Or are there deeper, far more structural reasons, why democracies are unable to mitigate inequality? On the contingent view, the inability of democracy to mitigate inequality can be explained by contingent features of the way in which democracy is organised. The structure of election finance, forms of party organisation, the susceptibility of media control, voter apathy, lack of information all contribute to making democracies less self-aware than they should be. Others, like Adam Pzeworski (2010) argue that there may be deeper structural reasons why addressing inequality is difficult. One major reason has to do with what I call 'small liberty effects'. In a society, which allows, some basic freedoms, even small differences can, over time accumulate and transform into great ones. The most powerful illustration of small liberty effects is illustrated in a classic paper by Mookherjee and Ray (2003). Their reasoning goes something like this. Suppose productive assets were equalised. But there were very very small differences in rates of return due to a variety of reasons. Some get a return on 0.02 per cent and others suffer a small loss of minus 0.02 per cent. After 50 years, such minute differences of return will translate into one group having almost eight times the wealth of others. And this is with minor differences (Mookherjee and Ray, 2003).

But there may be other reasons as well. Is it the case that the instruments of redistribution that democracies can use have severe limitations? And it might be worth considering briefly, the set of instruments democracies have used for this purpose and the politics around them in a country like India. The most obvious instrument is redistribution through taxation. But there is no serious politics structured around using this instrument for several reasons. First, of all countries like India have recent and vivid memories of the distorting effects of high taxes in the context of low enforcement capacity. There is a generalised scepticism about the efficacy of high direct taxes. How far this scepticism is justified can be debated in economic terms. But in the matter of taxes, there is an interesting ideological phenomenon also at work. The rich benefit from the fact that most people, at any level of society, do not like being taxed more; high taxes, even for the very rich are often seen as a slippery slope for legitimising high taxes for all. So while most democracies have some forms of progressive taxation, there are limits to how much they can tax. Second, in the context of globalisation and mobility of capital, there is scepticism about the efficacy of very high tax rates. Third, and this is a point I will return to later, taxes provide redistribution, through the instrumentality of the state. Often there is scepticism about a state's capacity to use taxes wisely. Indeed the case for lower taxes and an ideological delegitmisation of the 'public sector' as it were, go hand-in-hand. And certainly the historical performance of states gives grist to the mill of those who are sceptical that more resources must be poured into the state. But even when the state works the welfare effects of the state are likely to be higher than its equality effects. So broadly speaking, there appear to be political limits to taxation as an instrument of redistribution.

The second major instrument of redistribution was collectivising productive assets, particularly industrial capital. This instrument has simply turned out to be an unviable historical option. The third instrument of redistribution is the focus of one particular asset, land. Certainly after independence it was thought that land redistribution would be the major instrument of producing equality. But, and this is a global phenomenon, democracies have not been very successful at radical land reform. Most of the cases of successful land reform have been either through revolution or colonial powers destroying a landed aristocracy as the Japanese did in Korea. Land reform in democracies has been, at best ameliorative rather than radical. But at the present conjuncture, in the context of our uneven development, the politics of land is playing out very differently. At one level the issue of land is absolutely central to conflicts in our society. Many major fault lines in our society involve land, whether it is tribals desperately trying to secure use rights to their traditional lands, to farmers contesting land acquisition, to conflicts over shaping urban zoning. State regulation of land has also become central to the political economy of Indian democracy. There is a joke that after liberalisation the state controls only three things: land, liquor and learning. And these are three areas where the visible hand of rent seeking is tremendously powerful. Historically, of course land reform has been associated with better economic outcomes: states with relatively more egalitarian distribution of land produced a more egalitarian politics. But in a way this fact only highlights one of the paradoxes of land politics: you already need a certain degree of asset equality to shape politics in a more egalitarian direction. The politics of land itself has turned out to be greatly path dependent. Politics itself seems a rather weak instrument for producing asset equality. But while land remains an issue of great social contention, it is, with some exceptions, not the locus of an egalitarian politics for several reasons.

As Partha Chaterjee and many others have pointed out, in much of rural India, the quest is now to get off the land. The fragmentation of land holdings (combined with large scale shifts in life style aspirations) are making working on land less desirable. While regularising the rights of tenants and share croppers can have empowering effects, particularly in states like Bihar, the blunt truth is that access to small land holdings is not seen as considerably empowering. In rural India, the greatest fault lines are often between the interest of small farmers and landless labour; in some states the greatest complaint about NREGA raising wage rates has come from small and marginal farmers. In short, often the conflicts between 'adjacent' classes are more consequential and immediately severe than those between the top and the bottom, making politics less a matter of attacking privilege than holding onto small distinctions. Land politics in India is very complicated. But here I simply want to make one point. It is the axis of conflict. But it is no longer the main fulcrum of distributive politics. Parenthetically, one can make a stronger argument is that land assets are the means by which inequality is being reproduced and exacerbated rather than reduced.

Land acquisition has also become a mechanism for exacerbating inequality in India in three ways. First, property rights were weakened in India to facilitate land reform. Ironically, weakened property rights, which were meant to help the poor, ended up dispossessing them even more. Second, what farmers think of land acquisition depends, amongst other things, upon two factors: location and their existing assets. Again, ironically, farmers in an area with a real estate boom or high circle rates like Haryana are more likely to be willing to part with their land than farmers in poorer states. It is not an accident that land acquisition is harder in backward states like Orissa, West Bengal and parts of Uttar Pradesh (UP). The poor get a poorer deal in a poor state. High growth states like Gujarat have less of a challenge. As the recent conflict in UP has shown, large farmers also have a greater capacity to bargain, compared to small farmers, and are likely to get better deals. So dispossession is also unequal in its effects. Finally, there is one aspect to inequality in land discourse that is deeply insidious. There is some focus on monetary compensation and promise of jobs. But let us face two ugly truths. In most areas, we have not invested enough in the skills of dispossessed people for them to get meaningful jobs. Studies are showing that, particularly in backward areas, companies do not employ local labour: partly because of skills deficit, partly because of fear that local labour will unionise easily. But there is also an aspirational dimension. Even in Singur, it was startling to see the government promise jobs as janitors to those dispossessed. Contrast this with what the mayor of a Chinese city is supposed to have told those displaced. He admitted that the adults will have to sacrifice, but the promise was that the children of those displaced would have the same opportunities as those of the most privileged. And the state would ensure that. Whether or not this is entirely implemented is not the point. The point is whether any Indian politician looks at the children of the dispossessed in the eye and promises them something genuinely aspirational: a first rate, instead of a third rate school; a dream of a great job, instead of jobs low in the hierarchy. Land acquisition is often an occasion for reproducing social distance rather than closing the gap. It is important to be reminded of this backdrop because land conflicts are not just over compensation. The compensation issue has become a distillation of a complex set of issues: low trust in the state, resentment at inequalities that your encounter with the land lottery can only exacerbate, and a politics that rests on the conviction that power is arbitrary and access to it is simply a means of making money. But cumulatively land politics is exacerbating inequality.

The fourth instrument for producing some kind of distributive justice is the state itself. On this view the primary mechanism through which redistribution happens is not transfer or collectivisation of assets, but through the state provision of public goods, particularly health and education. At one level there is something powerful in this narrative. Welfare states have been the instrumentality through which the lives of the poor have been improved. But the welfare state has a very complicated relationship to the politics of equality along several dimensions. First and most obviously, the effectiveness of welfare states depends upon a number of factors, including state capacity. In India, that state capacity is very unevenly developed across time and space. State capacity is often a function of structural features like ability to generate revenue; but it is also a product of contingent political formations. But the unevenness and distrust of state capacity has meant, at the very least, that support for public provisioning is still very limited in India. One striking illustration of this is the fact that our discourse on universal entitlements is so under-ambitious. There is a powerful narrative that United Progressive Alliance (UPA) wanted to project universalising a set of basic entitlements from the right to education to employment. But you often get the feeling that these rights are so tepidly defined, and even more haphazardly implemented that they are fighting yesterday's battles, not tomorrow's challenges. The Right to Education for example has been enacted just at the moment where formal enrolment in a school is no longer a major challenge. What is a major challenge is ensuring quality education for all. Yet the focus of the legislation is largely on the infrastructural inputs. While many of the byelaws of this legislation have to be drafted, there is a real danger that this Act could hinder rather that support the pursuit of quality education. Similarly in Food Security, what is being proposed lags behind the practice of many states, including Tamil Nadu and Chhattisgarh. Tamil Nadu has universalised food security much more effectively than the Centre is proposing to do. So while welfare schemes are amelioratively helping people, their relationship to the politics of equality is much more tangential than should be the case.

There is another issue in the politics of welfare that needs some attention. Historically the Indian state has been relatively bad at targeting. To take just one example, under-inclusion and over-inclusion in BPL (below poverty line) lists is often as high as 50 per cent. Just the history of targeting failures in India suggest that there is an administrative case to be made for universalisation.

For policy purposes the BPL is a disingenuous construct. Normatively speaking, this line is an exercise in bad faith because it arbitrarily separates those who can avail benefits from those who cannot. The difference between those immediately above and below the poverty line is miniscule, almost irrelevant from a practical point of view. Yet that cut-off arbitrarily determines access to benefits. A BPL line, rather than being an expression of a commitment to equality, is a subtle exemplar of discrimination. The cut-off also bears no relationship to the particular objectives of public policy. It also does little justice to the fact that the poor are unevenly deprived along different attributes. A list has to be made with reference to objectives; but here the existence of the list defines the limits of the programme. The BPL is a classic case of state inversion that confuses ends and means. Second, the process of creating BPL lists produces a strange intellectual contortion. First, there is a survey that supposedly caps how many poor people there are. Then criteria are evolved to identify which particular households fall within the set. This exercise is a bit of sleight of hand: the identifying criteria selected should be such that they do not yield a figure higher than the cap that has been predetermined. If you go by criteria, caps make no sense. If you are committed to the caps, the criteria look arbitrary. Another instance of the state engaging in circular reasoning unhinged to any objectives. Third, there is the practical difficulty of implementing any criteria for selection. Again distinguished economists and planners have performed a heroic task of identifying easily implementable criteria that do not rely on complicated and dubious surveys. But objectively verifiable criteria that do not over-include or under-include are hard to design. Then the state resorts to including whole groups, or sometimes districts, in a blunt way that again makes the list discriminatory. It is small wonder that the states are deeply dissatisfied with the Centre setting the parameters of the criteria; the Centre in turn is suspicious that allowing the states to do their thing is a recipe for anarchy. But the most unconscionable practical consequence is the horrendous rate of under-inclusion and over-inclusion that has characterised these lists, often in excess of 50 per cent. The lists marginalise the poor rather than empower them.

So why does the state continue to persist with so flimsy a construction, one that is normatively dubious and practically difficult? In some schemes the state has made a departure, by making goods universal or by allowing self-targeting. But the mystique of the BPL remains strong. In part, its hold may be attributed to state inertia; the state often continues along inherited ways of structuring the world even when circumstances have rendered those strategies futile. Part of it is ideological: to show that something is being done for the poor, you first have to set the poor apart as a category, and make them a special object. How can we be seen for standing up for the poor, if we are treating them as equal citizens rather than as special wards of the state? It is also a way of ensuring that schemes for the poor by being exclusively for them, receive little attention from others. Ironically, all subsidies which the privileged enjoy, like petrol, are mostly couched in universalistic terms. Part of it is a false fiscal scare. On this view, if you don't target, and universalise schemes, the costs may turn out to be prohibitive. But this assumption is mostly false. As states that have universalised PDS (public distribution system), like Tamil Nadu, have demonstrated, there is self-targeting that limits the fiscal burden. Finally, there is also political expediency. The ministry of agriculture and food and state governments would rather let a catfight break out over who gets included or excluded, than focus attention on the real issue at hand: how do you design delivery systems with minimal leakage? The messiness of the BPL lists shifts the blame to civil society. If food is not reaching the poor, it can be blamed on the fact that people are gaming BPL lists; whereas the real culprits are delivery mechanisms that include everything from FCI to the ownership of food shops. Again, states that have done well with PDS focus less on futile controversies over lists, and more on structures and technologies of delivery. What lists are needed depends upon the objective of the programme. But at this historical juncture, it is clear that the BPL lists are serving very little purpose. For most schemes that matter to the poor they are unnecessary; these schemes can either be universalised or criteria can be evolved that bear some relation to the purpose of the scheme, rather than rely on an antecedently given list like BPL that we have not got right in over five decades. It will also remove this great scramble in the states to make poverty their sole revenue generation industry. Government needs to make a distinction between two kinds of waste. There is a form where the state incurs slightly higher costs, but the objective is fulfilled; universalisation of PDS will probably take this form. Then there is the form of waste where neither does the state save money, nor is the objective of the scheme fulfilled. But the BPL abets this more insidious kind of waste, as our unconscionable nutrition outcomes show.

There is great hope being placed in the fact that Unique Identification (UID) will help overcome some of these problems. The UID is certainly a necessary instrument for an effective state; the state needs to identify its citizens, and poor citizens in turn need an identity. But it is more likely that UID is more useful for universal schemes than targeted ones. UID will certainly help solve one problem in a universal scheme: identification of citizens. What is less obvious is whether it will be able to solve the challenge of targeting. As a matter of intellectual history, universal identification has gone hand-in-hand with the creation of universal rather than targeted welfare states. But this is a technical discussion. For our purposes what is important is this. BPL lists have two consequences for the politics of justice. First, it is usually the case, as the saying goes, that schemes for poor people are poor schemes. As a matter of simple political economy, schemes in which the privileged do not have a stake, are not subject to great accountability. But second, instead of producing widespread support for strengthening welfare schemes, it has produced more a politics of getting access to state resources by manipulating the categories of access, which again paradoxically ends up pitting the poor against the slightly less poor.

There is a final point to be made about welfare states in relation to the politics of equality. Where welfare states function well, they can certainly contribute to the improvement in the lives of the poor. In that sense, they are necessary aspects for the politics of equality. But welfare in this sense does not constitute the politics of equality for a couple of interesting reasons. In principle access to health and education and other public goods that form part of the welfare basket should enhance the capabilities of citizens to take advantage of opportunities. But these goods also enhance what one might call individuation. They allow the pool of citizens who are capable of being upwardly mobile. But they do not address the challenge of structural inequality.

One way of seeing this point is to see how ideologies of education play out in relation to equality. As a normative point, it cannot be debated that all citizens must have access to high quality education. But the comparative history of the relationship between education and equality is a little sobering in the following respects. First, access to equal opportunity in education is quite compatible with high levels of inequality. All that equal opportunity does is widen the pool from which successful candidates are drawn; it does not, by itself erase inequalities between different classes. Or rather, to be more precise, equality is more a function of compensation patterns for different jobs than it is of education itself. In an openly competitive system, where the job market does not have the right kind of distribution across incomes classes, equality of educational opportunity is quite compatible with inequality. For equality depends upon the penalties associated with not coming out on top. The more egalitarian an occupation structure, the less severe are the perceived penalties for not coming out on top. Europe has in part escaped the neurosis, a meritocratic competition can induce because there is greater background equality. In short, education alone may not produce a politics of equality. The real debate we need is on the kind of occupational structure we see emerging. What is the relationship between education and that occupational structure?

Meritocracy also has two peculiar psychic consequences. One of its unintended consequences is that it inculcates the idea that those who are left behind are somehow less worthy; and it creates a new form of inequality in turn. There is also an argument to be made that over the last twenty years or so, it is precisely meritocracy that has ideologically underpinned an ideology of great inequality. As some social observers have noted, people who rise through the system based on an idea of merit also have a greater sense of entitlement to all the fruits of their effort. What is interesting about income inequality in places ranging from the US to China is not the fact that it exists. It is that people at the top in particular and society more generally also came to the view that those at the top deserved what they have. They deserved it in part because they rose by the dint of their own talent. There is an odd sense in which privilege has to justify itself, but merit does not. Since the idea of equality of opportunity in education is so aligned with the idea of meritocracy (or rather the two legitimise each other), education is often not seen as the locus of equality.

This little excursus on meritocracy is interesting in relation to the politics of justice for another reason. In upper classes which have a sense that they have risen on the dint of merit, there is the possibility that there is less support for an egalitarian politics. This is because a society where achievement is linked to education attainment also gives those who achieve a sense of entitlement. It is perhaps easier to shame an aristocracy by claiming their wealth is undeserved; it is harder to induce guilt in those whose self-perception is that they have attained wealth by legitimate means. The expansion of a professional middle class may be conducive for supporting expansion of education. But this class, may at the same time have less patience with any politics of redistribution because it is the very ideology of education that supports their sense of entitlement.

There is therefore something of a crisis in articulating an egalitarian politics of social justice. Traditional Marxists believed that there is a subject or bearer of egalitarian politics, namely the proletariat. But there is no such natural subject, in part because all classes are now placed in very complex and contradictory relationships. There 'instruments' of equality have very limited reach. And even when they are successful in delivering certain goods, they often enhance the ethic of individuation, mobility, and competition rather than a politics of equality. It is therefore possible to articulate a discourse of improvement, but there is no locus of social justice.

II

If this is the case, then a profound challenge opens up for Indian democracy. At the moment when our republic was founded, Ambedkar very famously articulated the life of contradictions India was about to enter. On the one hand our constitution promised political equality. On the other hand actual social life was going to be marked by deep social and economic inequality. In some respects, this contradiction was not unique to Indian constitutionalism; it has been a feature of most democracies. In fact the kind of political equality that modern constitutions introduce is often seen as Janus faced. On the one hand these constitutions instantiate a normatively attractive conception of political equality. One central feature of this conception is that who one is should not matter to what political or even legal rights one has. The modern conception of citizenship is, in many ways, founded on this ideal. But this very attractive normative feature is also seen as, in some respects threatening. For this doctrine of equality is, as many have pointed out, as much a doctrine of anonymity. To repeat, who one is, is irrelevant to what rights one has.

Why is this conception of equality a threat? The worry is that this anonymity, while it opens up certain formal avenues of access, can actually also throw a veil over inequality. Indeed, Tocqueville had argued that in societies governed by formal equality (or anonymity), it is harder to mobilise an egalitarian politics. So, as Ambedkar had rightly worried, constitutional anonymity can leave real structures of inequality intact. This is a general challenge faced by democracies. But in a society marked by the particular form of inequality India had, this fear of constitutional anonymity was real and powerful. The challenge was to address this fear, while at the same time retaining the attractive normative features of constitutional anonymity. It was in this context that the recognition of caste as an axis of equality became central to Indian politics. The idea was that whatever constitutional anonymity might do, it must not render this particular form of inequality invisible, particularly in the case of Dalits.

But I want to draw attention to two features of this politics and the impact it has had on the politics of social justice. The first, I have discussed at some length in *The Burden of Democracy*, but the gist of the argument bears repeating here, because it explains some difficulties of egalitarian politics in India. But later in this section I will draw out some new implications of this argument to address one interesting analytical question about the salience of caste over class politics in India. Although I must make full disclosure and state emphatically that I worry about the new forms in which caste is being entrenched in Indian political discourse. But here I try and analyse why caste defines the contours of what we think of as equality so insistently.

Democratic aspirations are in some senses tied to the idea of equality. The idea of equality is complex and immediately invites the question, "Equality of What?" Income? Wealth? Political Equality? Opportunity? But understanding the political trajectory of Indian democracy does not require beginning with an answer to this question. In any society, especially democratic ones, the meaning and scope of equality will be fiercely contested and will be the basis for ideological divisions. Rather, it is the psychological impulses that lie behind the demand for equality; the existential burdens that any demand for equality seeks to address that leave their imprint on politics. The variety of structures, caste, class, patriarchy, that maintain and reproduce inequality are all too familiar, and Indian society exemplifies many of these to an unconscionable degree. But inequality is not simply a structural condition in which people find themselves; a condition measured by such objective indicators as Gini coefficients or development indices. Inequality is resented, and becomes salient for politics, because it is experienced existential burden that inflicts complex psychic costs by diminishing a sense of self. Not all forms of inequality are unjust. And the ways in which the experience of inequality shapes the self is a complex subject. But fundamentally inequality imposes the profoundest existential burdens when it is seen as denying individuals the minimum regard due to them, or when it constantly puts them is situations that are experienced as humiliating.

It is now a commonplace observation, thanks largely to Rousseau who most vividly wrote about the psychic burdens of inequality, that most human beings, unless they have been dehumanised to an unimaginable degree, place some value upon themselves. This does not mean that they are selfish; it is rather that they place some value upon themselves and wish that this value be somewhere affirmed.

The institutions and practices of most inegalitarian societies deny individuals this basic form of recognition, the recognition that they are valuable in some sense, that they have some moral standing. In most societies, this quest for having one's worth affirmed will take debased forms. The only way in which you can secure others' acknowledgement is either by seeking to dominate them, or by putting a convincing show of attributes and accomplishments that are capable of winning the acknowledgment of others. This is because the only way you can get acknowledged is by having power over them, by being able to say, "I know I am worth something, because I have power over you." Those not in a position of being able to dominate secure acknowledgement in other more self-debasing ways. They say something like, "Pay attention to me, because I can make your comparative sense of self-worth even more pronounced by debasing myself for you, by flattering you." Inegalitarian societies where there is no public acknowledgment of individual, self-worth will be characterised by both a fierce competition to dominate, and paradoxically, an exaggerated sense of servility. These are the two strategies of securing acknowledgement. Both desire to dominate and a kind of self-abasement, Rousseau suggested, would lead us to lead inauthentic lives: lives that were not governed by values, our concerns that were properly our own. Such societies would also give individuals frequently reasons to consider their self-respect injured: inegalitarian societies will routinely humiliate its members.

The aspiration to democracy is in part an aspiration to have one's moral worth acknowledged. The charge that an arrangement or a set of procedures is 'undemocratic' carries moral resonance, not simply because it describes a faulty procedure, but because it is accompanied by the sentiment that in being undemocratic someone's moral standing has been slighted. Acknowledgment by others of your moral worth is at least partly constitutive of an individual's sense of self-respect. A sense of self-respect is necessary to have a firm sense of one's own value, to have the conviction not only that life is worth living but worth living well. The absence of self-respect can be corrosive; it can make most pursuits meaningless.

In some senses, equal voting rights are a dramatic expression of individual's moral worth. But unless the collective arrangements of society give individuals the minimum bases for social self-respect, of which the equal right to vote, is just one aspect, society is likely to be characterised by an odd combination of a fierce competition for domination on the one hand, and abject servility on the other, and when neither succeeds, violence as a way of announcing one's moral standing. What institutions and objectives can satisfy the minimal requirements of acknowledging people's moral worth is a debatable one. But at the very least, freedom from abject necessity, removal of invidious and humiliating forms of discrimination, some equality of opportunity and access to a set of goods that are minimal requirements for being a capable agent in the modern world. The great liberal hope, embodied in the Indian constitution, was that ameliorating serious material deprivation, and an effective equal standing in the eyes of the law would go some way towards mitigating the desire to have one's worth affirmed, either by dominating others, or by having one's own sense of self fashioned by what we think might get others attention. Indeed, arguably, if the basis for social self-respect is adequately protected, the existence of other inequalities might matter less, because they could not be used as a base from which to dominate, despise, or negate others.

Conceptually speaking, there are many different ways in which, equality of moral worth can be affirmed. One might say, for instance, that we are equal in the eyes of God. Within Indian history, religious traditions, and traditions of dissent, these modes have always been available; but they did issue in effective and enduring demands for ordering the texture of social relationships. It is not indeed an impossibility to assert both that we are equal in the eyes of God and that a hierarchical social organisation such as caste is defensible; indeed the theoretical radicalism of so many claims to equality in the past was compromised by their practical conservatism. It can be granted that Indian history provides at least some conceptual resources for affirming equality. But the introduction of democracy is radical. Democracy is a way of affirming human dignity by granting individuals' civic standing. In a democracy the desire for having one's moral worth affirmed, for emptying social space of humiliation is given open social legitimation and expression

But, paradoxically, the struggles to affirm one's moral worth do not necessarily take the form of a demand for justice. Indeed, if Rousseau's diagnosis is plausible, the desire for having one's worth acknowledged can express itself in all kinds of debased forms, ones that require debasing others. Indeed, the paradox is that while individuals and groups can be acutely conscious of society's indifference towards them, they can, in turn be acutely indifferent towards others. Indeed, you would almost experience this to the case in highly inegalitarian societies. The only meaning empowerment has in such a society is power over others, some claim of power or privilege or access that sets you apart, rather than a generally shared sense of empowerment as such. The paradox is that the more unequal the background institutions and practices of society, the more likely it is that politics will be a struggle to displace the holders of power rather than an ambition to bring about social transformation. The struggle to move ahead will not be a common struggle for justice—for little commonality exists—but a competitive quest for power. A society that is adept at humiliating its members is, as Rousseau convincingly argued, more likely to make them adept at humiliating others than it is to teach them about justice. This perhaps explains one of the paradoxes at the heart of Indian politics. There are few other democracies where the universalist language of injustice, rights, even constitutionalism is so profusely used and has become part of so many political mobilisations. But it is a stratagem for particular individuals or groups to gain access to power, not an acknowledgment of the due claims of all. Discourses of law, constitutionalism, rights, justice, obligations, do not signify that a particular set of values is being taken as authoritative and these set genuine moral constraints for individuals. Rather, they are the languages in which particular grievances are expressed or interests advanced without the least acknowledgment of reciprocal or parallel interests and grievances of others. A sense of justice towards someone presupposes a sense of reciprocity, it presupposes that you acknowledge others. The more the social distance, the less likely that such reciprocity obtains. It is quite possible for a democracy to experience great clamour for recognition by particular individuals and groups without these resulting in diffusion of norms of justice. This follows the general pattern of the ways in which Indian society has been democratised. Democracy in India has advanced through the competitive negotiations between groups, each competing for their interests, rather than the diffusion of democratic norms. It is, in some senses, a contingent outcome of social conflicts, not necessarily a deep-seated norm. The purpose of political mobilisation has not been to make the state more accountable but to get access to or share in its power.

This conception of politics was most dramatically manifest in the way in which citizens often thought of the state. Given the commanding presence of the state, underwritten by an ideology of state-led development, access to state power became, for good or for ill, the principal means of improving the life chances of individuals. In an economy with slow and sluggish growth, averaging under three per cent, the state became a disproportionate provider of opportunity. Even access to opportunities and resources outside the state were mediated through state influence. Indeed, in one sense, politics through access to state power has become the swiftest route towards social mobility. In a strange kind of way, compared to the market, or educational institutions, politics of all kinds, from the most ambitious aspiration for power to the interest in gaining smallest benefits, came to be seen as a surer route to social mobility. Access to the state gave jobs and a likely class status that was better than anything available outside the state; the discretionary power the state conferred on all its officials, was experienced by many as empowerment, or at least an escape from the subordination that resulted from being at the receiving end of that power. Access to state power was about the only way of ensuring that one counted for somebody. Big scams do not tell the real story of the connection between corruption and social mobility. It is the thousands of petty fortunes that are made through the state that seemed to most citizens a surer bet of improving their class status than the uncertainties of a market. One of the peculiar features of Indian society has been that political power became almost the sole means of social mobility. Is there any other sphere of activity that is less stratified and more representative of Indian society than politics?

But the consequence of the growth of the state and its undoubted success in producing a kind of social mobility is attended by a paradox. This paradox is, namely that once the state is seen as a means for social mobility, it is not, for the most part seen as the provider of public goods. The state is adjudged to be successful, the more opportunities for large numbers of private individuals it can create through its own spending: if the number of government jobs expands for instance, even when not required, this is adjudged to be a political success, regardless of the opportunity costs this form of job creation imposes on others. The state exists primarily to satisfy the private interests of collusive interest groups. Although it is undoubtedly true that the dominant proprietary classes will have a disproportionate share of the state's resources, there is enormous fluidity in the nature of social groups that have at different times gained access to the state. But the net result was that almost never has that state been governed by a public philosophy; it is rather a high stakes competitive game in which individuals or groups seek advantages on particularistic lines. The raison d'etre of politics, the aims of public representation are no longer to respond to fundamental issues impinging upon common life but to organise the state's power in such a manner that its resources can be channelled in the direction of particular groups or individuals to protect their exclusive interests. The cumulative impact has been a view of the state and constitutional fabric that see them as institutions to be manipulated according to particularistic interests. One can appropriate Hegel's melodramatic phrase, "the state exists no longer." What Hegel meant in his context that the state and constitution were being manipulated to serve particular interests that the decisions that emanated from it did not carry the necessity of principle, but only the arbitrariness of expedience. To be sure, there are restraints internal to expedience, but how effective these restraints are will be a matter of some concern. It is extraordinary that the association of the state with the 'public' or the state with the 'common' the two sustaining associations of the state are wearing so thin.

But this politics continues because it has also acquired great normative depth. And it is this normative depth that I want to focus on, in the remainder of this talk. What I mean be normative depth is this. This de facto competition of groups to gain access to state power is now being given constitutional depth in different ways. First, as Sudipta Kaviraj (2005) pointed out several years ago, India had a discourse of equality in which equality was not about transcending caste. It was rather about claiming equality on the basis of caste. The measure of equality becomes the share of caste power in institutions like the state. The most extreme version of equality on the basis of caste is the legitimacy of what you might call the mirror theory of representation. On this view institutions are legitimate only in so far as the distribution of power within them mirrors, broadly speaking the relevant social cleavages in society. To a certain extent, the attraction of this ideal is understandable. If groups are systematically excluded from structures of power, there is prima facie a case that a society is operating on mechanisms of exclusion. There was consensus that these mechanisms very visibly and oppressively operated in the case of Dalits. But slowly this narrative was expanded to include other 'Backward Castes'. And one of the strange ironies of modern India is that the historical narrative of subjugation and marginalisation that was specific to Dalits has now been appropriated by other groups.

A society like India requires some form of affirmative action. What form that should take, who the state should target, why we should target them and how we should target them is an important subject that is best left for another occasion. Here I simply want to focus on some of the political and normative underpinnings of the kind of emphasis on reservation that we have institutionalised, and the implications of these assumptions for the politics of social justice. One way of bringing out the peculiarity of these assumptions is to ask the question how will the demand for equality be expressed? How will society ensure that constitutional anonymity does not throw a veil over inequality. One other possible criterion for ensuring this that has often been debated in the public sphere is the use of economic criteria. There was an understanding at the time of independence that this criterion would not cater to the specific form of injustice and discrimination Dalits faced. But using this criterion could help address other forms of Backwardness.

But we have come to believe that using economic criteria or class as a basis for reservation or affirmative action does not express a politics of social justice. Part of the reason often cited for this administrative: caste is thought of as a more easily identifiable characteristic than income. Part of the reason is that the caste/class overlap was very strong particularly in the case of Dalits. But this overlap is becoming much more complicated, particularly amongst non-Dalits, as the caste and occupation linkage is becoming weaker. But there is also a deeper reason at work. Reservations based on anything other than ascriptive criteria like caste are not seen as expressing a politics of equality for the following reasons. The first reason can be best highlighted by a little semantic experiment. Think of what the phrase "equality of classes" might mean. As applied to distributive justice, it can mean only the abolition of classes; otherwise the phrase equality of classes is a little bit of an oxymoron. But for reasons mentioned in part one, we do not have any instruments for the abolition of class. But the phrase "equality of caste" is not, in this sense an oxymoron. It requires neither the abolition of caste. And the degree to which we have achieved equality of caste can be crudely measured by the share of different caste groups in structures of power.

Just continue this line of thinking for a second. What are the differences between how we represent caste mobility and class mobility? If a poor person becomes middle class, this may reflect a salutary fact that society has opened up avenues for opportunity. But precisely by virtue of this mobility the person is able to change his class. And a society with great class mobility is a desirable one; at the very least is a potent expression of the thought that where one is born does not determine the opportunities one might have. But class mobility is compatible with two things. First, class mobility presupposes the continued existence of classes and inequality—all it suggests is that individuals can change their position. And the individuals who are so able to change their position no longer represent the class they came from.[1] A poor person becoming middle class, is an instance of a poor person becoming middle class. In class mobility, your position on the axis of deprivation being measured changes. Such a movement provides a measure of mobility; it is not seen as providing a measure of equality.

But caste operates somewhat differently. A Mala or Maddiga becoming rich may change their class status. But they remain a Mala or a Maddiga. They can still represent the caste from which they came in the calculus of power sharing. They may have become rich or powerful, but their position on the axis of deprivation being measured (in this instance, caste) does not change. In fact, one of the ethical dilemmas posed by reservation is the way in which it perpetuates a compulsory identity on citizens through officially sanctioned categories: once a member of a particular caste, always a member of a particular caste. But this normatively disturbing feature of the way in which we want to perpetuate caste as a compulsory identity also makes it attractive as a locus of social justice. This is because caste now comes to be a measure of equality in virtue of an immutable characteristic. In a way 'caste' answers the question "Equality with respect to what" in a way no other characteristic does, precisely because of its constructed immutability. Equality with respect to 'class' would require the abolition of class. Equality with respect to caste does not require this abolition. This immutability can also be combined with a simple measure: simply count the 'representatives' of each caste in the share of power. Again, with class this is impossible to do, because the mere act of access to power transforms the individuals' structural relation to class.

This institutionalisation of caste as the basis of equality has some interesting consequences. First, it is a form of legitimising class difference. Since we have limited instruments to achieve deep equality, class is now seen almost as a legitimate form of inequality.

1. I do not mean that they cannot have views that are sympathetic to the poor, or that they cannot identify with the poor or act on their behalf. The reference to representation here is not a reference to substantive views in this sense. It is simply that on the dimension of class they have become someone else.

Caste has become the form in which the politics of social justice has come to be sublimated.

Second, in India, there is no serious discourse on the relationship between justice and discrimination. This is in part due to the fact that the category of discrimination was specific to the Dalit experience. But the appropriation of the Dalit narrative by other communities has meant that power sharing rather than discrimination has become the central normative category in our thinking on justice. And in a way for 'upper castes' as well there is a tacit assumption that since a share to power has been reserved, discrimination is no longer a category one needs to think about.

Third, because equality can now be claimed only on the basis of an immutable identity, there is a growing clamour for the state to institutionalise these. Almost everyone knows that the politics of social equality depends on particular categories of identity being recognised and codified. The latest demand for a caste census is an inevitable outcome of this recognition. Social classifications recreate and solidify the realities rather than merely representing them. But the focus of politics of justice has shifted to what are the appropriate identity categories that need to be so codified. This will, in coming years take new forms. For instance, there will be greater political pressure to create new subdivisions within broad categories like Dalit or OBC (other backward classes). The demand for these subdivisions is inherent in the logic of equality on the basis of caste.

Fourth, identity politics and other forms of politics centred around welfare and justice are often posed as alternatives. Recent Indian history has shown that identity politics is the form in which the politics of social justice is expressed. And there is no reason to believe that the force of identity politics is going to diminish in the near future. Its forms may change, the categories deployed will be contested, and there will be a demand to expand this politics to new domains, including the private sector. But its central axis is going to remain demanding equality on the basis of an immutable characteristic.

The politics of social justice is at a deep impasse. The fear that constitutional anonymity must not draw a veil over inequality has led to the constitutionalisation of caste, as it were. It has provided a ready locus and measure of equality. But its price has been a move away from the ideals of Indian constitutionalism and the essence of democracy in two respects. It has reinforced the tyranny of compulsory identities and has reduced justice to crude and limited measures of power sharing. But caste becomes the locus of a politics of equality in part because there is deep structural pessimism about addressing other forms of inequality. India is going through a profound change, and the gains in both growth and poverty reduction are very real and widespread. But these changes do not, by themselves, address the politics of social justice.

India's growth has opened up new possibilities. It has certainly given the state more resources and potential for institutionalising welfare schemes. It is also producing new forms of improvement and mobility. But it has also increased the potential for rent seeking. Perhaps the best that we can hope for at the current conjuncture is 'small equality' effects that growth and welfare can produce. But how we will resolve the contradictions that Ambedkar talked about, still remains an open question. Were will be the locus of a politics of justice? Will the historical logic that made caste the dominant paradigm in which we think of justice continue? And will it crowd out the essential challenge we face. This challenge is best summed up in the words of the Chinese thinker, Qin Hui. He put it in a striking formulation, "What is excessive now is not liberalism or social democracy, but oligarchy and populism. It is therefore essential to critique both oligarchy from a liberal standpoint and populism from a social democratic standpoint." When I read these words I wonder whether there can be any better formulation of the challenges for Indian democracy. And I wonder how far we are from meeting these challenges.

References

Kaviraj, Sudipta (2005). "Democracy and Inequality in India", in Zoya Hasan and Francince Frankel (eds.), *Transforming India*. Oxford: Oxford University Press.

Mookherjee, Dilip and Debraj Ray (2003). "Persistant Inequalities", *Review of Economic Studies:* 369-93.

Pzeworski, Adam (2010). *Democracy and the Limits of Self Government.* Cambridge: Cambridge University Press.

10

RAJEEV BHARGAVA

Political Responses to Religious Diversity in Ancient and Modern India

It is frequently said that the way a society treats its vulnerable members, particularly its minorities tells a lot about the degree and quality of its civilisation. To love members of one's family or caste, even one's neighbours is easy and natural. The moral temper of people is tested best in their encounter with strangers and radical others.

The fact of India's rich diversity is widely registered, as also the general evaluation that its historical record in managing religious diversity has not been bad. Less understood is how this was achieved in the past or reproduced now. Even lesser known is what this really means, what the extent and depth of such achievement is.

In this paper, I hope to explore the conceptual resources in India to properly deal with religious diversity. What are contemporary India's moral expectations in response to religious plurality? What was ancient India's normative assessment of religious differences? Most societies today are characterised by religious diversity. Does India's experiments with religious diversity hold a lesson for other similarly placed societies? Do we have a decent answer to how one should politically deal with problems generated by religious diversity?

Religious Diversity and Domination

What does religious diversity mean? We might first distinguish between diversity of religion (external) and diversity within religion. (internal).

External diversity exists when different co-existing religions, each with a distinct identity of its own, exist within a single society. Examples include Israel with Jews, Muslims and Christians or contemporary European Societies with Jews, Christians, Muslims, Hindus and Sikhs and India which has always had multiple religious communities.

Internal diversity also takes two forms. The core beliefs, values and practices of any religion are invariably interpreted and elaborated differently by different sub-groups within a religion. This increasing internal differentiation creates a horizontal diversity that could cut very deep, creating schisms that often lead to bitter wrangling and sometimes violent conflict. Examples include Protestants and Catholics, the many denominations within Protestantism, or within Islam, Shias, Sunnis, Ismailis, Ahmedis, etc. Likewise, Hindus could be seen to be differentiated into Vaishnavites, Shaivites and so on. Such internal diversity is fairly well recognised. Less acknowledged is what might be called vertical or hierarchical diversity. Sometime during the course of the evolution of religions, some people are barred from participating in its mainstream rituals and practices. Over time, such groups are compelled to develop their own beliefs and practices that stand within an overall relation of subordination to the mainstream. They possess less or no value in relation to dominant practices and beliefs. Such powerless groups develop their own distinct modes of religiosity within an overarching system from which they have little escape. Thus people of the same religion engage in diverse practices that are hierarchically arranged. For example, caste-ridden Hinduism makes a distinction between pure and impure practices. Practices performed by certain castes are pure, and members of other castes are excluded from them. For instance, women or Dalits may not be allowed entry into the inner sanctum of temples and in many cases even into the precincts of an upper-caste temple.

This example already brings home a point that I ought to have made at the very outset of this discussion. Every form of diversity, including religious diversity, is enmeshed in power relations. If so, endemic to every religiously diverse society is an illegitimate use of power whereby the basic interests of one group are threatened by the actions of another. It further follows that inherent in religiously diverse societies is the possibility of both interreligious and intrareligious domination—a broad term that encompasses discrimination, marginalisation, oppression, exclusions, humiliation and the reproduction of hierarchy. (Two other forms of domination are also possible: the domination by the religious of the non-religious and the domination of the religious by the non-religious.)

To sum up, most societies are marked by religious diversity in each of the four forms specified above. Endemic to these diversities is intra- and inter-religious domination. A society deals well with religious diversity when it manages to continually reduce both these forms of domination. Its record in managing diversity is bad when it allows or fosters institutionalised religious domination. However, the reader may notice that though its success in handling religious diversity presupposes that it has the conceptual resources to do so, its failure does not automatically entail that it has no such resources. To be sure, without such resources, a society is destined to fail. But institutionalised religious domination might grow because such resources are neglected, ignored, deliberately suppressed and so on.

Modern India

Modern India provides one such instance of a society mishandling the cohabitation of its many religious groups, despite the vast resources it possesses to ensure that they all flourish. This happened before India's freedom from colonial rule. But it continues to be so, even after India refurbished its cultural resources to nourish diversity after independence. Allow me to elaborate this point.

As India came close and closer to its independence from British colonial rule, sadly it became more and more deeply divided. By 1940s, vocal sections of the Muslim elites had raised the demand for a separate nation-state, Pakistan, paranoid that a nation based on universal adult franchise would not only be Hindu but invariably have a Hindu state, detrimental to Islam and to sub-continental Muslims.

This demand was part of and in response to the majority-minority syndrome, a condition of spiralling estrangement between Hindus and Muslims, one where animosities groups circulate freely, adding layers upon layers of mutual grievances and where antagonistic games are played with no other end in mind except defeat and humiliation of the other. Not that Muslim elites alone were to blame for the syndrome. Far from that. Sections of Hindus had also built an exclusivist ideal of a purely Hindu nationalism, had begun to use a supremacist language and constructed a deeply divided memory of the nation's past. They branded all Muslims as invaders, forgetting that many converts to Islam were probably one of the many original inhabitants of the land. Anyhow, prospects of inter-religious domination loomed large, fears that did not go away with the formation of Pakistan because although reduced, Muslim population was still substantial, about 12 per cent of the population, 50 million in absolute numbers then and 120 million now.

The syndrome had another significant consequence. The 19th century had witnessed in India the growth of a number of freedom and equality-centred reform movements among both Hindus and Muslims. But the majority-minority syndrome set off by inter-religious rivalries forestalled these reforms, indeed intensified anti-reform tendencies. As B.R. Ambedkar, the great leader of Dalit put it, "When groups regard each other as a menace, all energies are spent on meeting this menace. The exigencies of a common front against one another generates a conspiracy of silence over social evils. Internal dissent and conflict is squashed in favour of the idea that everyone must close ranks or the community will weaken." A very real possibility existed that the legitimate interests of vulnerable sections among Hindus and Muslims would be neglected, partly because any articulation of their demand would escalate internal conflict and weaken the overall unity of each community. In other words, prospects of intra-religious domination loomed large too.

The leadership of the newly independent country was faced therefore with a choice: either to tolerate, indeed to consolidate both these forms of domination by the establishment of a (upper-caste) Hindu state or to combat them by instituting a secular state instead.

It is to the credit of Indian leaders then that they chose the second option and in doing so developed a distinctive conception of secularism with a genuine trans-cultural potential, suited particularly to a context of deep religious diversity, and different from all available western conceptions.

Although not available as a doctrine or theory, such a conception was worked out jointly by Hindus and Muslims in the subcontinent and can be found in the best moments of intercommunal practice in India and in the country's constitution, appropriately interpreted.

Eight features of the Indian model are striking and relevant to a wider discussion of secularism.

First, multiple religions are not extras, added on as an afterthought, but present at its starting point, as part of its foundation. Second, it responds simultaneously to both inter-religious and intra-religious domination. Third, it has a commitment to multiple values—peace and toleration; liberty or/and equality, not conceived narrowly as pertaining to individuals alone but interpreted broadly to also cover the relative autonomy of religious communities as well as their roughly equal standing in society. This it is able to do by simultaneously granting individual and community-specific rights. Fourth, it is not entirely averse to the public character of religions. Although the state is not identified with a particular religion or with religion more generally (there is no establishment of religion), there is official and therefore public recognition granted to religious communities.

Fifth, it rejects the idea that the state must intervene in religion only to control or suppress it (a conception born in France and developed in Ataturk's Turkey and more fiercely in the former Soviet Union and China). Nor does it erect a wall of separation between state and religion—an interpretation of the idea of separation developed in the United States where religion was to keep off the state to the same degree and in the same manner as the state keeps off religion. The two are meant do their respective jobs best when they do not enter into each other's domain of jurisdiction. In India, there are meant to be boundaries, of course, between state and religion but they are porous. This allows the state to intervene in religions, to help or hinder them without the impulse to control or destroy them. The state has multiple roles, such as granting aid to educational institutions of religious communities on a non-preferential basis but also in legitimately interfering in socio-religious institutions that deny equal dignity and status to members of their own religion or to others (for example, the ban on untouchability; the obligation to allow everyone, irrespective of caste, to enter Hindu temples; and potentially to correct gender inequalities), on the basis of a more sensible understanding of equal concern and respect for all individuals and groups. In short, it interprets separation to mean not strict exclusion or strict neutrality but rather what I call principled distance.

Sixth, this model shows that we do not have to choose between active hostility and passive indifference or between disrespectful hostility and respectful indifference toward religion. We can combine the two: have the necessary hostility as long as there is also active respect; the state may intervene to inhibit some practices, so long as it shows respect for other practices of the religious community and does so by publicly lending support to them. Seventh, by not fixing its commitment from the start exclusively to individual or community values or marking rigid boundaries between public and private, India's constitutional secularism allows decisions on these matters to be taken either within the open dynamics of democratic politics or on case to case basis by contextual reasoning in the courts. Eighth, this commitment to multiple values and principled distance means that the state tries to balance different, ambiguous but equally important values. This makes its secular ideal more like a contextual, ethically sensitive, politically negotiated arrangement (which it really is), rather than a scientific doctrine conjured by ideologues and merely implemented by political agents.

A somewhat forced, formulaic articulation of Indian secularism goes something like this. The state must keep a principled distance from all public or private, individual-oriented or community-oriented religious institutions for the sake of the equally significant (and sometimes conflicting) values of peace, this-worldly goods, dignity, liberty, and equality (in all its complicated individualistic or non-individualistic versions)—in short, helping to make society free from intra- and inter-religious domination. Indian secularism then is an ethically sensitive negotiated settlement between diverse groups and divergent values.

Principled Distance

Let me elaborate in somewhat greater detail two key features of Indian secularism, namely, principled distance and its contextualist character. Indian secularism admits fairly strict separation at the level of ends: the state has no religious ends. At the level of personnel and institutions, this is part of what is meant by distance. But at the third level, it maintains a flexible approach on the question of inclusion and exclusion of religion and the engagement and disengagement of the state, which depends on the context, nature, or current state of relevant religions. This engagement must be governed by principles undergirding a secular state, that is, principles that flow from a commitment to its stated values. This means that religion may intervene in the affairs of the state if such intervention promotes freedom, equality, or any other value integral to secularism. For example, citizens may support a coercive law of the state grounded purely in a religious rationale if this law is compatible with freedom or equality. Equally, the state may engage with religion or disengage from it and engage positively or negatively, but it does so depending entirely on whether these values are promoted or undermined. A state that intervenes or refrains from interference on this basis keeps a principled distance from all religions. This is one constitutive idea of principled distance. This idea is different from strict neutrality, in which the state may help or hinder all religions to an equal degree and in the same manner; if it intervenes in one religion, it must also do so in others. Instead, it rests on the idea that treating people or groups as equals is entirely consistent with differential treatment. This idea is the second ingredient in what I have called principled distance.

What kind of treatment do I have in mind? First, religious groups have sought exemptions from practices in which states intervene by promulgating a law to be applied neutrally to the rest of society. This demand for noninterference is made on the ground either that the law requires them to do things not permitted by their religion or that it prevents them from doing acts mandated by it. For example, Sikhs demand exemptions from mandatory helmet laws and from police dress codes to accommodate religiously required turbans. Elsewhere, Jews seek exemptions from Air Force regulations to accommodate their yarmulkes. Muslim women and girls demand that the state must not interfere in their religiously required chador. Jews and Muslims seek exemption from Sunday closing laws on the ground that this is not required by their religion. Principled distance allows, then, that a practice that is banned or regulated in one culture may be permitted in the minority culture because of the distinctive status and meaning it has for its members. For many republican or liberal theories, this is a problem because of a simple, somewhat absolutist morality that gives overwhelming importance to one value, particularly to equal treatment or equal liberty. Religious groups may demand that the state refrain from interference in their practices, but they may equally demand that the state interfere to give them special assistance so that they are also able to secure what other groups are able to routinely get by virtue of their social dominance in the political community. It may grant authority to religious officials to perform legally binding marriages, to have their own rules or methods of obtaining a divorce, to promulgate rules about relations between ex-husband and ex-wife, to arbitrate civil disputes, and so on. Principled distance allows the possibility of such policies on the grounds that to hold people accountable to an unfair law is to treat them as unequals.

However, principled distance is not just a recipe for differential treatment in the form of special exemptions. It may even require state intervention in some religions more than in others, considering the historical and social condition of all relevant religions. For the promotion of a particular value constitutive of secularism, some religions, relative to other religions, may require more interference from the state. For example, suppose the value to be advanced is social equality. This requires, in part, undermining caste hierarchies. If this is the aim of the state, then it may be required of the state that it interferes in caste-ridden Hinduism much more than in, say, Islam or Christianity. However, if a diversity-driven religious liberty is the value to be advanced by the state, then it may have to intervene in Christianity and Islam more than in Hinduism. If this is so, the state can neither strictly exclude considerations emanating from religion nor keep strict neutrality with respect to religion. It cannot antecedently decide that it will always refrain from interfering in religions or that it will interfere in each equally. Indeed, it may not relate to every religion in society in exactly the same way or intervene in each religion to the same degree or in the same manner. To want to do so would be plainly absurd. All it must ensure is that the relationship between the state and religions is guided by nonsectarian motives consistent with some values and principles.

Discerning readers would know how different this conception is from mainstream western versions, particularly those which developed in the United States, France and much of western Europe. Unlike India's subtle understanding of separation as principled distance, in America, separation is interpreted as mutual exclusion of religion/church and state for the sake of freedom and equality understood wholly as attributes of individuals. By mutual exclusion is meant this: Neither religion nor the state would intrude into the other's jurisdiction. They will both keep off each other's domain by virtue of an unbreachable wall, as Thomas Jefferson once put it. The state will neither help nor hinder religion which will remain in the hands of individuals and their associations, a product of their choices.

Indian secularism is different from the French model too which has its own specific understanding of separation as one-sided exclusion for the sake of republican equality. In order to enter the public/political domain as equal citizens, everyone must leave behind their religious identities in private. Those who fail to do so face a robust interference by the state. Though, religion has no power to get into the affairs of the state, the state retains all its powers to intervene in matters of religion—all this for the sake of unified political community.

Finally, Indian secularism is also radically different from conceptions of secularism in the rest of western Europe which does not even pretend to have equality or impartiality in the domain of religion. Different European states continue to remain entangled with their own respective national religion. They do separate from religion for the sake of liberal and egalitarian values outside religion but continue to offer exclusive support to the dominant religion. The consequence of this is the perpetuation of deep religious inequalities and the continuation of discriminations and exclusions for the less powerful religions.

This model which fosters critical respect for all religions by protection of the rights of religious minorities and with a policy of principled distance did not drop fully formed from the sky. It has developed in India historically. This goes against the idea propagated by many scholars that secularism is a Western ideal, a unique product of Western Enlightenment and Protestantism.

As the Indian example shows, this necessary link between secularism and Christianity is exaggerated, if not entirely mistaken. It is true that the institutional separation of church and state is an internal feature of Christianity and an integral part of Western secularisms. But as we have seen, this church-state disconnection is a necessary but not a sufficient condition for the development of secularism even in societies with church-based religions. It is clearly not a necessary condition for the development of all forms of secularisms. Moreover, as I have argued, the mutual exclusion of religion and the state is not the defining feature of secularism. The idea of separation can be interpreted differently. Nor are religious integrity, peace, and toleration (interpreted broadly to mean 'live and let live') uniquely Christian values. Most non-Christian civilisations have given significant space to each. Therefore, none of them is exclusively Christian. It follows that even though we find in Christian writings some of the clearest and most systematic articulation of this doctrine, even the Western conception of secularism is not exclusively Christian.

All right, one might say, secularism is not just a Christian doctrine, but is it not Western? The answer to this question is both yes and no. Up to a point, it is certainly a Western idea. More specifically, as a clearly articulated doctrine, it has distinct Western origins. Although elements that constitute secularism assume different cultural forms and are found in several civilisations, one cannot deny that the idea of the secular first achieved self-consciousness and was properly theorised in the West. One might then say that the early and middle history of secularism is almost entirely dominated by Western societies. However, the same cannot be said of its later history. Nationalism and democracy arrived in the West after the settlement of religious conflicts, in societies that had been made religiously homogeneous or had almost become so (with the exception of the Jews, of course, who continued to face persistent persecution). The absence of deep religious diversity and conflict meant that issues of citizenship could be addressed almost entirely disregarding religious context; the important issue of community-specific rights to religious groups could be wholly ignored. This had a decisive bearing on the Western conception of secularism. However, for non-Western societies, such as India, the case is different. Both national and democratic agendas in countries such as India had to face issues raised by deep religious difference and diversity. In India, nationalism had to choose between the religious and the secular. Similarly, the distribution of active citizenship rights could not be conceived or accomplished by ignoring religion. It could be done either by actively disregarding religion (as in all political rights) or by developing a complex attitude toward it, as in the case of cultural rights, where it had to balance claims of individual autonomy with those of community obligations and claims of the necessity of keeping religion 'private' with its inescapable, often valuable presence in the public. By doing so, Indian secularism never completely annulled particular religious identities.

Indeed, in addressing these complex issues, the idea of political secularism was taken further than it had been evolved in the West. Mainstream theories or ideologies in modern, Western societies have taken little notice of these features. Some are wary of interfering in religions. Others want to keep away even from subsidising them. But this compounds several problems. Communities in desperate need of help from impartial but powerful institutions remain unsupported. And powerful sections within religious communities that need to be stopped from harassing the more vulnerable members of their own community are unfettered. Many western societies today are struggling to deal with their postcolonial religious diversity. They lack the resources to deal with the problems endemic to this diversity. These societies are trapped in conceptions that have outgrown their usefulness. They would do well to look sideways to other conceptions because the later history of secularism is more non-Western than Western.

Diversity in Ancient India

Unfortunately, Indian scholars have themselves been slow to fully recognise the distinctiveness of Indian secularism. They assume that secularism comes only in one form, that the form it has assumed is western, born out of a dialectic between Protestantism and Western Enlightenment and it is too thickly intertwined with the religious and cultural history of a few western societies to have any relevance to India. This view is mistaken because the distance between state and religion grows either because a society resists and offsets the vast illegitimate power of its own religion by transferring some of it to a separate institution, such as the state or because the presence of multiple religions in society necessitates that other powerful institutions such as the state do not align themselves to any one religion for fear that this might result in war, persecution or injustice. India has very little experience of the first. It has never been home exclusively to one religion. Its religions have never had a powerful church. But it has an enormous experience of the second. It has developed multiple ways to distance political institutions from religious powers. In what follows, I provide one such example from ancient India.

Ancient Response to Religious Diversity: Asoka

We have habitually associated Asokan empire with 'religious toleration' but probably never paid attention to what this means or how significant his achievement was. Here I examine 2 of his many edicts to explore this issue. The 7th edict begins with "The beloved of the gods wishes that all *Pasandas* ('followers of a school of thought or teachings') must dwell everywhere, in every part of his kingdom."

This seems like a simple, quite inconsequential statement and has been treated as such by commentators who have a rather sanguine view of social and religious conditions in Asoka's India. Thus Vincent Smith claims that "the Dharma which he preached and propagated unceasingly with amazing faith in the power of sermonising, had few, if any, distinctive features." The doctrine was essentially common to all religions. When we apply to Asoka's policy the word 'toleration' with its modern connotation and justly applaud the liberality of his sentiments, another qualification is needed, and we must remember that in his days no really diverse religions existed in India. Buddhism and Jainism both were originally mere sects of Hinduism—or rather schools of philosophy founded by Hindu reformers—which in course of time gathered an accretion of mythology around the original speculative nucleus, and developed into religions. The same sentiment is echoed by Radhakumud Mookerjee who says, "It is to be remembered that Asoka's toleration was easy enough among the different denominations of the time, which were all but offshoots of the same central faith and did not differ among themselves so completely as the religons of Jesus, Zoroaster, or Mahomet introduced later into the country. Thus it was not difficult for the emperor, with due credit to the liberality of his views, to discern 'the essence of the matter in all sects' and honour it duly."

To be sure, some commentators recognised that Asokan edicts are written in times of intense sectarian strife. For instance, D.R. Bhandarkar says that people in Asoka's times had lost sight of the essentials of their faith and begun to focus excessively on rituals and theology. In these matters, there was unending acrimonious wrangling. Therefore, "When Asoka lived and preached, religious fanaticism and sectarian spirit were rampant." Yet even he seems not to link this wish of the beloved of the gods to have his subjects co-inhabit to rampant sectarianism or to realise its real import. Why should Asoka have said this? What could be the context in which he is compelled to say this? We get no sense of this from existing literature.[1] At any rate, it is not clear what form this strife took? Were sects expelling one another from territories where each was dominant? Had they segregated one another? Was something akin to what we call now 'ethnic or religious cleansing' attempted in that period? But if intense sectarian strife existed, there must at least have been some violence between sects, even if it was not purely motivated by doctrine. It is again hard to tell unless we try and imagine vividly what the background conditions were to some of these key edicts.

The 12th edict implores that all *pasandas* restrain their speech, a specification of a more general self-restraint, *samyama*, mentioned in the 7th edict. This is seen as a virtue, even a civic virtue. But why restrain only speech? Why is this the core, the *saara* of all *pasandas*? Why burden it with so much importance? What is the link between restraint on speech and co-existence? Does speech have the power to disrupt co-existence? We all know that it can but under what conditions is it so acutely significant as to become one of the central problems of a society and the chief concern of its royal edicts? Does speech have the power to push everyone over the edge or are people already so much on the edge that even speech can push them over it? Surely, it is easy for a reasonable person to tolerate people with whom she has minor differences. The difficulty of tolerance arises only when people with major, virtually irreconcilable differences encounter one another. What then is the context in which speech is virtually the sole carrier of deeply uncomfortable, major differences?

Once we properly examine the context of the edicts, we begin to get a sense of the importance of the edict. For a start, an internal conflict existed within followers of Vedic teachings, between those who indulged in expensive and elaborate rituals and those who found this baroque quality entirely unnecessary, wasteful, and distracting from ones primary objectives. Second, between those who believed in the necessity of propitiating gods and those who gradually moved

1. There is virtual consensus that this was a period of bitter sectarian strife. Bhandarkar says "It is plain that there was friction and bitter spirit between these (Ajivikas, Nirgranthas and Buddhists) sects" and "When Asoka lived religious fanaticism and sectariarianism was rampant." See Bhandarkar (1925).

away from this view and felt that the only significant action (*karma*) was the sacrifice (*yajna*) itself.

A third conflict also existed. Several commentators attest to the presence of pre-Aryan people in India. One such group was probably skeptical about the idea of a creator of the universe, believing that the world in which they lived was real and that salvation in this world was possible by exacting practical discipline.[2] They were generally pessimistic about other forms of liberation in this world and had little conception of any other world. The *Munis* are infrequently mentioned in the Vedas, but that is probably due to their radical difference with the Vedic tradition and their consequent marginalisation. It does not mean that their existence in this period was rare.[3] Thus a third major conflict existed between the Vedics and the pre-Vedic *Munis*, one ritualistic, believers in gods, seeking this-worldly goods and pleasures, and very largely materialist, the other renouncing the world of this-worldly pleasures and rituals, rejecting beliefs in gods and seeking liberation deep in the forests through rigorous practical discipline.

In addition to the three conflicts mentioned above, at least two conflicts went much deeper: (a) between pre-vedic and Vedic immanantists on the one hand and transcendentalists who developed the *Upanishads* and evolved the notion of the radical distinction between *Samsara* and *Brahman/Atman*. (b) An even deeper conflict between two different ethics, one Upanisadic, which has a transcendental metaphysics but no (or perhaps a weak) conception of transcendental morality and the other which opposes transcendental orders of the real, outer or inner world, but develops a strong idea of

2. See Pande (1957, 1995). Also see Crangle (1994). Crangle says "Early Vedic practices involve, by and large, a worldly attitude whereby the worshipper seeks to appease gods by performing various ritual sacrificial ceremonies. The Rig Veda, however, mentions some opposed to Aryan rituals.... These were unbelievers, riteless people... Outstanding in this regard were the Munis. The Rig Vedas offer the earliest literary evidence for the existence of *Munis*."

3. D.D. Kosambi (1959) also mentions the existence of non- Aryan people called *nagas* who were settled in parts of what now are Bihar and Uttar Pradesh. They did not speak the Aryan language and appeared not to have any contact with the Aryans. This appears to confirm G.C. Pande's (1995) claim that a group of wondering ascetics called *Munis*, marginal to Vedic life, also existed in the region.

transcendental morality, one that allows judgements from outside any this-worldly point to be made on both self- and other-related actions of every subject. Allow me to elaborate.

The key difference between the Rig Vedic and the Upanishidic world lies in the birth of the idea of radical transcendence and therefore of a duality between this cycle of birth and death in this world (*samsara*) and *Brahman* or *Atman*, the ultimate reality pervading the whole universe or our deepest inner, imperishable selves. *Samsara* is radically separated from *Brahmana* or *Atman* in that the latter can be achieved only by totally negating the former. True Liberation (*moksha, mukti*) lies in escape from the cycle of *samsara*. *Moksha* cannot be attained by performing sacrifices. But nor could *Moksha* be obtained, contra the *Muni* and early Jain tradition, by physical austerities even for thousands of years. Offerings (*dana*), sacrifices, recitations of Vedas, and performance of austerities may earn merit but only steadfastness in pursuit of the knowledge of *Brahman* would help us achieve *Moksha* or true immortality.

Both *Brahman* and *Atman* are wholly outside the given, immanent and mundane world (*samsara*) and manifest a point from which one can, to use Benjamin Shwartz's phrase, "stand back and look beyond" and contemplate it. Hence the appropriateness of the term 'radical transcendence'. Hence also the aptness of the use of axiality. The Upanishads provide the axial turn in Indian civilisation. Here we have the birth of a major potential conflict between vastly different weltanschauungs. For nothing that the vedic people or the *munis* think to be significant is truly or ultimately important for Upanishadic thinkers.

Nonetheless, there is one sense in which the break between the pre-Vedic/Vedic and the Upanishadic followers may not have been total. This has to do with the necessary place of others in an ethic of self-realisation. What follow are very tentative remarks, the principal import of which is that higher order other-related values or principles (lets call this morality higher, separate and transcendental) are negligible or secondary in pre-Buddhist thought in the Indian subcontinent. Allow me to elaborate. For Vedic Brahmanism, Dharma has less to do with what we owe one another. Neither sacrificial rituals nor Gods are invoked for the good of the generalised others, say for the *Munis*. In both its individual or collective forms, this is a self-focused ethic of fulfillment or realisation. The content of this ethic does not change with the introduction of the idea of radical transcendence. The early moment of the axial turn in Indian civilisation does not appear to make the generalised other central to its ethic of individual or collective self. To be sure, notions of justice, right and wrong exist, but these are probably in the hands of the Kshatriya king, matters decided in any given context by his will or judgement. Dharma in its Vedic or post-Vedic, Upanishadic senses has very little to do with what we must, by some transcendental necessity, owe one another.

All this begins to change with developments in later Upanishadic thought and more clearly with Buddha. With Buddha's teachings, the transcendental point, to use Gananath Obeyesekhre's (2002) phrase is "ethicised" (in my terminology, one might say, moralised). From now on, judgements of the rightness or wrongness of action are 'mediated and delayed'. They may even be enunciated after one's death. This is the birth of transcendental morality—a transcendental evaluation of the rightness or wrongness of action in relation to others which affects a person's life not in this world alone but his destiny after death, outside this world. This also entails a shift in the meaning of Dharma. Dharma from now on also begins to mean this radically transcendental morality. Quite clearly, there must have been not only a conflict between ancient ethics and this new ethic inspired by Buddha but also a contest over the meaning of key terms, such as Dharma. We now have two radically differing notions of Dharma, one a particular ethic of a single-cosmos oriented (this-worldly) self-realisation and the other, a transcendental morality for all concerned with right inter-personal conduct. Indeed, even the term 'inter-personal' is not quite correct, because the conduct in question includes how human beings behave towards non-human animals. 'All' means all humans and animals, virtually all living species. The protest over ritual sacrifice was perhaps more against the sacrificial killings of animals. This made eminent economic sense but is not reducible to it. For the Kshatriyas, war had become a mode of life and perhaps the greatest benefit yielded by *yajna* sacrifice was success in war. The Kshatriyas needed animals that they stole from ordinary pastoralists. War on the other hand meant not only the arbitrary killing of humans and animals but also the destruction of people's livelihood. Thus, both pastoralists and small farmers may have risen in protest against war and sacrificial killing.[4] Buddha's teachings thus instantiates a major transvaluation of Vedic values, a 'dynamic best captured in Assmann's notion of normative inversion whereby one group's rights and responsibilties are turned by another group into prohibitions and scandals.'[5]

I hope to have shown the deeply mistaken character of the view that religious interaction in Asoka's period of rule was relatively trouble-free and that he must have had an easy time finding a common ground among followers of different schools of thought. It is well known that shared philosophical and cultural assumptions provide no immunity against intense conflicts. The assumption that offshoots of an entity conflict weakly with their parent is even more untenable. Buddhism may have been an offshoot of 'Hinduism' but conflicted with it at many levels, on many issues. As for Jaina philospliy, it is not even entirely clear what epistemic gain ensues to see it simply as an offshoot of Hinduism. Thus, Vincent Smith and Radhakumud Mookerjee clearly underestimate the depth of conflict in Asokan times. Thapar and Bhandarkar are right that this was a period of intense and bitter sectarian conflict. However, in my view, even they are unable to home in on the novelty of what was at stake in Asoka's period. By vividly representing the central conflicts of those times, this account now gives an entirely different gloss on Romila Thapar's (1961) remarks that this is a period of intense sectarian struggles and to her claim that 6th century BCE was 'the century of universal questioning'. It also helps us to see the real

4. "There were sound economic reasons for Asoka's change to rule by morality, from the precepts of a book which not even its greatest admirer could accuse of being moral." Kosambi, p.223.

5. See Pollock *op. cit.*: 404.

issues at stake in those struggles—a conflict between notions of weak and radical transcendence as well as between immanent and transcendental moralities. The 6th century BCE must have been a century of massive intellectual and emotional turmoil with gigantic social implications, the like of which had never been witnessed earlier. It appears that the need of the times was a public or political morality—a clear statement of not only how we must treat ourselves (found in *Brahmanical* philosophies of that time), but also a firm and well-grounded statement on how we treat each other and all living creatures (not explicitly found in *Brahmanical* philosophy but found in Buddhism in a radically transcendent form, a transcendental morality) but one that could arbitrate between these multiple, radically different, often incommensurable rival conceptions so that each could co-exist by discovering or evolving a morality that is learn from one another.[6]

The Real Significance of the 7th Edict

I hope by now we also possess a much better understanding of what exactly is so novel about the harmless looking statement in the 7th edict. Given the many-layered, incrementally deep conflicts involving several different groups and the necessity imposed by trade and urban conditions for them to cohabit, Asoka had to evolve some way to hold them together. Buddha's teachings had provided him with conceptual resources to imagine something that would be more than ad hoc and tactical, something long-lasting and endorsable from within each *pasanda's* perspective.[7] They had given him the hope in the development of public norms from below and the redundancy of orders from above. One of them was that all *pasandas* must dwell everywhere in his empire.

6. Kosambi proposes that a number of sects with subtle metaphysical differences arose in protest against the "monstrous cancerous growth of sacrificial ritual in the tribal kingdoms." The greatest fruit of the *yajna* sacrifice was success in war; fighting was glorified for its own sake as the natural mode of life for the ksatriyas, while the brahmin's duty and means of livelihood was the performance of vedic sacrifices (p.166).

7. Sadly, this might have been the primary reason why his empire was so brief, ephemeral and anomalous. Equally, this surely is the only reason why Asoka's Dhamma continues to be remembered more than 2,000 years later.

Among historians, only D.D. Kosambi appears to have grasped the true importance of this statement. Kosambi believes that the edict is meant to communicate primarily to leaders of each *pasanda* rather than directly to *pasandas* themselves. Through the 7th edict, Asoka effectively grants these leaders permission to travel freely everywhere in the kingdom to provide them an opportunity to teach and convert each other. Asoka impartially grants this privilege to religious teachers of all *pasandas*. It is likely that the edict became necessary because mutual interaction and the attempt to preach one's own ethics to others had begun to cause severe friction, leading to the birth of local rules forbidding one *pasanda* from communicating with or worse entering into the territory of another *pasanda*—something akin to what Sudipta Kaviraj in a different context has called back to back existence. Instead of perpetuating mutual exclusion and the resulting homogenisation of each settlement, Asoka, it seems, gives assurances to the leader of each *pasanda* that they must feel secure everywhere and encourages free interaction and dialogue amongst them, albeit now regulated by moral norms.

As mentioned above, he is able to do so by virtue of a major conceptual transformation, facilitated by a change in the background conditions, perhaps even in the social imaginary. A new form of society far more heterogeneous than the original simple tribe-community had come into being. Living together here was terribly different but at the same time no longer on optional extra but inevitable, a natural part of one's environment. To respond to the crisis generated by radical heterogeneity, a new legitimating ethic had become necessary. Buddha's teachings made possible a different conception of Dharma. It needed a great leap of imagination to arrive at the view that what we call Dharma can be used not only for personal self-fulfillment or the fulfillment of the needs of specific groups but rather to ease the newly emergent problems of a new form of society that simply could not do without diverse groups. It is a discovery of the first magnitude that Dharma or religion can be used to ease the difficulties of early society, to make the common life of diverse elements of society easier. It necessitated that a collective ethic substitute correct ritual by good deeds for the sake of others.

Moreover, Buddha's teachings opened up the possibility of the radical socio-political restructuring of the world and the self by politico-moral action from above. Buddha's ethic included the pivotal importance of moral action. Once one stands outside the whole cosmos and is able to see its limitations, and once the transcendental point from which one examines the cosmos is viewed as emanating a moral vision, it becomes possible to imagine a profound restructuring of society and polity in accordance with that vision. Once again, D.D. Kosambi is imaginatively on to this point when he says that more than a personal conversion of the emperor, there appears to have taken place in Asokan times a deeper conversion of the whole previous state apparatus. The king not only preaches a new morality but is able to launch radically new political and administrative measures that includes public morality as an essential ingredient, and provides a framework within which radically differing ethics can co-exist and nourish one another.[8]

VI

Search for a Common Ground

What, despite profound differences in world-views, could the basis of such co-existence be? How may people not just live together, interact face-to-face, but live together well? For Asoka, a morally desirable living together is possible if everyone follows the Dhamma. Edict 12 says, "The beloved of the Gods does not wish to overvalue gifts and sacrifice. More important than these is the reverence one's faith commands or the number of its followers or its core ethical values. Even more important than these ethical values are the essentials of all faiths and *pasandas*. It is these essentials

8. Finally the rules governing ordinary people and the ruler himself stemmed from the same moral source. This was quite unlike the statecraft recommended by Chanakya where an entirely amoral ruler committing all kinds of crimes against subjects and neighbours reigned over a morally regulated population.

that constitute the common ground of these seemingly conflicting conceptions."[9]

What then is the common ground among rival conceptions? For Asoka, Dhamma constitutes the all-important common ground, the essentials, of all *pasandas*. What then are these essentials? Interpreters here give differing answers: Dhamma is sometimes seen as virtue, religious truth or simply piety. But the most convincing answer, consistent with what is mentioned above and provided by Obeyesekre and Tambiah is that Dhamma is akin to transcendental morality. If so, it is fair to say that for Asoka, rites and rituals have no meaning unless embedded within an ethical perspective and the ethical import of these gifts is overridden by their lack of moral significance. This is why they may be offered only as long as they are not injurious to anyone (humans as well as non-humans). No animal may be killed in order to be sacrificed. Nor should there be any *samaja* (assembly) for such a purpose, implying that other kinds of assemblies, especially the *Sangha*, are permissible.[10]

What then is the content of *dhamma*? The fundamental principle of dhamma is *vacaguti*, variously interpreted as restraint on speech or control on tongue. It is significant that the edicts recommend that there be restraint on speech but have little to say on restraining actions. It is almost as if the spoken word is not only more important than the written word but also more significant than physical action. Here again, it is crucial to retrieve the surrounding context of Asokan edicts.

VII

The 12th Edict: Restraint on Speech

We can't recover that world but we can imagine one where virtually nothing is written or read. Writing and reading have not

9. See Zimmer, 'Asoka, rather than trying to uphold one view or the other—and thereby identifying himself with one school or the other—sought to emphasise what he held to be the 'essence' common to all sects and schools. Doing otherwise would have been to encourage a more vociferous conflict of ideas and practices among these sects and schools, thereby compromising the concord and cohesion he was trying to build up within his kingdom.'

10. Nikam and Mckeon (1962).

yet taken possession of our psyche.[11] Speech has no visual presence; it can't be seen. Every word is spoken. Language is rooted and resides almost entirely in sound. Text, meaning something strung together, is also only spoken and heard. Everything is thought aloud and communicated. The spoken word carries the entire burden of our emotional life, all that uplifts or gets us down, brings us together or pulls us apart. The entire complex of Art, Philosophy, and 'Religion'—poetry, our deepest metaphysical thoughts, acts to honour gods and goddesses are all spoken, recited, sung, chanted and heard. All these are composed, transmitted, stored, reproduced and enriched orally. One might even say then that life itself is lived in sound. And, perhaps, destroyed in sound too.

Not only life but also public life is lived and extinguished in sound. Indeed, the public domain is constituted almost entirely by the spoken word and can therefore be disassembled by it too. After all, when words flow off the tongue effortlessly, they also tumble out inadvertently and what is worse, carelessly. But then, words that matter must be enunciated with great care, even greater thought, for once uttered they can't be withdrawn. It is important in such cultures to differentiate such unguarded speech from one that carries weight or is valued. If they are to perform all the functions that the written word serves for us now, such treasures must be stored and remembered in memorable forms. To be remembered without being written and to be effective, this speech must be crafted with great economy, and be crisp, rhythmic and rendered with great power.

11. This is denied by many scholars who wrote early in the 20th century. Mookerjee (1928) writes that literature and culture seem to have filtered down to the masses so as to produce a comparatively large percentage of literacy. Smith (1920) points out that the existence of edicts in the vernacular shows mass literacy. Such views are naive. The epigraphic habit had barely begun to form in Asoka's time. The rulers had begun to play with the new technology, no doubt. Asoka can even be credited for having realised the enormous future potential of writing and to have been among the first to have used it for dissemination and 'moral conquest'. But mass literacy at that time is inconceivable, because there was little need for it. Besides, a large heterogeneous empire dictated that edicts be written in different languages. Nothing about wide spread literacy can be inferred from it. To say that the edicts were written in the vernacular would entail that Greek and Armaic were vernacular languages, which is absurd. It is best to go along with Stanley Tambiah (1986) on this issue. He writes, 'The intellectual milieu in which early science and philosophy advanced was essentially oral, small scale and face to face. If this was true of early Greece, it was emphatically true of India in the Axial Age."

Only thus will it transform into a powerful mode of action. Words in oral cultures have always had enormous power. They can beckon gods to help us tide over problems, create something out of nothing, empower or disempower others, turn them into stone, even kill them. Words can be weapons or an elixir. They can soothe or cause grievous hurt. In oral cultures, words have magical potency.

One can hardly overestimate the immediacy and vibrancy of social interaction and, more pertinently, the agonistic energies in predominantly oral societies and its publics. Verbal duels, speech fights, word-wars, verbal tongue lashing of adversaries in intellectual combats—all these are commonly found in societies largely unaffected by writing. Moreover, vitriolic reciprocal name-calling exists frequently with fulsome expression of self-praise and excessive bragging about one's own prowess.

Given this context, one can now understand why oral speech acts appear to have more weight than all other forms of action. It is almost as if the greatest harm that might be inflicted on the other is through speech rather than physical action. It is not clear from the edict what the level of physical violence in that society was, if social interaction was already civil enough for people to even conceive that they could injure or kill one another over philosophical or religious differences. At any rate either 'hate speech' was considerably more significant than physical violence or else physical violence was largely confined to the territorial aggression and politics among the Kshatriyas. Quite certainly the antagonistic energy in speech was unmatched even by physical violence. Generally people knew how to do things with spoken words. They poked fun, ridiculed, abused, cursed, mocked, scoffed at, were satirical and sarcastic, belittled and humiliated others —all by subtle manipulation of the spoken word.

VIII

Two Forms of Self-Restraint

We do not have much evidence of the verbal battles and hate speech of that period but the edicts imply that verbal wars in that period were intense and brutal. They simply had to be reined in. But what kind of speech must be curbed? Edict 12 says that speech that without reason disparages other *pasandas* must be restrained. Speech critical of others may be freely enunciated only if we have good reasons to do so.[12] However, even when we have good reasons to be critical, one may do so only on appropriate occasions and even when the occasion is appropriate, one must never be immoderate. Critique should never belittle or humiliate others. Thus there is a multi-layered, ever deepening restraint on one's verbal speech against others. Let us call it other-related self-restraint. However, the edicts do not stop at this. They go on to say that one must not extols one's own *pasanada* without good reason. Undue praise of one's own *pasanda* is as morally objectionable as unmerited criticism of the faith of others. Moreover, the edicts add that even when there is good reason to praise one's own *pasanda*, it too should be done only on appropriate occasions and even on those occasions, never immoderately. Undue or excessive self-glorification is also a way to make others feel small. For Asoka, blaming other *pasandas* out of devotion to one's own *pasandas* and unreflective, uncritical, effulgent self-praise can only damage one's *pasanda*. By offending and thereby estranging others, it undermines one's capacity for mutual interaction and possible influence. Thus there must equally be multi-textured, ever deepening restraint for oneself. Let this be self-related self-restraint.

Elsewhere, in the 7th edict, Asoka emphasises the need not only for self-restraint, *samyama* but also *bhaavshuddhi*, again a self-oriented act. *Bhaavashuddhi* is frequently interpreted as self-purification, purity of mind. However, this term is ambiguous between self-purification within an ethic of individual self-realisation or one that at least includes cleansing one's self of ill will towards others. My own view is that in the context of the relevant edicts, the moral feeling of good will towards others or at least an absence of ill will towards others must be a constitutive feature of what is meant by *bhaavshuddhi*, a crucial part of the more general purification

12. "There should not be condemnation of others without any ground. Such slighting (*lahuka*, from *laghu*) should be for specified grounds only." See R.K. Mookerjee, Asoka, p 159.

of *bhaava*. Self-restraint and self-purification are not just matters of etiquette or prudence. They have moral significance.

Given all this, and in order to advance mutual understanding and mutual appreciation, it is better, the edict says, to have *samovaya*, concourse—an assembly of *pasandas* where they can hear one another out, communicate with one another. They may then become *bahushruta*, i.e. one who listens to all, the perfect listener, and open-minded. This way they will not only have *atma pasanda vraddhi,* the growth in the self-understanding of one's own *pasanda* but also the growth of the essentials of all (*saravadhi* or *saaravraddhi*). The edicts here imply that the ethical self-understanding of *pasandas* is not static but constantly evolving and such growth is crucially dependent on mutual communication and dialogue with one another. Blaming others without good reason or immoderately disrupts this process and, apart from damaging *Dhamma*, diminishes mutual growth of individual *pasandas*.

The edicts add that no matter how generous you are with gifts and how sincere your devotion to rituals, if you lack samyama, *bhaavshuddhi* and the quality of *bahushruta*, then all the liberality in the world is in vain. Conversely, one who is unable to offer gifts but possess the aforementioned virtues lives a *dhammic* life. Thus one whose speech disrespects no one, who has no ill will towards others and who does no violence to living beings is truly *dharmic*. Dharma is realised not by sacrifice but by right speech and conduct.

IX

Is this Toleration?

Thapar (1961: 139) says, "the 7th edict is pleading for toleration among all sects." Likewise, the term "religious tolerance" is also used by Tambiah (1977). Is the term 'toleration' or 'tolerance' appropriate in this context? In the classical 17th century meaning of the term, to tolerate is to refrain from interference in the activities of others even though one finds them morally disagreeable, even repugnant and despite the fact that one has the power to do so.[13] Here one puts up with, even suffers the morally reprehensible activities of others. The powerless other escapes interference of the powerful because the latter shows mercy towards them, a virtue in the powerful exercised in relation to those who do not really deserve it. Lets call this a hierarchical notion of toleration, given the asymmetry of power between the two groups and the attitude of superiority that one has towards the other. A second conception exists: Two groups, equally powerful, may also tolerate one another. Each has power to interfere in the activities of others and each finds the other morally repugnant but both refrain from doing so because the mutual costs are too high. This is modus vivendi toleration. Clearly the Asokan case does not fall within either of these two conceptions.

A third conception is also non-hierarchical. Here A and B refrain from interfering in each other's activities out of indifference and because they don't particularly believe that one is more powerful than the other. True, they do not heartily approve of each other. The acceptance of one another may be somewhat grudging, more out of resignation than enthusiasm. It may also be true that this new disposition is a result of the dilution of the perceived power of the larger group, softened by the force of principles or reason or commerce or due to the disuse of collective power in matters concerning ultimate ideals. Neither really cares for another, as long each keeps out of the other's way. This is live and let live attitude, one that is found in post-industrial, individualist, liberal societies. Everyone, in this conception, has a right to be, as long as he or she causes no harm to others. I may disapprove of what you do but as long you do it in your privacy and not in my face, I don't really care. The Asokan case does not fall under this conception either. If none of these conceptions is able to cover the Asokan case, then why use the term?

The basic idea of toleration is that A does not accept B's views or practices but still refrains from interfering in it, even though one has the power to do so. A fourth conception may not violate this basic

13. See for example, Mendus (1989).

idea and yet be distinct from the other three conceptions. Parents often put up with the blemishes of their children which they would not suffer in others. We choose to overlook a fault in our lover, even in our close friends that we would not excuse in others. We might endure deep difference in world-views in fellow citizens because we value fraternity. In all such cases, we put up with dislikeable states of doing or being in others even if we have some power to do something about them simply because we have love or love-like feelings for them. Here one tolerates not despite hate but rather because one loves the other. A mixture of love, friendliness and fellow-feeling is in the background or becomes the ground of a different conception of toleration.

Unlike other conceptions which presupposes the idea that oneness with significant others as well as God is achieved by abolishing/ignoring/belittling the radical other, i.e. by eliminating plurality, here, in the second conception, oneness is attained by accepting all radical others as equally significant because they variously manifest one supreme being or concept. Thus to tolerate is to refrain from interfering in the life of others not despite our hatred for them, nor because we are indifferent to them but because we love them as alternative manifestations of our own selves or deeply care for some basic norm common to all of us. We may not be able to do or be what they are, we may even dislike some of their beliefs and practices but we recognise that they are translations of our own selves or of gods within each of us. This binds us together in a relationship of lasting affection.

So suppose that A accepts the value of many but not all of B's beliefs and practices but recognises that beliefs and practices he does not accept follow from some of those he does or that some beliefs and practices he is unable to endorse follow inescapably from B's different background, then out of respect for some of his beliefs and practices, A would put up rather than interfere with those with which he disagrees. Asoka's views, I believe to have shown, fall broadly within this fourth conception. If so, one might use the term 'toleration' in this context, as long as one is careful not to confuse it with the other three, more standard conceptions.

But in the end it is perhaps better to avoid using the term 'toleration'. No matter what its surrounding context, toleration focuses solely on a set of other-related self-restraints. But Asokan edicts clearly go beyond this by also making it necessary to observe a set of self-related self-restraints. In mutual toleration, each observes identical forms of self-restraint: I don't interfere in your beliefs and practices and you don't in mine. But the edicts speak instead of what we might call correlative self-restraints. One is not asked to refrain from excessively criticising others and one self. Instead, one is asked not to immoderately and without good reason be critical of others or indulge in the correlative practice of self-praise, quite a different thing altogether. It is by simultaneously observing both forms of self-restraint that one completes a moral act. It is better to say then that the edicts outline original norms of civility and principled co-existence among radically differing *pasandas* in a deeply heterogeneous society.

The distinction between the two forms of self-restraint is important because it helps us to more clearly see why Asoka's political morality is not reducible to but goes beyond toleration in every sense of the term. An example here from our own time might illustrate my point. India is a country where a majority of its people either call themselves or are taken to be Hindus. Though not entirely, the ethos of many of India's social and political institutions is saturated by one or the other strand of 'Hinduism'. So, regardless of our evaluative judgment, it would not be entirely incorrect to say these institutions are somewhat Hinduised or wear a Hindu look. Yet, India also has Muslims, Christians, Parsees, Buddhists, Jains, Sikhs, atheists and people with many other not so easily definable outlooks. Sections of Hindus may find their practices disagreeable, morally discomforting, or just downright strange but they tolerate them. They may collectively have power to interfere in them, even banish them, but they refrain from doing so. Indeed, legally they have no other option. These religious communities have rights not to be interfered with in their religious and cultural practices. But the minorities will not be able to effectively exercise their rights, if Hindus do not possess the capacity for other-related self-restraint.

Most Hindus do as a matter of fact exercise such restraint. But is this sufficient for a morally justified co-existence between Hindus and minority communities? Suppose then that community-specific rights of minorities are respected but Hindu self-assertion becomes more pronounced. Let us say they build new temples around every corner, ensure that these are mightier in size than mosques and churches, fund new radio and television channels that stream Hindu teachings and no other, introduce text books that speak largely of and glorify Hindu gods and goddesses, change national and state symbols in order to make them explicitly and exclusively Hindu and so on. What would its impact be on the psyche of the minorities? Most likely, it will increase their sense of social and cultural alienation. It will force them to feel left out of many public domains. It might even lower their self-esteem.

Alternatively, Hindus can show some self-related self-restraint, so as not to show off, to not always wear their religion and culture on their sleeve, to not always advertise their wares, as it were. Indeed, to persistently announce in public than you are the boss in your own country might be a sure sign of deep-rooted insecurities and anxieties, one that is both potentially damaging to others and to oneself. Abandoning this self-related self-restraint might then adversely affect everyone, destroy the very fabric of contemporary Indian society.

Conclusion

I have argued that Asoka's conception and policy of Dhamma can not be properly understood unless we vividly imagine the background conditions within which it emerged. The ambition of a new public morality widely endorsed by all affected groups could not have been possible without the pressing need to come up with a novel initiative in conditions of acute conflict among rival world-views. At the centre of these struggles were bitter disputations between predominantly one-world oriented practioners of ritual sacrifice and those who opposed such violent rituals and sought a new transcendental, world-negating morality for all. The availability of new conceptual resources forged during these disputes made it possible to devise a new policy that, though not guaranteed to succeed, gave the hope for a durable principled co-existence between groups engaged in fierce verbal disputes. This new political morality placed at the centre a series of self and other-related self-restraints. Only the simultaneous exercise of these new voluntary constraints could ensure amicable collective living. This policy might be called 'toleration' but only by a massive change in its dominant meaning. On standard interpretations, toleration involves the privatisation of ill will or hatred. Both must be neutralised if not expunged. However, this new notion implies no such thing. Quite the contrary, for it presupposes in the background something closer to good will and respect. But in the end, even this might not be appropriate. Till we discover a suitable Prakrit, Pali or Sanskrit term, it is best to call it civil.

References

Bhandarkar, D.R. (1925). *Asoka*. Calcutta: Asian Educational Services. p.112.

Crangle, Edward Fitz Patrick (1994). *The Origin and Development of Early Indian Contemplative Practices*, Weisbaden: Harrassowitz Verlag. p.28.

Nikam, N.A. and Richard Mckeon (1962). "Rock Edict, XII", *The Edicts of Asoka*. Chicago University Press.

Mendus, Susan (1989). *Toleration and the Limits of Liberalism*. Macmillan.

Mookerjee, R.K. (1928). *Asoka*. McMillan. p.102.

Obeyesekhre, Gananath (2002). *Imagining Karma: Ethical Transformation in Amerindian, Buddhist, and Greek Rebirth*. Princeton University Press.

Pande, G.C. (1957, 1995). *Studies in the Origins of Buddhism*. Motilal Benarasi Dass. pp.257-62.

Smith, Vincent (1920). *Asoka, The Buddhist King*. Oxford: Oxford University Press. p.139.

Tambiah, Stanley (1977). *World Conqueror and World Renouncer: A Study of Buddhism and Polity in Thailand against a Historical Background*. Cambridge Studies in Social and Cultural Anthropology (Book 15). Cambridge: Cambridge University Press. p.64.

———. (1986). "Reflexive and Institutional Achievements of Early Buddhism", in Johann P. Arnason, S.N. Eisenstadt, Bjorn Wittrock (eds.), *Axial Civilizations and World History*. p.461.

Thapar, Romila (1961). *Asoka and the Decline of the Mauryas*, Oxford: Oxford University Press. p.4

11

SATISH DESHPANDE

Caste and Castelessness in the Indian Republic

Towards a Biography of the General Category

The theme of my paper has been at the centre of public attention for a long time, and specially in the last two decades, namely caste. Despite being at the centre of our attention, however, caste continues to elude us in fundamental ways—or at least so it would seem. I would like to explore some of the ways in which it has proved to be elusive, and the reasons why this has happened.

The quickest way to map the terrain I wish to cover is to recount a joke that has been circulating on the internet. Popularised five or six years ago when the 93rd Amendment to the Constitution introduced reservations for the Other Backward Classes (OBCs) in elite educational institutions, the joke goes as follows: India decides to send a space exploration team to the moon. Feverish negotiations begin immediately on the composition of the team, and after much haggling it is decided to include nine OBCs, six SCs, three STs, and, if there is any place left, two astronauts. This simple joke unintentionally offers us a deep insight into the central predicament of caste today. The insight is contained in the fact that the 'astronauts' are not identified by their caste but only by their qualifications (as astronauts), whereas the quota-*walas* are identified only by their caste and not by their qualifications. In short, the joke correctly assumes that 'we' will know the caste of the astronauts without being told, but will agree that it is irrelevant in the face of their qualifications, while simultaneously agreeing that though the quota-*walas* too would presumably have qualifications, these are irrelevant in the face of their caste. To put it differently, upper caste identity is such that it can be completely overwritten by modern-professional identities of choice, whereas lower caste identity is so indelibly engraved that it overwrites all other identities and renders them illegible, along with the choices that they may represent.

This, to my mind, is the central predicament of caste today—its hyper visibility for the so-called lower castes and its invisibility for the so-called upper castes. Having started out with the common goal of transcending caste—an objective that no one dared to question publicly and everyone seemed to share—we appear to have reached a dead-end where society is split into two unequal and implacably opposed sections. For one section, caste appears to be the only available resource with which to try and improve life-chances in a game where the playing field is far from level. This section, which constitutes the large majority of the population, includes many disparate groups that nevertheless share an interest in caste-based politics. For the other section, which is far less numerous and much more homogenous, caste has already yielded all that it can and represents a ladder that can now be safely kicked away. Having encashed its traditional caste-capital and converted it into modern forms of capital like property, higher educational credentials and strongholds in lucrative professions, this section believes itself to be 'caste-less' today. Not only is there no dialogue possible between the two sides, they are trapped in a perverse relationship where each is compelled to unravel the arguments knitted by the other.

What I would like to emphasise here is the mismatch in the public perception of the two groups. The story of the political encashment of caste is often told—indeed it has dominated public discourse over the past two decades. This is a noisy and raucous account, full of the rough and tumble of political contestation, and it has also attracted ample attention from social scientists, as attested by concepts such as 'dominant caste' or 'the Congress system'. The other story—that of the 'extra-electoral' coup effected by the upper castes through the transformation of their caste with the grain of the dominant common-sense—which is for obvious reasons monopolised by the vocal upper caste minority—this story is almost unseen and unheard. That is, it is seen and heard in other garbs—it appears to be a story about something other than caste, like the story of nation building for example, or the story of a great and ancient tradition modernising itself.

I want to suggest to you that one reason why caste has proved elusive is because we have not recognised the consequences of this asymmetry. While it is of course necessary to address the question of the lower castes and their demands for social justice, we will not get a purchase on the contemporary complexities of this institution unless we pay close attention to its taken-for-granted side, namely the 'naturalisation' of the upper castes as the legitimate inheritors of modernity. In brief, my contention is that caste can be understood only if we pay as much attention to it when it is invisible or infra-visible as we do when it is hyper-visible or ultra-visible. Whether it is represented as a chosen goal or claimed as an actual achievement, castelessness holds the key to caste.

Therefore, my objective today is to attempt an initial account—a brief biography—of the emergence and rise of the notion of castelessness and its main form-of-appearance in everyday life, namely the 'general category'. Needless to say this is a preliminary and incomplete effort, a rehearsal rather than a performance. Such an effort must begin by asking how a journey originating in a common starting point—the desire to 'abolish' caste—could lead to such sharply divergent paths. There are two obvious places where answers may be sought. First, we must examine the starting point to check whether it was in fact common or shared, and the extent to which this was so. Second, we must examine the particulars of the initial part of the journey to check whether something happened along the way that magnified existing differences among fellow travellers or else manufactured new divisions. The next two sections attempt to take up each of these options in turn. Part I examines the apparently universal goal of 'abolishing' or transcending caste and its many distinct strands in the decades leading up to independence. Part II deals with the ways in which the new Republic tried to give expression to the variously understood objective of 'abolishing' caste in its constitutional ideals, legal norms and policy practices. The concluding section (Part III) speculates on the current and possible future trajectories of the 'general category'.

PART I

The Provocation of Caste

The case of caste offers a paradoxical union of the over-familiar and the poorly understood. As the unique institution that indelibly marked Indian society as fundamentally inegalitarian and therefore unfit for modernity, caste was the universal provocation. No Indian and certainly no Indian wishing to claim modernity in any way, could remain indifferent to it. The broad tenor of the response was also pre-given by the encounter with modernity, that is to say, something had to be done about caste—it could not be allowed to continue 'as is'. And this generalised urge to change or act upon caste was typically expressed by the term 'reform', which, as Susan Bailey (2008: 155) has noted, "proclaimed the existence of a community or confraternity of the enlightened, working in harmony towards improvement and 'uplift' in the life of the nation." This apparent commonality was, however, very deceptive because of the divergence between implicit intentions and explicit rhetoric. Public statements about caste were more constrained by the normative pressures of modernity than communitarian intentions, which could always manage to create some space for maneuver. What this meant in practice was that the language in which political and social programmes were expressed was far more convergent than the divergent projects that these programmes actually contained. Even when these disparate positions eventually seemed to congregate around firmer and more specific terms like 'abolition', they continued to subsume wide variations in perspective and intent.

Thus, when tracked through sites such as the Indian National Congress and its official resolutions, for example, it is clear that the public language in which caste was addressed acquired the motif of 'abolition' very late and only through a slow and reluctant process. As Ambedkar has documented in his famous essay, "What Congress and Gandhi have done to the Untouchables", even after talk of 'abolition' became common, it remained facile and was rarely accompanied by a concrete understanding of caste and the practical course to be followed to achieve its abolition. Moreover, caste appeared to be unique in the sense that it was the only all-encompassing institution that was slated for abolition rather than reform. The obvious comparison is with religion which, even when it harboured numerous social evils, could still be presented as possessing an indispensable residue that was well worth preserving. Finally, while 'everyone' had religion including the colonisers and the moderns, caste was uniquely ours and it was without question 'un-modern'.

In this sense, therefore, when speaking of the 'abolition' of caste, reformist public rhetoric was leaning far ahead of its constituency which was still located well to the rear of the rhetoric. This ideological overhang is most clearly visible in the early stages of the campaign against caste, namely the last quarter of the 19th century and the beginning of the 20th. The most prominent voices here are still those that are seeking the reform of caste groups qua castes. The practical measures advocated here require nothing more than the simplification of an over-intricate system and the dissolution of proliferating sub-castes in favour of a larger, more effective collective caste identity. Examples of such campaigns were many, calling for rationalising and modernising, say, the *kayasths* or the *brahmins* as a caste by promoting interdining and intermarriage among sub-castes and urging sub-castes to rise above petty rivalries and claims to precedence. Associated measures might include those that were part of the larger social reform agenda such as education of girls, raising the age of marriage, doing away with arcane taboos and superstitions, and so on. So, what might be stated as a campaign to abolish caste was actually one designed to prepare castes to meet the modern world as castes.

A second set of agendas were less parochial and attempted to address the severe disabilities that the caste system imposed on the lower and especially the lowest castes. These efforts matured at the national level into the 'constructive programme' of the Indian National Congress (INC) launched in 1922 soon after Gandhi's virtual takeover of the Congress. One of the major themes of this programme was the campaign against untouchability, easily the most visible and damaging practice associated with caste. However, it is important to emphasise the self-imposed limits that this programme functioned under. One way of mapping the gradual and reluctant widening of the ambit of the anti-caste campaign within the Congress is to trace the evolution of Gandhi's positions on caste. Gandhi, too, began with what was essentially a rationalisation and reform programme whose overall objective was to simplify the needless intricate system of castes into the four broad *varnas*. The legitimacy of the latter—construed as *varnashramadharma*—remained an article of faith with Gandhi that he gave up only towards the end of his life, after sustained interaction with powerful opponents like Ambedkar, Periyar and radical anti-caste groups like the Jat Pat Todak Mandal.

At the start of this political and moral journey, we have Gandhi declaring in 1921, just before the launch of the 'constructive programme' that: "The caste system is the natural order of society... I am opposed to all those who are out to destroy the caste system". From there, by a gradual process helped along by the constructive programme and escalating in 1932 after the Poona Pact and the launch of the Harijan uplift campaign, Gandhi had arrived, by the mid-1930s at the view that "Caste must go". Gandhi's faith in the basics of the caste system, which he understood in terms of the doctrine of *varnashramadharma*, endured for nearly a decade and a half of his career as an anti-caste activist. During this period, all that Gandhi desired was the purification and simplification of the system that would help it to rediscover its *sanatana* or eternal virtues. Despite some discomfort with the unjustifiable reliance on birth to determine *varna* or station in life, it is instructive from a contemporary vantage point to see just how far even such a committed political reformer was willing to go in his support for caste. Similarly, striking instances of reformist political beliefs co-existing with extreme anxiety about 'losing caste' were seen among early Tamil brahmins supporting the Congress and other pro-change groups in the south (Pandian, 2007). The clearest evidence for the gradualism that attended Gandhi's slowly evolving views are visible in the intercaste marriages that he began to advocate in the 1920s. As Mark Lindley has shown, intercaste initially only meant inter-subcaste and strictly intra-*varna* marriages. This slowly expanded in the late 1920s to intra-*savarna* marriages that could be across the three twice-born *varnas*. It took a significant and clearly difficult interregnum before Gandhi could bring himself to advocate the marriage of twice borns with the Shudra castes. Ultimately—after the 1936 publication of Ambedkar's famous text *The Annihilation of Caste*, the undelivered text of the Presidential Address to the Jat Pat Todak Mandal—Gandhi graduated to his most radical position of advocating intermarriage between Harijans and caste Hindus. By 1946, two years before his assassination, he publicly declared that the only marriages that could take place in Sewagram Ashram would be those involving a Harijan bride or groom. The point of this excursus into the biography of the most famous campaigner against caste in pre-independence India is to show that 'abolition' could have many meanings that evolved over time.

Finally, there was a third version of 'abolition' that stood at the far end of the spectrum, a position represented by Ambedkar with his stated goal of 'annihilation'. For him, mere intermarriage was necessary but far from sufficient to uproot caste. Unlike his more moderate allies in the Jat Pat Todak Mandal, who were enthusiastic advocates of intermarriage, Ambedkar wanted to attack the ultimate foundations of caste which he believed were located in Hindu religion and specially its revered scriptures. It was precisely his call to disown the scriptures that alarmed his hosts in the Mandal and led to the withdrawal of their invitation to address their national convention in 1936.

In short, the moral pressure faced by the institution made abolition the preferred motif for programmatic public utterances on caste. However, this apparent unanimity of purpose concealed a broad spectrum of attitudes ranging from revitalisation and rationalisation to annihilation. Ambiguity of language was desirable and even sought after because of the pervasive nature of caste. It was (and is) no easy matter to 'abolish' an institution that affects almost all areas of social practice—an institution so broad and inclusive that it constitutes a 'way of life'. In the final approach towards independence, therefore, these varied positions tended to find expression in similar sounding phrases and slogans that were intentionally vague and imprecise. It is no surprise, then, that the Constitution makers should have carried these ambiguities into the founding document of the new Republic.

But civil society was not the only active force working on caste during this period—the colonial state too was an important actor. Indeed, an influential strand of scholarship has argued that caste as we know it today is, in the words of Nicholas Dirks (2001: 3), "a modern phenomenon, that it is, specifically, the product of an historical encounter between India and Western colonial rule." Possibly the most consequential intervention of the state was its effort, via the Census of India, to enumerate caste. As has been argued first by Bernard Cohn and then by Arjun Appadurai, Nicholas Dirks and others, the very effort to enumerate caste led to important changes, with the institution becoming progressively more and more 'substantialised' and fixed than it had been previously. In the 1930s, the enumeration question was also tied to the question of electoral politics as provincial legislatures were formed and a gradually expanding electorate was demarcated, beginning with literate and property-owning individuals and ending with universal adult franchise. Two events are particularly relevant from this decade, the Census of 1931 and the negotiations around separate electorates that culminated in the so-called Poona Pact of 1932.

The Census is particularly relevant from the point of view of the emergence of 'castelessness' as a possibility and as a conscious political and social desire. Writing in the chapter on "Caste, Race and Tribe" in the Census Report of 1931 (Ch. XII: 430), J.H. Hutton, the Census Commissioner, observes that:

> As on the occasion of each successive census since 1901, a certain amount of criticism has been directed at the census for taking any note at all of the fact of caste. It has been alleged that the mere act of labelling persons as belonging to a caste tends to perpetuate the system, and on this excuse a campaign against any record of caste was attempted in 1931 by those who objected to any such returns being made. It is, however, difficult to see why the record of a fact that actually exists should tend to stabilize that existence. It is just as easy to argue and with at least as much truth, that it is impossible to get rid of any institution by ignoring its existence like the proverbial ostrich, and indeed facts themselves demonstrate that in spite of the recognition of caste in previous decades the institution is of itself undergoing considerable modification.

He goes on to wonder whether, by aggregating castes across regions wherever feasible, the census "may claim to make a definite, if minute, contribution to Indian unity." He also speculates about the relative importance of different possible motives for the campaign against the recording of caste data in the census, including "a bona fide desire to see caste abolished", as different from "entirely other considerations of a political nature", and also the sectarian desire to see an expansion in the numbers of particular communities and groups. But his most interesting revelations concern the 'no caste' category which was specifically provided for in the census of 1931, "as distinct from the individuals who on account of ignorance or accident failed to state any caste at all". Nearly 19 lakh people seem to have made use of this category in 1931, with 98 per cent of them being from Bengal. Although this amounts to a little less than 0.8 per cent of the total population of Hindus in India, it is still true nevertheless (as pointed out by Kingsley Davis, 1951) that the number of 'no caste' returns in 1931 is greater than that in any previous census.

There is evidence to suggest, therefore, that the possibility of refusing a caste identity—at least in response to the colonial state—was already well established by the 1930s. However, we need other sources of socio-historical evidence to evaluate the precise nature of this response and the reasoning that lay behind it. On the other hand, the census results can also be said to demonstrate the pervasiveness of caste as a ubiquitous form of identity. As Kingsley Davis has shown, the vast majority of Indians were willing and able to state their caste, including most of those belonging to small sects like the Arya Samaj or Brahmo Samaj that were actively opposed to caste. Caste was reported extensively by Muslims—indeed, well over 80 per cent of them reported castes, with 133 castes being exclusively Muslim. Caste was also reported by Sikhs and to a lesser extent by Christians (Davis, 1951: Chapter 18).

Equally important, if not even more so, is the question of the electoral significance of caste identities. With the Muslim demand for a separate electorate having already crossed the point of no return by the 1930s, intense attention was focused on the depressed classes. Gandhi and the INC had particularly high stakes in this issue because of the way the numbers stacked up. According to the 1931 Census, Hindus accounted for 68.2 per cent of the population of India, while Muslims made up 22.2 per cent. Given that the 'exterior castes' (mostly corresponding to the depressed classes) accounted for as much as 21.1 per cent of the Hindu population, the grant of a separate electorate to them would reduce the Hindus to a minority. More importantly, this would be a major blow to the moral authority and hence the eventual political power of the Congress as the representative of 'India' rather than only a caste Hindu minority. While there were strong inequities marking the relationship of even the so-called 'interior castes' (or Shudras) with the twice-born minority within caste Hindus, these divisions could be papered over and prevented from emerging into the open. The disabilities imposed on the depressed classes were so severe and shocking that no amount of propaganda could hide them. Thus, the distinctness of the untouchable castes was already an established empirical and political fact.

It is this fact that Gandhi was addressing in his negotiations over the question of separate electorates for the Depressed classes being demanded by Ambedkar. By embarking on a preemptive fast unto death—the very first time that he had taken such a radical step—Gandhi ensured that Ambedkar would have no option but to succumb. The Poona Pact of 1932 thus cemented the claims of the Congress and specifically of Gandhi to represent all of India. Hence, helping to conceal the fact that the leadership was exclusively upper caste and the even more closely guarded 'public secret' that these castes represented a very small minority of the Hindu population. The muting of caste identities was thus a necessary precondition for the construction of a Congress 'majority'—a development of immense significance in the emerging era of electoral democracy.

However, a peculiar and paradoxical twist was imparted to this by Ambedkar's vigorous championing of the untouchable cause. The Poona Pact agreed to significantly increase the guaranteed political representation (in the form of reserved seats in the legislatures) for the depressed classes, but a very heavy price was paid for this 'concession', as Ambedkar realised only too clearly. Separate electorates could be seen as articulating a demand for a full share in the nation, a demand that underlined the equal claims of the untouchables. Although this was not immediately obvious, the grant of reservations reduced the depressed classes to the status of supplicants for whom a special concession was being made by the majority that 'owned' the nation. This effectively positioned the upper caste minority (which was in control of the majority) as the de facto owner of the nation, with the power to grant favours to this or that sub-group. It is this mindset that has shaped upper caste common-sense on issues of caste and specially reservations. Its effects are visible even today whenever there is a controversy on these issues. This is also the origin of the hypervisibility of the lower castes, with the untouchable castes being at the extreme end of hypervisibility. Until the eruption of the 'interior castes' in their avatar as the 'OBCs' in the Mandal conflagaration of 1990, it was the Dalit-Upper Caste axis that was central to questions of visibility and invisibility.

PART II

Caste, Constitution and Citizenship in the New Republic

It is to be expected that the birth certificate of the nation reborn as a republic—the Constitution of India—will bear the marks of the contradictions that have shaped it. Among the most significant contradictions are those that concern the vexed institution of caste. The central tension is between, on the one hand, the need to 'abolish'—or at least to delegitimise—caste as an institution that affects all citizens; and, on the other hand, the commitment to redress the disabilities of caste imposed on one section of citizens, namely the lower castes. These conflicting demands—requiring in the first case that caste be de-recognised, and in the second case that it be recognised—have to be accommodated within the overall framework of a 'passive revolution', that is, a revolution from above whose fundamental tendency is to minimise the impact of change on already entrenched enclaves of power and privilege. As the manifesto of the passive revolution, the new constitution must be faithful to both terms. Being in some sense a revolutionary constitution, it is full of radical good intentions. But it is also a passive or an orphan constitution in the sense that "there is no class backing the Constitution with its iron will", as Madhava Prasad (2011: 45) has written, so that it lacks "the will to change" and offers only "the letter of the law...without the spirit." The legal career of caste in the passive revolution is thus shaped through the disparate effects of Constitutional intention, judicial interpretation and the policy initiatives of the new Republic.

In colonial and pre-colonial India, caste identities were compulsory for all—only those who renounced the world could be caste-less (Burghart, 1983). Nationalist efforts to exorcise the embarrassment of caste succeeded to some extent in valorising a worldly ideal of castelessness, but they were unable, and also largely unwilling, to mount an all out assault on caste. This ambivalence is translated into the Constitution through the inclusion of, on the one hand, the rights to equality and non-discrimination, and on the other hand, the charge on the state to show special consideration to the STs (scheduled tribes) and SCs (scheduled castes), to 'SEBCs' (socially and educationally backward classes), and more generally to the 'weaker sections' of society. The two kinds of entitlement are neither equal nor symmetrical. Being a fundamental right, the right to equality and non-discrimination takes precedence and is preemptive—the state's duties towards the lower castes and weaker sections may be discharged only as 'permissible abridgements' of this always-already established right.

Thus, the Constitution promises to redress the injustices suffered by the SCs and STs, and also to ameliorate the disabilities and disadvantages suffered by the SEBCs, but these promises are contained in the Directive Principles of State Policy that are not justiciable. The relative weight to be attached to these Principles in comparison with the Fundamental Rights may be a matter for judicial interpretation, but the preeminence of the latter is never in any doubt. Moreover, to keep its promises to the SCs and STs (and the SEBCs, who are a different category in principle but similar in practice) the state must first recognise them as castes, and this in itself is sufficient to confine such initiatives within the bounds of a benevolent exception to the prior and stronger commitment of the state to not discriminate among its citizens on the basis of caste.

By contrast, the biggest boon that the state grants to the upper castes is a guarantee of anonymity in caste terms. This effectively means that, regardless of the extent of their past or present privileges, their caste identity can never be used directly to prohibit or limit access to any public resource. In other words, the upper castes cannot be prevented from cornering a disproportionate share—or even all—of a public resource because they belong to caste A or B; their share can be limited only by setting aside portions exclusively marked for castes X and Y. But as we have seen, such an exclusive setting aside—or reservations—are already designated as exceptions to the norm of non-discrimination and equality. From the perspective of the upper castes, therefore, the constitutional guarantees of equality and non-discrimination amount to a licence to capture unequal shares of public resources. This licence is limited only by two things, first the rules of the market or open competition, and second, the exceptional device of reservations. The most significant aspect of this licence is that it can be worked without having to name one's own caste.

Although the commitment to redress caste injustice was integral to the social contract upon which the nation was founded, the new constitution constrained the victims of caste to demand justice as a caste-marked exception, while its beneficiaries were empowered to demand perpetuation of their advantages as a casteless norm. Neither route leads towards the annihilation or even the diminishing of caste; but in dominant common sense, one route is presented as having already passed this destination, while the other is accused of leading us away from it. In our time, it is the unbridgeable divergence of these two routes—and their unshakeable internal certainties—that make the 'annihilation of caste' seem more like a disabling dream than an empowering utopia.

Barely six months after the Constitution of the Republic of India was formally adopted, the Madras High Court upheld in July 1950 the plea of two Brahmin petitioners, Champakam Dorairajan and R. Srinivasan, claiming that their fundamental right to equality and non-discrimination guaranteed by the Constitution were being violated by caste and community quotas then in force. Although the specific order being challenged—known as the Communal G.O.—predated constitutional reservations, these petitions also impacted the new legislation. The unanimous verdict of the Full Bench of three judges striking down the Communal G.O. sent shock waves through Parliament, which saw its much publicised social justice initiative nipped in the bud when the Supreme Court concurred with the High Court in April 1951. The Law Ministry (then headed by B.R. Ambedkar) and the government (headed by Jawaharlal Nehru) responded swiftly with the First Amendment to the Constitution, protecting reservations in higher education with the same special proviso already included for job reservations. The First Amendment was passed in June 1951, less than two months after the Supreme Court verdict, but the state was put on the defensive.

In reality the courts had been victorious in defeat. They had managed to firmly establish the primacy of the meritocratic norm over the aberrational status of social justice initiatives, at the same time that they made explicit and endorsed a new kind of agency that the Constitution implicitly offered to the upper castes, an agency based on the universal-normative position of 'castelessness'. This was, however, a presumptive castelessness—that is, it did not require the upper castes to 'give up' their caste in reality; it simply assured them that they would be presumed to be casteless as long as they did not invoke their caste explicitly. In effect, the new Constitution forbade the state to name or act against caste-based privileges or advantages as long as they wore the garb of secular modernity. Constitutionally and legally, caste was henceforth to be recognised only as a source of disadvantage or vulnerability, not as a source of privilege or advantage. And when it was invoked as a liability (as in social justice legislation), it was promptly imprisoned in the straitjacket of a regrettable and hopefully shortlived exception to the meritocratic norm.

The arguments in the Dorairajan case in the Madras High Court bring this out very clearly. The court is told that if the Communal G.O. had not existed and selection to the roughly 400 seats in government engineering colleges were made solely on 'merit', i.e., in terms of the marks obtained in the qualifying examination, then Brahmins would have obtained 249 seats instead of the 77 they were allotted under their communal quota. The court sees this as clear evidence of injustice against Brahmins, with no attempt to reflect on how a Republic committed to ending caste inequalities ought to deal with a situation where a historically privileged community numbering 3 per cent of the population would corner 62 per cent of the seats in a state-subsidised engineering college. Nor does the court evince any interest in the facts that, once admitted, all candidates would receive the same instruction, and would be held to the same academic standards. Justice Viswanatha Sastri is both eloquent and unequivocal in his defense of caste-based advantages:

> It may be that through the fortuitous operation of a rule, which in itself is not discriminatory, a special advantage is enjoyed by some citizens belonging to a particular caste or community. This advantage is not taken away by Article 15(1). If, for instance, students belonging to a certain community or caste by reason of their caste discipline, habits & modes of life, satisfy the prescribed requirements in larger number than others, it is not permissible to shut them out on that score.... It would be strange if, in this land of equality and liberty, a class of citizens should be constrained to wear the badge of inferiority because, forsooth, they have a greater aptitude for certain types of education than other classes (Madras High Court, 1950).

Clearly, what is at work here is not the 'general category' as such, but rather its immediate ancestor, namely an explicitly caste-marked identity that has suddenly been freed of its particularistic burden by the 'fortuitous' advent of a historically unprecedented category—the unmarked universal citizen. Pictured in this liminal moment at the cusp of tradition and modernity, and posed (so to speak) with its progenitors, the new Republic and its freshly minted constitution, this figure is clearly recognisable as *Brahmin* even as it proudly wears the new clothes of the citizen. These are clothes; they are not—or not yet—a disguise or costume, and the upper caste subject is at this early moment in its career remarkably uninhibited about exhibiting signs of caste belonging. But already, even at this inaugural stage, there is an awareness that 'in this land of equality and liberty' the public declaration of upper caste identity has been made voluntary. Unlike the compulsory marking of lower caste identity which the new Republic continues and intensifies, upper caste identity may now be declared or not at will. Most important, the privileges and benefits that accrue to the upper caste identity may now be accessed anonymously, while its political-moral debts and liabilities are written off by the new Constitution.

The broader consequence of these changes is that the welfare of the upper castes need no longer be pursued in visible fashion through the mediation of public politics; it can now be made congruent with impersonal collective goals like nation building, development, or later in the story, by equally anonymous forces like the market or globalisation. While it is not perfectly symmetrical, the situation of the lower castes is a study in contrasts—the pursuit of their interests requires the mandatory mediation of public politics, and their needs must usually be articulated as particularistic demands. In brief, upper caste interests go with the grain of development and the market and appear to involve the exchange of equivalents, whereas lower caste interests appear as transfer payments that must be justified as exceptions. But what is taking shape here is not casteless egalitarianism, but rather a 'democracy' of castes qua castes, as Suditpa Kaviraj (2011: 291) has suggested.

It is important not to exaggerate the legal or policy impact of the 1950-51 judgements. Their immediate effects were largely overturned by the swiftly enacted First Amendment. Also, the Dorairajan-Srinivasan case had little to do with the Constitutional reservations for the SCs and ST; it was part of an ongoing local contest between the *brahmins* and the 'non-*brahmins*'. The main impact of these early judgements was ideological, and in this respect it was considerable. By creating the conditions for the infra-visibility-ultra-visibility division, the category of the unmarked citizen helped to mystify the category of caste and its social relations. In fact, it authored and disseminated a new kind of common sense where the very definition of caste was truncated and equated with the lower castes. This was in keeping with similar effects produced by other universal-modern categories invested with power—for example, patriarchal commonsense reduced gender to women, while white supremacy limited race to non-whites or people of colour. The unmarked universal became the abode of normal, naturalised power, its transparent invisibility being a sign of its privilege in contrast to the compulsory markings that subaltern identities were forced to display. It took four decades and the emergence of the key category of the 'OBCs' (other backward classes) before the infra-visibility of the upper castes qua castes—or at least its normal-natural status—could be named and challenged.

PART III

After Mandal: The Crystallisation of the 'General Category'

One of the defining events of the 1990s—probably the most momentous decade in the life of our republic—is the social revolution now known simply as 'Mandal'. The Mandal moment marked the long delayed arrival on the national stage of the critical category of the OBCs. Given its electoral weight and socio-political significance, this was like an avant garde play where the Godot-like protagonist arrives very late and disrupts the narrative, forcing the audience into hurried retrospective revisions of the storyline. I will focus here on only those aspects of Mandal that are immediately relevant for the 'general category'.

Although it might seem rather obvious in retrospect, the first consequence of OBC assertion for the 'general category' was not immediately recognised. It took some time for the realisation to sink in that, with the OBCs too being added to the 'reserved category', the 'general category' had now become an euphemism for the upper castes. In fact this had been true since the advent of the Republic, because the OBC participation in the general category was actually negligible—this being the very fact that had triggered the Mandal upsurge in the first place. Until this moment, the fiction of the 'general' being the all-inclusive universal had been easy to maintain, given that reservations were locked into the exceptional mode from the beginning. The constitutional attempt to be 'caste blind' had worked against the public naming of caste (outside the reserved categories), thus offering anonymity to the upper castes and OBCs.

One of the curious facts about Mandal—perhaps also the reason why it gets elevated to a rare instance of national catharsis—is the way in which it seemed to drive home lessons that should have been learnt already. Thus, the basic trajectories of OBC politics had already been traced in many regional contexts, notably in the southern states, for whom Mandal was just so much dejá vu. Despite this, the national media and even academia seemed to realise for the first time that the upper castes who had been accustomed to regarding the general category as their ascriptive birthright were actually a minority, while the reservation categories constituted the vast majority of he population. Even though the absence of reliable statistics on the OBCs fuelled scepticism and controversy, this conclusion was hard to resist. With the publication of separate statistics for the OBCs by the National Sample Survey Organisation at the end of the decade, many doubts could be resolved, and the logic of numbers was strengthened. What this brought to light was the long forgotten 'power sharing' or consociational argument for reservations. If power flowed from aggregated majorities in a democratic polity, then it was hard to explain why the distribution of opportunities could be allowed to be so far skewed in favour of a minority that it supported stark forms of durable inequality. And though the traditional meritocratic arguments continued to be advanced, they seemed to lose their lustre. Mandal provoked a re-evaluation of the symbolic and practical scope of the general category.

One instance of such a revaluation is in the so-called Mandal case of 1992. Here the Supreme Court consciously invokes the history of the checks and balances played out between non-discrimination, equal protection of the law, and the special charge on the state represented by the SCs and STs on the one hand, and the other unspecified 'weaker sections' and/or the SEBCs. Coming full circle from the ratio of the Madras High Court in its Dorairajan and Venkatramana decisions of 1951 that quashed the Communal G.O., the Court reiterates that the unreserved or general category cannot be treated as a de facto quota for upper castes. It states unequivocally that those reserved category candidates who qualify to be included in the general category must be included in it—they must not be forced into the quota seats, nor can the size of the quota be reduced because of such inclusion in the 'merit category'. Although, once again, this is not new (various High Courts as well as the Supreme Court itself had reached similar conclusions several times since 1958), there is something about the context that adds weight to this re-evaluation.

However, the most recent national level assertion of castelessness is that provoked by the proposal to enumerate caste in the 2011 Census. It is here that we see the media and civil society organisations mounting campaigns claiming precisely a casteless identity. Similar proposals to count caste in the 2001 Census had been summarily rejected by the then Home Minister, L.K. Advani. The discussion at that time had remained largely confined to the pros and cons of gathering such data; castelessness did not emerge as a visible and vocal identity. Despite efforts to delay, block or otherwise scuttle the proposal, efforts which were ultimately successful, it did seem for a while that caste was actually going to be counted in the 2011 census. It was this prospect that energised the upper caste elite and crystallised its claims to castelessness. For the first time, the weight of the anti-caste enumeration campaigns was placed more on the claim of castelessness rather than on other consequentialist arguments. One of the best known instances of protest came from the veteran actor Amitabh Bachchan who declared on his blog that Census enumerators who came to his home would be told that the caste of its inhabitants was 'Indian' and nothing else. Soon after, a new civil society initiative led by similarly inclined upper caste elites calling itself 'Meri Jati Hindustani' was launched. As its name suggests, the campaign urged citizens to join in the effort to scuttle the counting of caste by insisting on returning themselves as 'hindustani'.

One sees the emergence here of a voice and a sensibility that is beginning to believe in its own castelessness. That such claims invariably emanate from the upper castes (and that too from the elite among them) continues to elude proponents. Once they are successfully interpellated by the ideology of castelessness, upper caste subjects see their caste identities as incidental or irrelevant to the claim. They can thus assert with some sincerity that it is mere coincidence that everyone who makes such a claim happens to be upper caste. This is the generation that is in most cases far removed from the process of the conversion of traditional caste capital into secular modern casteless capital that previous generations effected. It is objectively true that for such individuals—who, it must not be forgotten, may still constitute a minority within their own caste group—caste plays little or no role in their lives. It is for this group that family seems to have replaced caste as the source of social capital (Beteille, 1991). Long accustomed to a comfortably homogeneous environment populated almost entirely by people like themselves, this group is unsettled by the recent arrival of hitherto excluded and therefore strange and unknown social groups in their vicinity. It is the double coincidence of the maturation of a sense of castelessness and the arrival of strangers in the social neighbourhood that confirms and amplifies this response.

This is a good time, then, to be working towards a biography of the general category. The problem of false universals is already known to us from feminist theory and from critical race theory. We can use the insights of this literature to understand how the general category has fared as a universal in our context. We can also examine the possibility of reclaiming and re-positioning this category in the light of what we have learnt. Can we imagine a different avatar of the general category as a 'true universal'?

It is in the nature of utopias to be ill-defined. So it is hardly surprising that Dr B.R. Ambedkar's cherished ideal, 'the annihilation of caste', remains to this day an inspiring but vague destination without a reliable route map. But located as we now are within the postnational condition, with the Nehruvian naivetes of yesteryear a distant memory, it is time perhaps to interrogate this utopia more closely. If one meaning of annihilation must be to render caste irrelevant as a determinant of life chances, then it is necessary to understand not only how a particular caste habitus might block or limit these chances, but also how another such habitus might enlarge or amplify them. Recent social science research offers us some accounts of the former but almost nothing on the latter. When it comes to the positive and productive facets of caste we have only broad correlations between outcomes; we lack detailed accounts of processes and modalities, the concrete ways in which an upper caste identity secretes and synergises the dispositions and embodied competences that add up to that abstract term, 'advantage'. To understand the productive side of caste, we need not one but many detailed biographies of the 'general category'. In the last analysis, then, the call to interrogate the upper caste self is not about the end of illusion as it might first seem, but about the revitalisation of what is perhaps our most intimate utopia.

References

Davis, Kingsley (1951). "The Demography of Caste", in *The Population of India and Pakistan.* Chapter 18. Princeton University Press. Prepared under the editorial sponsorship of the Office of the Population Research, Princeton University. Pages xvi+263.

Dirks, Nicholas (2001). *Caste of Mind: Colonialism and the Making of Modern India.* New Jersey, USA: Princeton University Press.

Pandian, M.S.S. (2007). *Brahmin and Non-Brahmin Genealogies of the Tamil Political Present.* New Delhi: Permanent Black.

12

GOPAL NARAYAN GURU

Two Locations of Injustice
Present and Posterity

The recent demand made by members of the self-proclaimed Dalit Indian Chambers of Commerce and Industry (DICCI) to exploit natural resources[1] for strengthening their position as capitalist can add to the scepticism of some of the environmentalists who have been critical of Dalits for undermining the need for conservation of ecology and environment.[2] At the larger level of theoretical imagination, some of the theorists of intergenerational justice might find DICCI's demand deeply problematic. These theorists arguing the case for conservation of natural resources from the normative point of view would suggest that protection of natural resources is vitally important for ensuring justice to the future generation (Mazor, 2010; Gosseries and Meyer, 2011). The environmentalists and ecologists in general would share the theorists' larger normative concern. However, one may find DICCI's attempt to premise capitalism on the exploitation of natural resources suggestive of one kind of injustice that according to the former is likely to implicate into its regressive logic not only common Dalit themselves but also their future generation, should the latter fail to exploit natural resources that are now considered by such 'Dalit' to

1. This demand was made by one of the Congress party leader at the Central level. This was repeated by the Chairperson, DICCI, Karnataka Chapter. As has been reported, the chairperson said, "Dalit have been denied right to natural resources for centuries. They should get equal share of resources (land, water and minerals) on par with upper castes", *http:/www.thehindu.com51062210 ece.*

2. Many environmentalists focus only on the conservation of resources and obliquely oppose the capture of natural resource by anybody including Dalits. The environmentalists working at the village level were very vocal opposing the Dalit struggle for common land. They opposed it on the ground that this land is required for social forestry.

become capitalist. Interestingly, one also finds in DICCI's position on environmentalism concern an unity of purpose with the corporate who also see the exploitation of natural resources a bright future for the accumulation of profit. Only difference between the two is while the Dalit want to exploit natural resources in order to gain foothold in the company of capitalist, the latter would like to put its Mythical Wamana's cosmic foot not only on the mountains, rivers and forest but on the common creatures like human beings and animals making the latter ecologically vulnerable. DICCI seeks to locate injustice in the mutually related problems—lack of opportunity to exploit natural resources and inability to become capitalist, while the environmentalists locate intergenerational injustice in the over-exploitation or ruthless destruction of ecological and environmental resources.

Speaking from the third position, I find the dialectic between the common Dalits and nature very difficult. It is difficult because both the nature and common Dalits share the same traumatised and tormented space. Both nature and common Dalits are exploited, suppressed and are rendered equally vulnerable to the assault and vagaries of these two social forces. Both nature and Dalits have their respective adversaries—corporate greed in case of the former and social dominance of the twice born in case of the latter. To use Ambedkar's formulation, capitalism is the enemy of nature while Brahmanism and capitalism both are the enemy of common Dalits. If common Dalits are as vulnerable as the nature, then on what ground can one defend DICCI's demand for right to the exploitation of natural resources? Is historical denial of such right provide a sufficient ground on which one can mount objection to injustice? If the state (this is what is the best for the DICCI) grants this right will it effectively address the question of exclusion and alienation that has affected Dalits generations after generations? To put differently, on what ground therefore, DICCI is making a claim for the compensatory discrimination? DICCI members thus seek to convert the collective injustice of bygone Dalit generation in order to buttress their claim in this generation. As we shall see in the following analysis, such demand is fraught with contradiction to the extent, that DICCI members are using the historical injustice of the past generation but at the same time their aspiration to become capitalist does not guarantee justice to the future generation of the common Dalits. Internal exclusion or continuous injustice across social situation, is built into such conception of rights which is based on individual aspirations. In fact, they will have to address the following question on an urgent basis: Will the DICCI members, therefore, have the state to allot the common grazing grounds, thus destroying the livelihood source of both Dalits and cattle? Needless to say, such logic would forge unity of purpose between DICCI and classical corporate houses both in India and abroad. Finally, should the members of DICCI find justification for such right to exploitation of natural resources in the idea of ethical relativism, which seeks to justify Dalit right to nature's exploitation in relation to corporate right to exploitation of natural resources? To put it still simply, if others are exploiting natural resources then why object to Dalit demand for such exploitation? A quick answer to these questions could be given in the following manner: If one finds commonality between Dalit and nature in terms of the state of constant embattlement, then the category of Dalit is not available to DICCI members at least on strong moral grounds. To put differently, DICCI members if they want to persist with their claim to exploit natural resources have to necessarily walk out from Dalit identity into much desired identity—the capitalist. They cannot be both (Dalit and capitalist) at the same time. In fact, they, on moral (regulation) and ethical (cultivation, conservation, preservation) ground forfeit the right even to make some indirect suggestion about the intergenerational injustice.

However, this does not solve the problem; because the common Dalits are locked in multilayered contradiction with ecological and environmental concerns. Village commons or common grazing grounds seek to express this multilayered contradiction in which Dalits find themselves at the centre. Dalits of Maharashtra and northern parts of Karnataka for example, have been struggling to capture and retain their hold on the village commons like *gainran* (in Maharashtra) (Guru, 1996) and *gomata* (Karnataka)[3] land. At one level, the village community is opposing this Dalit capture of common land. At another level, Dalits face opposition even from the environmental NGOs who may like to use the common land for social forestry.[4] Yet at another level, the state government, in the age of globalisation, is making the common land available to the transnational corporate interests; thus offering land as surrogacy to harness the international profit. However, Dalit struggle to capture common land might be seen at least from the point of view of the environmentalist a definite attempt to disturb an environmental balance which according to the latter is the precondition for protecting the interest of the future generation. Thus rights of future generation become the ground on which the environmentalists would then oppose the Dalit claim to right to equality (in exploitation) of natural resources. While rights in terms of well-being of future generation provide ground on which the environmentalist can oppose the claims; common Dalits however, will have morally superior reason (attached to their bare survival) which could provide basis on which these common Dalits object to injustice rooted into the denial of access to bare minimum resources.

Dalits might seek to offer more considered response to environmentalist objection by offering the following arguments:

a) Rights become rights when they have beholder in a visible person. Visible person can physically exist only in the present generation and not in the future generation. For a future generation to have rights should exist and currently have interest (Mazor, 2010: 352). Dalits, in order to remain visible, need to physically exist at the first instance. And for such corporal existence, they require livelihood resources on the permanent basis. It is for the creation of livelihood resources, they would lay their claim on right to a viable piece of

---

3. Drishtri an NGO based at Bidar and led by Kamal Karker has been doing the work on Dalit land question in northern Karnataka. Drishtri conducted a few public hearings on the same land question at Bidar.

4. The Dalit land struggle was opposed by some government led NGOs in Maharashtra during the late 1980s.

land that could be subtracted for example, from the common grazing grounds.

b) They would further argue that, the environmentalist can not oppose Dalit right to common land because they as the part of the social contract have promised to share the common moral understanding that the latter would acknowledge the entitlement rights of every one including Dalits. The Dalit would further argue that their right to a piece of land in the larger pool of common land would also enable them to offer some security to their future generation. In a way, legal possession of common land in some form is aimed at being fair to the future generation as well.

c) They would provide a historical argument in order to justify their right to land from the common grazing grounds in the villages. They would argue that the contradiction between collective right to grazing ground and individual right to a small patch of land has to be understood in terms of the historical accumulation of their deprivation and their alienation from the decent (as we shall see in the following pages, Dalits only had negative rights sanctioned by the Manu Smiriti) livelihood resources which came to be dominated by the twice born caste in India. The history of exclusion from the livelihood resources start from the time when Dalits were segregated and decimated as "broken men" in Ambedkar's (1990) expression well outside the civilisational boundary of the caste based civil society in India. They were broken not only from the civilisation but also from the privileged water and land locations. In this regard, Dalits require no evidence to claim that it is the twice born who won the fertile land in the basin of major rivers in India. In some parts like Sagar *taluka* of Malnad region of Karnataka; one normally does not find a Dalit owning the areca nut land that is close to the water source.[5] Of course there are always exception to the rule as some rich Dalit with appropriate political background do have areca nut farms in Sagar *taluka*.[6] Dalits of this region do have fallow or *gomata* like land. Similarly, Dalits along with the OBC castes find themselves located

5. My own field observation of Sagar *taluka*, Shimoga district, Karnataka, 16 October 2013.
6. Conversation with *tapswi* and K.G. Mahabaleshware, 17/18 October 2013.

on the terrain of hills in the coastal Konkan in Maharashtra, while the top of the twice born have their houses and areca nut fields and water resource located right in the valley. We all know that in the mountainous terrain, fertile land and water resources lie at the basement of valley (Guru *et al.*, n.d.) But on the plan, the physical order in locations gets inverted, thus elevating the upper caste to the top of the geographical morphology of villages and pushing the Dalit at the bottom.[7] Thus, systematic separation of Dalits from the livelihood sources would make the Dalit 'encroachment' of common land valid.

d) It is also possible to argue, much against the view point of some of the ardent and earnest environmentalists, that Dalit right to common resources could be defended on the ground that common Dalits unlike DICCI, do not have profit making intention behind capturing the common land; in fact they look at this land as a resource that would ensure them a bare minimum provision for livelihood.

e) Finally, Dalits would like to justify their claim to the right on common land because it assigns essence to the very language of rights. Rights won through struggle carries a lot of moral significance and such rights enabling Dalit to participate in the larger life of the state with equal worth is constitutive of this essence.

Arguably possession of individual rights provides an initial condition to participate in the larger life of the state. It is the larger life of the state that definitely guarantees Dalits an opportunity to participate in the rational transaction of the state. Therefore, much against the skewed reading of state by some of the scholars on environmentalism (Baviskar, 2003), Dalits find state, does not appear as a mean functionary as some of the scholars would like it, on the contrary, it appears to be meaningful to the former. It helps Dalits to progressively move out from the culturally demeaning life of caste ridden community into its larger rational life that had approval from Ambedkar (1979).Within the framework of state and legality, the

7. This is a conversation with Prof Shyam Lal, Jaipur. Moreover, we can see this landscape in many villages in Varahd region of Maharashtra.

modern conception of rights has a triggering off impact on common Dalits. State restoration of right to land, though in a limited sense, but offers Dalits an opportunity to gain credibility and respectability. If Dalits have land regulated in their name, this state intervention according to many Dalits can then serve as a guarantee to get loan from the bank. However, bank transition is not without problems which are why Dalit had to start their own banks.[8] Moreover, land possession reduces dependency on the local lords as well, and this in turn can help Dalits to gain dignity.

f) Dalits would have a strong reason to establish their right over common land particularly in the context where it would help them to walk out from the framework of negative rights into the sphere of modern rights based on legal entitlement, for example to common land. As mentioned above, modern rights which flow from the social contract as concluded in the form of Indian constitution, have at least theoretically replaced the negative rights that the Dalits had to scrap like hide of the dead cattle and its bones to cast off cloth of the feudal lords and the leftover food, *zoohtan* of the feudal families.[9] Individual rights to common land would help Dalit to gain dignity as they would mix their labour with their own and natural soil rather than with the night soil of the upper caste. It is in this sense they would begin to find John Locke closer to their both existential (livelihood) and normative (dignity) concern. Lockean conception of labour would help Dalit to achieve dignified separation from the night soil.

Finally, Dalits through their labour and moral will power make the land resources mobile through its augmentation. Because, most of the land that Dalit have captured, for example, in Uttar Pradesh (UP) (Saharanpur) or in Maharashtra is fallow and degraded. The possession of common land would help Dalit to liberate from what David Ludden (2012) calls, proprietary authority. In India, village commons, for all practical purposes, have been under control of high caste village lord. To put differently, Dalit would free the land

8. Vilas Wagh esatablished Sidartha Bank for Dalit in Pune.

9. I thank Prof Rakesh Chandra for sharing this information with me. Moreover in Maharashtra, the Mahars, one of the leading Dalit castes, were given the small piece of land near the village, called hadki hadoli for flaying the skin of the dead cattle.

from the 'blocked dialectic' that does not allow common land as a resource to move from the upper caste to lower caste.[10] This blocked dialectic has its origin in the non-implementation of land ceiling act by the government of India. These are some of the arguments which are radically different from the arguments as put forward by members of DICCI, and hence on their merit would motivate us to reach consensus on the Dalit efforts to put individual possession of common land access before the collective common land for social forestry. Before we take on board, the possible objection that one may have outside the objection that the environmentalist can raise both about common Dalit and DICCI, it is necessary to defend as to why am I using injustice as the core word in the title of this essay.

In this case it is injustice and not so much justice that provide grounds for reaching easy consensus. The advantages one gets from injustice as the starting point is the following:

a) Taking our cue from Judith Shklar (1990), we can see merit in this privileging to that extent that injustice provides us powerful point from where we can very effectively interrogate the notion of justice.
b) Injustice as a starting point enables us to discern more clearly the wrong in our society (Annas, 1993).
c) Privileging discussion from the vantage point of Injustice would put us in better position to locate different levels of Dalit critique of mainstream conception of justice. The demand for reservation within reservation could be one example to appreciate this internal critique of the idea of justice.

However, the arguments that common Dalits can marshal in favour of rights to common land as against the collective good that is associated with conservation through social forestry, will have to meet the following objections that have come from the environmentalist with future orientation. First, as mentioned earlier, some environmentalist might object to Dalit attempts to

10. My own study of Taradgaon village in Phaltan *taluka* of Satara district and Raundala village in Akot *taluka* of Akola district. Both villages are in Maharashtra.

demand or capture grazing land on the ground that it involves the violation of cattle rights. In fact, some of the scholars held colonial power responsible for converting grazing land into cotton growing field.[11] Dalit could also be accused of being anthropocentric thus privileging human rights over animal rights. According to such thinking, introducing moral hierarchy that puts human rights before animal rights, however, runs the risk of making our understanding of rights anthropocentric. Eco-extremists taking their cue from Thoreau would see the rights of animals as equally morally worthy as the rights of human beings. Thoreau's such liberating actions no doubt confers dignity on the domestic species and reveal that a latent instinctual seed is preserved secretly within the skin of most creatures (Macauly, 1997). Common Dalits, however, would choose to meet this accusation of being anthropocentric by offering two counter arguments that the followers of Thoreau would want to take on board for due consideration. First, they would argue that the skin of animal may preserve instinct of compassion which the animals do, but the social construction of animal in India, so would Dalits further argue, also preserves the instinct of sacred and profane, which can be detrimental to the human rights of Dalits. They would like the defenders of animal to remember that the Hindu conception of sacred cow has sought to historically torture the social life of Dalit. And this history continues till the recent times. One finds an extension of such socially embattled history in Dalit killings that happened in 2002 in north Indian towns. For example, in Jhazzar town in Haryana state of India, five Dalits were killed under the pretext that they were responsible for flaying the skin of sacred cow. They might find anthropocentric perspective defendable in the situation where the high caste Hindus privileging sacred cow over the life of a Dalit treat them as 'profane'. For the defenders of orthodox Hinduism, the life of a Dalit in comparison to the life a sacred cow is [illegible]isable.[12] On many occasion, the upper caste seems to have used

11. Laxman, the study of common on Akola District during the British period.

[12.] This was the view that was expressed by the Vice President of the Vishwa Hindu Parishad (VHP) in 2002.

these sacred cows to destroy the standing crops that the Dalit grew on the common land in many villages in Maharashtra.[13]

The social struggle of Dalits led by Ambedkar at Mahad in Ratnagiri District of the then Bombay state in 1927, was aimed at securing the rights to drinking water. In fact, he at human level sought to convey the parity of right between animal and human. Ambedkar's famous argument was that how could the Hindus deny untouchable right to drinking water when the same right was extended to animals? (Khairmode, 1987). Ambedkar's struggle for water at Mahad is suggestive of the failure on the part of the defenders of animal rights in India to perform their duties to other human beings (Brennan and Lo, 2010). Caste system does not encourage us to be kinder in our behaviour and attitude towards other people. Conception of sacred cow does not morally motivate the upper caste to develop kindness towards Dalit. Moreover, Dalit would also argue that they like Thoreau's love for domestic animal. In fact, in case of Dalit treatment of domestic animal, compassion dominates reason as Dalits do not want to barter their animals for the sake of some gains. Finally, they would say that it is the duty of the state to provide fodder to cattle. In fact, the state government in Maharashtra has been forced to provide fodder to cattle from the drought affected area.

Third, however, some scholars who are reading Foucault would certainly find the Dalit perspective on state problematic. Taking their cue for Foucault, some of the scholars might find Dalit argument to participate in the larger life of the state quite problematic on the ground that the state as the Foucauldian would like to see, would push Dalits into disciplinary trap. As has been evident from the Dalit struggle for government land, the state accepts one's right to land only through the performitivity of violence. That is to say, Dalits have to provide the evidence that they were attacked and their standing crops were destroyed by the adversaries. The land rights get recorded and register only after the upper caste or the state machinery performs violence against Dalits. This of course is not the route that

13. Gopal Guru.

the Dalit would like to follow for getting land rights. Secondly, after the Dalits undergo the ordeal of physical violence, then they have to be ready for second round of violence which has a moral dimension to it. The state humiliates Dalit while legally acknowledging their rights to land (Chengara land struggle in Kerala and Gairan struggle in Maharashtra). To put differently, Dalits can redeem rights only through humiliation. The irony is that to create minimum livelihood resources for the future generations, the present generation Dalits suffer an element of injustice at the hand of the state. Finally, state intervention through social engineering as mentioned above has the capacity and intention to facilitate justice only at the symbolic level just helping a few families to possess a small piece of land. Such critique of the state may prevail on common Dalits to realise that the social engineering by the state in fact is ineffective in minimising the degree of injustice between two generations of Dalits.

Rights by implication generate an individualistic consciousness that tends to overlook the inherent contradiction in the structures underlies and renews the phenomenon of injustice. Common Dalits are likely to ignore the incipient process of injustice that grips generation after generation of vast number of people into its logic raising dust without substantially changing the level. The symbolic capture of land thus has serious theoretical implication for the very concept of injustice. It is in this sense, injustice becomes intergenerational or it is carried forward across generations. Let us look at this problem in its more complex theoretical expression. However, I would like to make a submission here that my theoretical take on injustice does not move ahead with the help of hypothetical cases. In fact, the support of my theory emanates from experience that is historically produced. The experience of injustice does provide conceptual background for theroising intergenerational injustice (Mazor, 2010: 385).

I find Sundar Sarukkai's formulation of intergenerational equality, quite helpful in making sense of injustice across generations in this birth. To put differently, eliminating injustice in one generation is impossible and hence reduction of the degree of injustice is the only wise thing that one could suggest. From the liberal perspective, achieving justice in one generation is an incremental project. In this project, the rotation principle at its base has the assumption that justice is intergeneration when redeemed across generations.

Drawing further on Sundar Sarukkai's (2013) critique of the concept of intergenerational equality is the *Adwaita* narratives of rebirth. In this regard it is important to bring in Gandhi here who, I argue, had ambiguous relationship with the conception of intergenerational injustice. It is possible to find parallel in Gandhi. From the Gandhian perspective, the impossibility of achieving justice in this birth is not possible. I would like to argue, that injustice has a spillover and it has its acknowledgement in Gandhi's (*adwaita*) thinking. Gandhi's rotation principle seems to operate in spiritual time and not lived time. This difficulty of removing injustice is expressed by Gandhi in the Karma theory which he according to me espouses symbolically. For example, look at his famous speech, "If I am to take rebirth then I would like to be reborn in 'Bhangi' family" (Bose, 1972). Karma theory is reproduction of injustice. Gandhi, however, does not give up the efforts to reduce the degree of injustice in the lived time in this very birth of Dalits. This is clear from the following ideas that Gandhi has suggested: "We do not want to produce a dead equality, where every person becomes or is rendered incapable of using his ability to the utmost possible extent. Such a society must ultimately perish" (Shklar, 1990).

Interestingly, one can also draw parallel, between the orthodox *Adwaita* philosophy and liberalism in its all incarnations through an hermeneutic act of inversion. Market driven and regulated liberal order through the logic of its invisible hand, at least theoretically promises the rotation of principle—thus for example, pushing the top of the twice born down and the Dalit up in a skewed opportunity structures. It is skewed from the point of view of the upper caste who would always want to be on the top of the opportunity structure. It is in this karmic sense, one is only temporarily located in the structures and that one has a bright chance to prop up in the radical reshuffle. It is like the orthodox *Adwaita*, where caste based injustice is temporary and every other person has a chance to go up and come down depending on the kind of karma one does. Should this karma theory create hope among the poor and who then should exercise their right of reproduction in this hope to get justice in this next generation? Of course, DICCI members use neo-liberalism and not orthodox *Adwaita* karmic framework for the articulation of rotation principle. The desire to take advantage of rotational principle, unlike Heykean invisible hand (Shklar, 1990) require the visible hand of either of the state helping the former to get hold of natural resources or the corporate to get some leverage in the market transaction.

I am making an argument that the rotational principle which claims to minimise the gap intensity of injustice between two generations of Dalits, has been only partially effective just raising the dust rather than moving poor Dalits out of their quarantined locations both in the rural as well as urban India.

Drawing further on Sundar's observation, I would like to argue that the problem of injustice at the experiential level is negated through the argument that rotation as a zero sum game can work out to the expectation of every one even Dalits. The sphere of injustice is ever expanding across Dalit generations. This continuation of injustice across Dalit generation is visible in the re-association with negative rights that the Dalits had given up in the initial years of India's independence. They are stuck up in the same place, same level of empty essence, and same negative sources of livelihood. Their rag-picking ironically depends on the mindless consumption of the urban middle class. Those who celebrate the emergence of rising middle class should stop for a while and think about the consequences of the levels of its consumption. The consequences of middle class consumption are that it requires a battalion of Dalit rag-pickers to clear the garbage from the urban middle class families. It is known as *Ghanta Gadi* in several cities in Maharashtra. The rag-pickers particularly from cities like Ahmedabad continue to get paid both in money as well as in kind like leftover food and cast off cloth of the modern feudal lords.[14] The rag-pickers have reproduced the system of negative rights that was rampantly prevalent during the feudal times all over India.

14. My field observation with members for Dalit Foundation Delhi.

The other area in the garbage economy has also forced Dalits reproduce the negative rights that were recognised through the symbols of 'broom' and 'muck basket'. In Hyderabad, most of the rag-pickers are from the lowest of the low-Rellies who keep coming from mainly two districts of Andhra Pradesh (AP)—Prakasam and Karnool.[15] These two districts are relatively backward districts. In the villages they are even beyond the margin of the villages, almost decimated to the quarantine quarters outside the village. When they come to the cities, only place that is available to them is near the open sewage or drainage. Only work that is available to them is the rag-picking for which they do not have to compete or go through the middle men or a contractor. In this regard it is necessary to note that these migrants do not treat this as the final option. They, in fact, always look for relatively better options. According to some scholars of poverty and plastic, "fluid reality of caste relation underlying the plastic scrap trade reveals that if a certain low caste status was initially a pre-requisite for engaging in this work, the very process of participating in this non-traditional, upgraded occupational chain has resulted in a marked reconstitution of that status" (Gill, 2010: 187). In her attempt to serialise the dirt, she further argues that plastic trade is physically distasteful but not necessarily as ritually polluting (Gill, 2010). However, as we shall see in greater detail in the following pages, Dalit women do not experience any 'upward mobility' as many of them, for example, in Chennai would not be able to shift from rag-picking to maid servant, which is just marginally decent. In such cities like Pune, many of the middle class households do refuse to employ these rag-pickers. The concentration of double dirt we are told desist the middle class household from employing these women.[16] Similarly, the *walmikis* (sanitation workers to put it in official parlance) have not been able to change their fate as generations after generations are pushed into manual scavenging.[17] The lack of opportunity has forced Dalits to frustratingly cling to scavenging and it was evident

15. Conversation with Vasanta Balgopal in Hyderabad on 8 October 2013.

16. Conversation with Sangeeta Thosar in Pune.

17. Conversation with social activists, in Jalgaon who requested anonymity.

when the scavengers refused to respond to the call for clinging to this obnoxious 'work'.[18] The tragedy that is associated with the reclaiming the right to scavenging is that it brings back the language of negative right that is defined in terms of mixing labour with night soil thus putting on hold the language of positive rights which is to be identified with mixing labour with natural soil as mentioned earlier. Similarly, the Dalit women rag-pickers' demand for identity card also amounts to the restoration of negative rights. Dalit women rag-pickers are seeking ID card from the Municipal Corporation in Pune with the hope that the possession of ID would protect themselves from the dirty gaze of civil society and the evil eyes of the state and private security.

Rag-picking is no doubt an obnoxious option and yet Dalits are forced to do it. Taking huge risk not for the self but for other's well-being certainly carries high degree of moral significance. Doing dangerous job also involves living dangerously on the margin or wretched slums. The obnoxious overlap between the two kinds of dangers has an annihilating implication, which removes the moral distinction between the subject and object. This in effect makes Dalit as the part of dirt. Eventually, Dalit becomes dirt and dirt become Dalit. There have been attempts by some rag-pickers led by some NGO from Pune to achieve this moral separation of Dalit from dirt. This separation is not structural but symbolic. They with this ID do not gain an advantage to appear in the public sphere with generic identity. In fact their identity gets permanently fixed. Dalit women rag-pickers are demanding special identity cards so that they could shed off the humiliating description that they are dirt. This identity as dirt does not help Dalits to appear in the public without the sense of shame. The negative description of Dalit as dirt results into what Patterson (1982) has called "social death" of the former. Manual scavenging, sex work and rag-picking are not decent opportunities as such spheres are not selected by choice and they are not competitive. Since these are odd jobs with obnoxious character by nature and lack glamour, credibility and competition, Dalit women have chosen to

18. Ibid.

use ID card as a viable means to separate labour from these night soil. While mixing labour with soil is recommended for radical rotation but mixing labour with night soil is against rotation.

In our observation of Ahmedabad metropolis in Gujarat, we have come across post graduate (PG) *walmiki* students who were pushed into the sewage and manhole cleaning.[19] We also read in the newspaper every year cases where Dalit get killed by the poisonous gas in the manhole. Such Dalits are treated as walking carcass and hence are beyond any civilisational interaction of the twice born civil society. It is in this sense such Dalits are put to social death. If these people do not have reverence for their life, then why should they exist and why should they procreate and endanger the life of their future generation? Why are they aiming at destruction while they are alive? Why do the rag-pickers and the manual scavengers have a perverted attitude to their life—a necrophilia, the term that can be borrowed from Eric Fromm.[20] To put it more provocatively, do such Dalits have a right to procreate if they cannot guarantee any decent break for the future generations? If Dalits are not able to become capitalist, such failure is going to make them the burden without capitalist aspirations. They treat capitalism a moral resource that can guarantee the former a sense of social worth. For such Dalits becoming market worthy is the sole precondition to acquire social worth. If they are the source of liability and burden, why do they through 'indiscreet' sense of reproduction would want to increase the social as well as individual burden? This is the question that comes from classical capitalist, middle class and even Dalit. In such indirect suggestion, one can easily sense the strong presence of Malthus who has made this suggestion long back. But such members of Dalit and non-Dalit should keep in mind the Marxian critique of Malthus (Foster, 2000). Malthusian premise was that poor Dalits have no right to reproduce. They might claim that their indirect suggestion has a moral significance as they connect right to reproduction with the duty to acquire capacity provide care to their children. To put

19. Gopal Guru, field observation, 2006.

20. Unamuno quoted in Fromm (2004).

it more bluntly, according to the Malthusian followers, the present generation's decision to produce children involves the grave risk as they cannot secure the future of their children. If this is the case, then do Dalits have right to reproduce? In the same logic of the line of capitalist thinking of which some of the Dalits is the unfortunate victim, one might then argue that Dalit women have no reproductive right as their children do not add to the capitalist consumption significantly. It is in this sense Dalit women do not produce socially necessary population so would the logic of new thinking in Dalit quarters would drag us to. Of course such thinking lacks razor sharp angle as has been given by Maria Mies who says, "international battle over women's bodies has entailed a dual strategy of discouraging poor women from the south from breeding poor people, while middle class women of the north are encouraged to breed because they add to consumption demand which drives capital accumulation" (Menin, 2011). So, why should Dalits produce?

Actually one can give fourfold answer to this rather difficult question. First, taking cue from Hayek some Dalits might argue that they have been stuck up in the same place and this is because of their misfortune on which they have no control and hence their decision to reproduction does not and need not have the backing of considered judgement (Shklar, 1990: 81). It is their misfortune that has to resurrect the negative rights as mentioned earlier. Second, the conception of threshold as has been conceptualised by scholars[21] and practised by Dalits would throw some light on the question as to why the poor in general and Dalit poor in particular reproduce? Social and emotional economic support is the threshold level that makes poor in general and Dalit in particular to think of reproduction. In order to substantiate this argument, such Dalits would provide an evidence of some parents who are seeking early retirement so as to make room for their wards, particularly son. In the state of Maharashtra, such cases are on the rise and accepted by the state. Relying on one's own sons is considered more advisable and valuable than relying on the state. Such people do not trust the state. This is

21. *op. cit.* Lukas H. Meyer and Dominic Roser, in ed, Axel Roseer, p. 220.

not to deny that some parents even from poor families do delay or completely stay away from reproduction. Poor people do take a moral call on the question of reproduction that is outside the vagaries of the state. Third threshold condition is related to the traditional norm that it is better to have children rather than not to have them at all. Exercising natural rights on fertility is the threshold in this case. In our society, parents with children are respected than those parents who cannot have children despite their decision to have children. Final threshold that the poor Dalit seem to decide is again related to the birth of a baby. They might have baby with deformities rather than baby still born. Obviously from certain point of view these are highly objectionable justification that are built up around the idea of 'threshold' and misfortune. We need to offer less problematic and more convincing justification.

We can argue that Dalit poor require to procreate so that kidneys and wombs could be supplied to those who can afford it.

Many self-enlightenment capitalist including Dalit are ready to make amendment to their rigid position and would not criticise Dalit in particular and poor in general to produce children. Because this production is in their interest. They still require man power for the growth of capitalism.

Conclusion

In conclusion, let me then make some concluding remarks, that in the age of globalisation Dalits do suffer from a self-defeating dystopia. This dystopia which is suggestive of regression in imagination of collective emancipation, is reflected in the demand that some of them are making to become a capitalist even by exploiting natural resources. According to such Dalits, exploitation of natural resources is a necessary condition to become a successful capitalist. In such a demand, one finds an unity of aspiration that the Dalits have achieved along with those who see in the physical mountain a virtual mountain of money.

I am going to further argue that Dalit right to exploit natural resources cannot be defended either on the ground of blanket claim to fight social exclusion or on the grounds of ethical relativism which would justify Dalit right to exploitation as the right which other have been exercising all these years. In fact, on moral and ethical grounds, the common Dalit need to take a lead to resist both forces from within and outside that are ruthlessly exploiting the natural resources for profit. Therefore, Dalits need to take a moral lead to defend not only ecologically balanced life but also environmentally sustainable life.

References

Ambedkar, Babasaheb (1979). *Writing and Speeches of Babasaheb Ambedkar.* Vol. 1. Mumbai: Education Department, Government of Maharashtra. p.27.

Annas, Julia (1993). "Women and the Quality of Life: Two or One?", in Martha Nussbaum and Amertya Sen (eds.), The Quality of Life. Delhi: Oxford University Press. p.27.

———. (1990). *Writing and Speeches of Babasaheb Ambedkar.* Vol. 7. Mumbai: Education Department, Government of Maharashtra. pp.274-75.

Baviskar, Amita (2003). "Communities and Conversation: The Practices of Eco-development in the Great Himalayan National Park", in Vasant Saberwal and Mahesh Rangarajan (eds.), *Battles Over Nature.* Delhi: Permanent Black. p.277.

Bose, N.K. (1972). *Studies in Gandhi.* Ahmedabad: Navajivan Publishing House. p.57.

Brennan, Andrew and Y.S Lo (2010). *Understanding Environmental Philosophy.* Durham: Acuman. p.34.

Fromm, Eric (2004). *The Dogma of Christ,* London, New York: Routeldge. p.132.

Foster, John Bellamy (2000). *Marxis's Ecology, Materialism and Nature.* Kharagpur: Cornerstone Publication. pp.94-95.

Gosseries, Axel and Lukas H. Meyer (2011). *Intergenerational Justice.* Oxford University Press

Guru, Gopal (1996). "Understanding Dalit Atrocities in Maharashtra", *Economic and Political Weekly.*

Guru, Gopal Subodh More and Shantaram Pandhere (n.d.). *Dalit Dignity Index.* Mumbai: Vikas Adhyaya Kendra.

Khairmode, C.B. (1987). "Biography of Babasaheb Ambedkar", *Sugawa* 2: 34.

Ludden, David (2012). "Investing in Nature around Sylhet into Geographical Hisory", in Mahesh Rangarajan and K. Shiramkrishnan (ed.), *India's Environment History.* Delhi: Permanent Black. pp.65-66.

Macauly, David (1997). "Bewildering Order: On Finding Home for Domestication and the Domesticated Other", in Roger S. Gottlieb (ed.), *The Ecological Community.* London and New York: Routledge. p.104.

Mazor, Joseph (2010). "Liberal Justice, Future hope and Natural Resources Conservation", *Philosophy & Public Affairs* 38(4): 381-408.

Menon, Nivedita (2011). *Subversion.* Permanent Black. p.91.

Sarukkai, Sundar (2013). "What Justice Can We Expect from Advaita?", Paper presented at the Kochin Conference on *Caste and Narayan Guru.* 18-21 July.

Shklar, Judith (1990). *The Faces of Injustice.* New Haven: Yale University Press.